Praise for *Dispatches from the Great Campaign*

"In this book, Jason Jones gives us his unique perspective on the world in crisis like a wordsmith pounding out a sharp edge with the forge and hammer of a blacksmith. He does not bring ivory-tower platitudes. He brings the grit and grace of a man who, day by day, can be found in the trenches working right alongside the vulnerable. Truly, when his feet hit the floor in the morning, the demons say, 'Oh no — he's up!' This book should come with a warning label: Jones's riveting words will challenge you to action."

— Bear Woznick, Author, *12 Rules for Manliness*

"Jason Jones is one of the few people I've met who is truly not afraid to go where others won't. Through this book, he becomes a powerful witness from the front lines of war, and his fight for human dignity across the world is unstoppable. What touched me the most is how deeply he cares about every country suffering from war and persecution, including my homeland, Ukraine. *Dispatches from the Great Campaign* is a book that calls us to reflect on the world God has entrusted to us, examine our Christian heart, and courageously consider what it truly means to defend life wherever it is under attack."

— Valentyna Pavsyukova, Founder and President, Chalice of Mercy

"Discover the inspiring story of Jason Jones, a man of God who seamlessly blends faith with global activism. Jason is a voice for the silenced and the oppressed worldwide, and his tireless work aims to bring peace and hope to those in need. Join him on this powerful journey of faith and justice."

**— Ryan Hendrickson, Sergeant First Class (Retired),
U.S. Army Special Forces (Green Beret); Author, *Tip of the Spear*;
Founder, Tip of the Spear Landmine Removal**

"Jason Jones has the heart of a humanitarian and the mind of a philosopher. His words, even if one does not agree with them, are not those of a commoner detached from the realities of which he speaks. Rather, they come from a man whose whole life represents the distillation of enlightened thought into heroic action on behalf of his fellow image-bearers. For that reason alone, he is worth listening to far more than most. He is a loving, clear, and prophetic voice crying in the wilderness of this spiritually desolate age. If his is among the voices we heed, we can still avoid the darkest of dark ages to come. If not, may God have mercy on us."

—Joshua Charles, Former White House Speechwriter, New York Times Bestselling Author

"Jason Jones combines the pastoral and the prophetic in a rare and remarkable outreach to the most vulnerable peoples of every tribe, tongue, and nation. He frames his mission with a moral lens, tying mistreatment of the vulnerable to spiritual consequences. And he does so inspired by Jesus' words: 'As you did it to one of the least of these my brethren, you did it to me' (Matt. 25:40)."

—Dr. Jules Gomes, Vatican Correspondent and Biblical Scholar

Gratitude for Jason Jones and the Vulnerable People Project

"In a time full of darkness, wars, hatred, and malice, I met the great Jason Jones, who is always there for vulnerable people. He raises their voices to be heard, their struggle to be known, their fear to be broken in the face of evil. He supports them with real actions, hope, love, and steadfastness. I am one such example — as a Christian Palestinian, I was displaced from my indigenous homeland. But Jason showed up, raised my voice, and gave me hope. He never left me alone in this battle, and he proved that there are still good people in this world and that there is always light at the end of the tunnel."

— Alice Kisiya, Palestinian Christian leader from Bethlehem

"I am deeply grateful to Jason Jones for his unwavering commitment to help those on the margins, regardless of ideology or border. This dedication to the common good takes courage and was especially evident in the aid he brought to the Rio Grande Valley and the vital support he provided to our organization."

— Karina Breceda, Director, Shelters for Migrant Women and Children

"I wish to express my heartfelt gratitude to Jason Jones and the Vulnerable People Project (VPP) team for rescuing the Sisters of the Sacred Heart of Jesus from Sudan amid a civil war. These sisters, who have served in education and social work since 1954, were trapped in Sudan during intense fighting in 2023. After we tried several avenues, God connected me with VPP — the only group willing to help.

"VPP acted swiftly, coordinating with Sr. Christine to plan the rescue. Despite dangerous conditions, destroyed infrastructure, and food shortages, Jones's team ensured a safe evacuation, even delivering insulin to one of the sisters. On May 20, Sr. Christine confirmed they were all safely in South Sudan. I praise God for VPP and the rescue-team members who risked their lives to save nearly seven hundred people.

"Jason, thank you for your radical love for the vulnerable and for being a bright light in this dark world."

— Chris Merli

"Jason Jones has dedicated his life to helping the most vulnerable people around the world, including families in Afghanistan during some of their darkest times.

His work is driven by deep compassion, courage, and an unshakable sense of responsibility. He stands with those who are often forgotten, offering real help and lasting hope. Jason has even helped Afghan soldiers who were facing life-threatening danger, providing them with shelter and safety when they had nowhere else to turn. Through his efforts, thousands of lives have been touched and transformed. This book reflects the heart of someone who truly serves others."

— Prince Wafa, Former Afghan soldier who served alongside the U.S. military as an interpreter and was rescued by Jason Jones

"The Vulnerable People Project reaches places and people often overlooked by governments and institutions, ensuring that the vulnerable are seen, protected, and empowered. In just three years, VPP has employed fifty-four security guards, supported eighteen priests and nuns, and stood with the Jewish community across Nigeria. Through solar installations, CCTV for churches and hospitals, clean water projects, and aid to flood victims and orphans, their impact has touched more than five thousand lives since 2022.

"This remarkable outreach is driven by the compassion of founder Jason Jones, who travels the world to uplift the forgotten. His commitment reminds us that dignity and hope are possible, even in the harshest circumstances."

— Fr. Viktor Ekanem, Vulnerable People Project liaison, Nigeria

"I am deeply grateful to my friend Jason Jones, whose incredible kindness and selflessness changed my life. He helped me reunite with my one-year-old son, personally bringing him from my country of Afghanistan to the United States — an act of compassion I will never forget. Jason is a true humanitarian who works tirelessly to help people around the world, regardless of race, nationality, or religious belief. His actions reflect a heart full of love and a deep commitment to making the world a better place. I'm honored to know him and forever thankful for what he has done for my family."

— Beneficiary of the Vulnerable People Project

Dispatches from the Great Campaign

Also by Jason Jones
from Crisis Publications:

The Great Campaign Against the Great Reset

Jason Scott Jones

DISPATCHES FROM THE GREAT CAMPAIGN

Defending Life on the Front Lines

Manchester, New Hampshire

Cover design by Updatefordesign Studio.

Cover image AI generated by cover designer (Flavius).

Crisis Publications
Box 5284, Manchester, NH 03108
1-800-888-9344

www.CrisisMagazine.com

paperback ISBN 979-8-88911-536-6
ebook ISBN 979-8-88911-537-3

Library of Congress Control Number: 2025938952

First printing

Contents

Foreword

In 2024, the Democratic Party ran on the most radical abortion agenda ever seen — and they lost almost everywhere. One of the reasons they lost is that, despite what the Mainstream Media may say and no matter how well attended the "Shout Your Abortion" rallies may look, Americans, no matter the labels or differing policy perspectives they may hold, respect life.

We are a nation that wants to protect the vulnerable and defend the weak, yet there is still work to be done. Jason, more than most, knows just how much more we must do here and abroad.

The Culture of Death has a chokehold on us. It starts at the abortion facilities and mail-order abortion websites killing the most defenseless among us. Abortion is not merely "one issue among many" but the first of many that we must engage in if we are to speak and stand for the most vulnerable.

Unlike other human rights activists, Jason doesn't push aside the child in the womb and the fifty million children who will be aborted in our world this year, to stand for just for the "trendy" vulnerable. Jason stands with all.

In fact, it was the promise he made after losing his first daughter to the violence of a forced abortion that has brought him to see every human as intrinsically valuable — not because of his or her age, location, ethnicity, or religion but because each was made in our Creator's image.

No matter the issue and no matter the prevailing opinion of the political establishment, Jason always speaks truth, uncomfortably calling all Americans, on both the Left and the Right, to stand for the vulnerable — for the child in the womb, the migrant at the border, the Muslim in China, and the Christian in Gaza.

Jason's articles collected here perfectly articulate his vision for a just and peaceful world. His commitment to defending each child in the womb builds an architecture of protection for all, one that can end the Culture of Death in America and throughout our world.

His thoughtful words and policy prescriptions demonstrate a deeply rooted integrity to always speak up for the dignity of every human person.

It's my hope that every member of the Pro-Life Generation will read these articles, see Jason's deep heart for each vulnerable person, and be encouraged in their lifelong fight to end the violence of abortion and always stand for the weak and the vulnerable, no matter who and where they are.

Kristan Hawkins
President
Students for Life of America

Introduction

What Does Being Human Mean?

To be human is to love your neighbor.

That may sound simple, even sentimental — but it's not. It is the most demanding command anyone has ever issued. It comes from Christ Himself. And it's the only thing that keeps me going.

I began this mission as a young atheist, driven not by faith but by fury — by the loss of my first child to a brutal act of violence. I didn't believe in God, but I believed in human dignity. And I knew, deep down, that it was something worth fighting for.

I launched into activism with the zeal of a soldier: If I could not save my own daughter, I would spend my life trying to save every other child from a similar fate. I would end every war, protect every migrant from exploitation, stop every drone strike, silence every tyrant, and pull every vulnerable person from the brink of despair.

And I still feel that way — far more often than I care to admit. I am still haunted by the desire to save every life. I still wake up with the weight of the world on my chest. And when I fail — as I always do — I am driven to the edge of despair.

But I've learned something in the midst of that struggle: This crushing burden isn't a sign of virtue. It's pride.

The need to save everyone, to be everywhere, to carry the cross of the whole world — that is not the call of God. That is the voice of my ego dressed in pious clothing. It is only in silence, in prayer, and especially in front of the Eucharist that I hear the real call: not to save the world but to love my neighbor.

I've come to understand that love is not passive, and it's not vague. It has order. It has discipline. It demands sincerity and sacrifice. I've realized that it's not my job to play God but instead to serve Him. And the way I do that is by loving the person right in front of me — with courage, humility, and fidelity.

That was the lesson I began to learn the day I lost my daughter. Her death opened up a moral universe I'd never seen before. It shattered my adolescent ideology and cracked open the first real question of my life: *What is a human being worth?* And through that question, I found God — not in a thunderclap, not in a vision, but in the quiet recognition that every life I'd ever fought for was a reflection of something infinite. And that something is a Someone.

I saw it in the children who died in John Brennan's drone strikes. I saw it in the frozen faces of refugees. I saw it in sidewalk vigils, in shelter kitchens, in war zones. I saw it in the hunted eyes of our Afghan allies — abandoned by the government they served, now hiding in safe houses that my nonprofit had to build across Central Asia.

And I saw it in the mirror.

That's when I understood: I wasn't fighting for abstractions. I was answering a call. I had been led — by pain, by pride, by promises made in the darkest hour — to the feet of a God I'd once denied. And now I knew what I'd been created to do: *to love God and to love my neighbor.*

This book is the story of that journey. It's the records of dispatches from the front lines of culture, war, faith, and memory. It's the record of a man who still often wants to be a savior but is learning, one day at a time, to be a servant. It's the story of a promise made to a daughter I'll meet only in eternity — and the vow to keep that promise, not with rage but with love.

To be human is to love your neighbor.

Even when you're tired.

Even when you fail.

Even when it's dangerous.

Even when it comes with a cost.

Even when he is your enemy.

That is our mission. That is simply what we were created to do.

Chapter 1

LIFE

The Day I Lost a Daughter to the Culture of Death

December 8, 2013

It was two days before my seventeenth birthday, a Saturday morning, the day after a football game in which I'd played. So I was tired and sore, but I could smell breakfast downstairs, and somebody was walking up the stairs. I was half asleep. The door opened; it was my girlfriend. I smiled, of course — but from the look on her face I could see that this wasn't called for. This was a serious moment. I steeled myself.

After a few long seconds, she looked up at me and said, "I'm pregnant." That woke me up quick. We sat there in my bedroom, two young teenagers. My room was still a boy's place, hung with football posters and with sneakers and baseball gloves strewn across the floor. But there I was, sitting next to my pregnant girlfriend. I knew all of a sudden I'd lost the right to keep on being just a boy. My girlfriend went to an all-girls Catholic school and looked ahead to college, while I was dreaming of college football and a career in the NFL. We each had a plan for our lives. It was time to scrap those plans.

We strategized together, figuring out how to take care of the new life we created. It felt completely natural and, incomprehensibly, even a little exciting. Our adult lives were starting much sooner than we had planned, but we'd figure it out. So here's what we decided: I could drop out of high school to join the army (a friend of mine had just done the same). My girlfriend would keep things secret, wear baggy sweaters, and take vitamins until I got back from basic training, and then we would be together — and I'd take care of all three of us.

So that's what we did. I went to the recruiter's office; I got the paperwork, which I needed my mother and my high school principal to sign. Now, out of 565 students at Amos Alonzo Stagg High School, I was number 565. So my principal was quite happy to sign that piece of paper. My mother, with five kids, was also quick to sign the paper, with very few questions asked.

When I got to basic training, I didn't go to church. I tried to once, but it was just too much for me to bear. In fact, I realized I'd rather do anything else. So I asked the drill sergeants, "When the rest of you guys go to church, can I stay back and clean something?" They agreed, so I took on pots and pans duty, which nobody wanted. I discovered that the station was right next to a freezer where the drill sergeants would hide ice cream bars. I realized that if I took those ice cream bars, packed them in buckets of ice, and snuck them upstairs, when the soldiers came back from church I could trade them. "You shine my shoes for a week? Okay, here's an ice cream bar. You polish my brass for a week? Okay, here's an ice cream bar. You make my bed …" And so skipping church meant that I didn't have to polish my brass, shine my shoes, or make my bed. Not the best start for my moral education.

I was almost finished with basic and advanced infantry training and getting ready to graduate and go home. I'll never forget the day — it was a Sunday when I was cleaning pots and pans while everybody else was busy praying. A friend came running in and said, "Jones, your girlfriend is on the phone, and she's crying." So I ran out, knowing that I wasn't supposed to leave my station or answer the phone. But I picked it up, and she was crying, as I have never heard a woman cry before. Ever. The only way that I can explain it is that her *soul* was crying. And she kept saying over and over and over again, "I'm sorry, I'm sorry, I'm sorry. It wasn't me." And then her father said, "Jason," over the other line, "I know your secret, and your secret's *gone*. She had an abortion."

As soon as he'd said that word, a sergeant reached over my shoulder and hung up the phone. So I punched him. Another drill sergeant grabbed me, but he saw that I was crying, just saying over and over again, "He killed my baby! He killed my baby!" They pulled me into my captain's office and threw me in a chair. At the sight of me falling apart like this, my captain — a big army ranger — looked pretty broken up himself. I managed to form some sentences: "Sir, call the police, my girlfriend's father killed my child." And he asked me to explain what happened. And as I did, he looked confused and he said, "Private, why would I call the police? Don't you know that abortion is legal?" And you know, I didn't.

Although I was just an E1 private making three hundred dollars a month, I did know one thing — that human life begins at fertilization. That information was not above my pay grade. And I knew that my child was a human being. My captain must have been pro-life, maybe a Christian, because he soberly and sympathetically gave me a SparkNotes version of *Roe v. Wade*. Then he handed me a roll of quarters for the phone and said, "I want you to go to the PX; I can't have you disturbing the whole battalion." I walked to the PX, hearing again the sound of my girlfriend sobbing, feeling our loss in my gut. The thought of that baby had kept me going, every grueling day of basic training. My heart was broken.

And my mind was reeling. What really knocked the wind out of me, what was really incomprehensible, was that what had happened to my baby was perfectly *legal*. That wouldn't sink into my head. It was too insane. I got to the pay phone, and I called her back. We stayed on until every quarter ran out and the mechanical voice said, "You have sixty seconds. Please deposit more change."

But I didn't know what to say, because she was still crying. And so I said the only thing I could think of that might comfort her. And I meant it. I said, "I promise you, that even if no one else cares about abortion, and if it takes me the rest of my life, I will end abortion for our daughter Jessica" (we knew that our child was a girl because the abortionist said to my girlfriend afterward, "By the way, your baby was a little girl"). And I know now that no one person can defeat the Culture of Death. But I really meant it at seventeen, that I would, through my own will, end abortion. And I believed it.

When I got back to my duty station — I was stationed at Schofield Barracks, Hawaii — I figured out how to get started. I said, "I'm gonna start knocking on doors" (I knew the Mormons and the Jehovah's Witnesses would knock on my mother's door, and she would talk to them). Just off Schofield Barracks there was all this housing, full of Filipino immigrant farm workers. I would knock on their doors, and the workers would open the door, "Haole, what do you want?" I was this skinny kid with a shaved head and ugly PX civilian clothes, and I'd say: "I wanna talk to you about abortion. Can we talk about abortion? Do you know it's legal?"

And they'd look at me like I was crazy, but sometimes they'd pour me Coors Light in a cup with ice, and we'd talk. Sometimes they'd slam the door in my face, but most of the time they agreed with me that abortion was a horrible crime that must be stopped.

This was my plan! I would just knock on doors for the rest of my life on my off time. That's all I could think of. Then one day I got an angry call at my barracks. This woman was *mad*. She demanded, "Are you the man going around neighborhoods saying you represent us?" She gave the name of her organization. I said, "No, Miss, I've never heard of you. I've never said I represent you."

She said, "Well, yes, you are." I responded, "Miss, I've never heard of you guys. How would I say I represent you? I've never heard of you." She said, "You're Jason Jones, right? You gave your number to so-and-so, right? And you're going door-to-door talking to people about abortion." I said, "Yes!" She said, "We're Hawaii Right to Life, that's what we do!" I stopped being defensive and was thrilled. "You mean there's a group? There are *more of us?*"

Before I got out of the army, one of my officers found out what I was doing. He'd heard rumors. He called me into his office and said, "Private, I am hearing something very strange. I hear that in your off time sometimes you go around neighborhoods harassing civilians about abortion." I said, "Yes, sir, I do that." He said, "Are you crazy?" I said, "No, sir." So I told him what I wanted to do — to end abortion in America.

He stared at me and thought for a moment and said, "Well, you know, as an officer I was taught that if we had a big goal, we needed a big plan. You start with your goal, and you work your way back, step-by-step. You need a plan. Go write a plan. This is a big thing you're trying to do."

So I went, and I wrote this hugely ambitious plan. I brought it back to him, and I said, "There's the plan, sir. This is how I'm gonna end abortion." He said, "This is a good plan. Work the plan. Work the plan for the rest of your life, and maybe you'll achieve your goal." When I got out of the army, I started to work the plan. And I have been working the plan ever since. Of course, God throws me plenty of curve balls, and the plan has to change to suit the political changes in our country. But everything I do, in every sphere of my life and career, is guided by the central purpose that I found at age seventeen, because of my lost daughter Jessica — promoting the incomparable worth of the human person.

I went to the University of Hawaii, started the pro-life student group, and became chairman of the Young Republicans. It was as a college student — still an atheist, a fan of Ayn Rand, actually — that I discovered just how much courage it can take to defend the value of human life. The purveyors of the Culture of Death on campus — the most vocal being the aging faculty and abortion industry hucksters — refuse to acknowledge that you're trying to defend the dignity and incomparable worth of the human person. The hippie reenactors will cast you as someone trying to ruin everyone's fun — to turn "harmless" hookups into life-changing catastrophes. Your mission is to get them to understand that "hookups" in dirty dorm rooms are not worth denigrating the dignity of the human person or denying transcendent moral values, such as justice, love, and compassion.

Now that I'm making movies in Hollywood, people come up to me and congratulate me for my courage. Do you know what I tell them? "Compared with a college campus, being pro-life in Hollywood is easy. You know who is courageous? Those pro-life student activists. They are the ones on the front lines."

It is essential that pro-life young people stay bold and stay active. One thing to remember is that for every person who joins a student pro-life group or speaks up for our cause, there are at least one hundred, maybe one thousand, more who silently agree with us. This is true even on the college campus — but especially true in the rest of society (including your future bosses, coworkers, and potential spouses).

Social science bears this out. In 2012, a Gallup poll found that only 41 percent of Americans identified themselves as "pro-choice," while 50 percent said they were "pro-life." Those are the best poll numbers that the pro-life position has had since Gallup started asking people this question in 1995, and the trend continues in our direction. The truth, that life is sacred, is graven in the human heart, and no lie can prevail against it forever.

I learned that lesson from reading one of the most powerful books I've ever come across, Pope John Paul II's autobiographical *Memory and Identity*. It was the last book he wrote before he died. In it, that pope wrote about the three great ideologies of evil that he faced in his life: Nazism, Communism, and the Culture of Death. And he pointed out that in his own lifetime, there was a point when Nazi ideology seemed unbeatable. The Nazis had conquered most of Europe, were menacing Britain, were rolling straight for Moscow, and were starting up their machinery for exterminating their enemies. People who lived under Nazi occupation had every reason to think its power would last indefinitely. But in fact, that regime was destroyed after only twelve years in power. So much for the Thousand-Year Reich.

Next, the pope pointed out how Communists, who did much of the fighting against the Nazis and then filled their shoes as conquerors and tyrants, looked absolutely unconquerable. Communism rolled over Eastern Europe and then conquered China and exported its agents and its armies to every corner of the globe, arming itself with nuclear weapons that could wipe out the human race.

Then in 1989, the Communist colossus collapsed from within. It had been built upon a bedrock of lies about the human person, so human beings eventually rejected it. We were born to know the truth, and something in our soul is repulsed by lies. This awakening takes work, and it takes time. But it is ultimately unstoppable.

Now a whole generation has grown up free in countries like Pope John Paul II's Poland — in time to face what the pope called the third great evil of our century, the Culture of Death. It seems too deeply entrenched to be dislodged. Our culture's elites embrace it as a gospel that can't be questioned. Our government funds and promotes it, not just here but around the world — as the Soviets once pushed Communism. As I write this, the federal government, through the Obama administration's HHS mandate, is threatening with closure any institution — religious or not — that will not comply with the Culture of Death by funding abortion-causing drugs in their employee health insurance plans.

The mission at hand can look challenging. But as Pope John Paul II would remind us, they looked even grimmer in 1940, and again in 1948. And those two empires of lies came tumbling down. So will this one — if we make it our life's work to share the dignity, beauty, and incomparable worth of the human person.

I understand now that I will never be able to keep that promise I made as a naive seventeen-year-old high school dropout to single-handedly end abortion. But I do know that all of us working together will see in our lifetime a transformation of our culture into a Culture of Life. That's why I love the work that Students for Life of America does. They do what is absolutely necessary for this transformation. They inspire and train this generation of abortion abolitionists — the generation who survived abortion themselves but are now targeted by the abortion industry to destroy the next generation. Students for Life of America knows that college campuses are the Ground Zero for this transformation, and they are one of the only organizations doing this critical work. It is an honor to stand beside them.

I know that if all of us commit our lives and resources to this, the greatest human rights cause of our age, we will see full legal protection for the human person, from the child in the womb to the child in her mother's arms, from the embryo to the elderly, in our lifetime.

Generation Life: The Politics of the Future Is Young, Diverse, and Pro-Life

November 13, 2014

There were many reasons people voted Republican last week. They worried about Obamacare, the border crisis, the explosion of Islamist violence around the world, and the plain lack of leadership that has marked the past six years. What I want to talk about is the *way* they voted Republican, the character, styles, and beliefs of the candidates who won — and those who lost.

Unless we understand the deeper roots of this recent triumph, we will see it squandered like similar landslides, such as George H. W. Bush's in 1988, and Newt Gingrich's congressional sweep in 1994. As Paul Weyrich warned in his prophetic "Letter to Conservatives," it is all too easy to waste electoral victories by ignoring the principles that drove them. If we want 2014 to mean much more than a windfall for political consultants, we must follow it up with concerted political action on behalf of conservative principles, and increased activism in the culture, from the movie screen and YouTube to college campuses and humble homeschools, advancing the moral values that make America's experiment in ordered liberty workable.

If Republicans want to leap across ethnic, sex, and generational boundaries to expand their support and continue to win, the message they should take from this election is obvious: nominate principled candidates who care about issues of universal human significance — the sanctity of human life, the integrity of the family, and liberty constrained by personal responsibility — alongside traditional Republican areas of strength, such as low taxes, smaller and more local government, and fiscal restraint.

As Jon Stewart admitted in a panic on *The Daily Show*, the most exciting candidates to win in 2014 were young, pro-life social conservatives. The first black woman elected by Republicans to Congress in U.S. history was the charismatic Mia Love of Utah, whose campaign website announces, "I am proud to say that I am pro-life. My commitment to pro-life policies is unwavering." In case you think her win was just some Utah quirk, pro-lifer Elise Stefanik defeated millionaire filmmaker Aaron

Woolf to become at thirty-one the youngest woman in Congress, representing a district in deep-blue New York state. In traditionally Democratic West Virginia, eighteen-year-old Saira Blair was just elected to the state House, making her the youngest lawmaker in the country. This "millennial" told Fox News, "I am pro-life, pro–Second Amendment, and I'm pro-Constitution because those are my uncompromising principles." So much for old white men being the only people who care about such issues.

Nor are the demographic changes fueled by immigration flipping states to Democrat candidates, as both the Left and the Republican establishment have long warned us was inevitable. In the increasingly Latino state of Texas, pro-life conservative Greg Abbott crushed partial-birth-abortion crusader Wendy Davis by more than a million votes, even though she outspent him by some $11 million.

Democrats who thought they could spin the defense of unborn life into a "Republican War on Women" were stunned when the state where they banged that piano key the loudest, Colorado, tossed out incumbent, favorite son, and abortion advocate Mark Udall in favor of pro-life Cory Gardner. In New Hampshire, by contrast, pro-choice immigration alarmist Scott Brown was beaten by Democratic incumbent Jeanne Shaheen — in a state whose other senator, Republican Kelly Ayotte, is solidly pro-life. So much for the claims of Republican establishment strategists that economic and security issues are winners, while human life is a loser.

Mainstream, secular survey organizations have shown that this generation of college students is far more pro-life than their parents. Groups like Students for Life of America and Live Action, led by heroic young women such as Kristan Hawkins and Lila Rose, are changing the way young people see the face of abortion. Instead of a liberating choice that empowers women to embrace their sexual freedom, young people are realizing that abortion is a cruel and destructive means for young men to evade their responsibilities and leave women to pay all the cost for an adolescent, male-driven "hookup culture."

If Republicans want to leap across ethnic, sex, and generational boundaries to expand their support and continue to win, the message they should take from this election is obvious: Nominate principled candidates who care about issues of universal human significance — the sanctity of human life, the integrity of the family, and liberty constrained by personal responsibility — alongside traditional Republican areas of strength, such as low taxes, smaller and more local government, and fiscal restraint. Help those candidates to campaign on these issues that cut across traditional lines of self-interest and groupthink, issues that, in fact, inspire magnificent coalitions like the one that formed the Republican Party in the first place, to elect America's greatest leader, Abraham Lincoln. It is men and women who invoked the Lincoln tradition in politics who secured the most enduring changes in America, not squirrelly pragmatists like Richard Nixon or Karl Rove. Machiavellian strategists might swing an election here and there, but by failing to address the deeper principles that are changing society itself, they ensure that their causes will flounder and be forgotten. The next Abraham Lincoln, the next Ronald Reagan, will be a leader who speaks to America's heart, soul, and conscience. Let us prepare the way for that leader by speaking from ours.

The Pro-Life Art of War

May 27, 2015

Imagine if same-sex marriage were prohibited nationwide and legal protections for homosexuals were consistently struck down or defeated — while sodomy laws were reimposed and enforced, with billions of dollars in funding from Congress. How effective would you consider the gay rights movement?

If the Second Amendment were reduced to a hollow, meaningless shell, and Americans' guns — even hunting and target rifles — were all confiscated by the feds, what would we think of the gun lobby?

If the United States abandoned Israel to its fate and started sending aid and arms to Hezbollah and Hamas, what would we say of the Israel lobby?

Fix each of those scenarios in mind, and let's ask the question: What should we think of the pro-life movement? The answer is tragically clear: For all the minds and hearts it has changed, it is a comprehensive political failure. American abortion laws are among the laxest on planet Earth — far less protective of unborn life than laws in secular Holland or Scandinavia.

In fifty states abortion is effectively legal for all nine months for any reason, including sex selection, and is funded by the government. (Well-intended restrictions on abortion after "viability" all include "life AND health of the mother" exceptions any doctor could drive a truck through — and laws against partial-birth abortion ban only one method, out of many, of destroying unborn children.)

In 2013, a Republican House of Representatives awarded more than $500 million to Planned Parenthood — which does one-fourth of America's one-million-plus abortions, a figure that has stayed at roughly the same level since *Roe v. Wade,* despite the hundreds of millions of dollars and decades of effort of sincere and hardworking pro-life advocates. It's not that we aren't trying.

Nor is our issue outrageous and unpopular. The defense of unborn life boasts the most passionate advocates, from the widest diversity of backgrounds and from every part of our society. It has a built-in network of support among Christians. Its appeal cuts across ethnic lines. As knowledge of biology and technology for viewing and treating the unborn improves, it's clearer and clearer to everyone, even pro-choicers, that the unborn child is both human and alive. Most have even stopped denying it.

And yet we get nowhere. Had the pro-life movement, to which I have dedicated my life, simply never existed, as it barely exists in Western Europe, would the number of abortions that have taken place in America have been much higher? Would the laws be any worse? It's honestly hard to say.

Such a massive failure on so many fronts cannot be blamed on misguided tactics. Besides, we have tried a wide variety of tactics over the decades, to little effect. The problem must be strategic. Perhaps it's a question of how pro-lifers understand the nature of our very movement, and our concept of politics.

Up till now, most hardworking, sincere pro-life leaders have conceived of our movement as something like the children's crusade — a tragic medieval episode that saw thousands of underage, unarmed Christian peasant boys take passage to the Holy Land, confident that God would honor their sincere trust in Him by granting them victory. Of course, what really happened was that the pilgrims were beaten and robbed along the way, and those whose ships did land were sold into slavery by the Arabs. That's pretty much what has happened to pro-life voters over the years, come to think of it. We can thank our own strategy for that. The good-hearted soldiers in the trenches, who pray outside clinics, volunteer at crisis pregnancy centers, and work to get out the vote, deserve better generals and a more realistic battle plan.

Having pure intentions, and even God on our side, is not enough. (God never promised that it would be, by the way.) If one's going to fight in what is actually a war, one has to be well armed, strategic, and ruthless, and we pro-lifers have been none of these things. Nor have we been ready to learn from other movements that did succeed — such as the pro-gay, pro-gun, and pro-Israel movements that have made profound impacts on American public policy.

What can we learn from those winning movements to resurrect our own? Here are just a few victory lessons we can take away:

1. When we're talking about changing laws and protecting the innocent, we're not just a moral movement. We're a political pressure group, and our job is first, second, and third to move the needle on policies and legislation. Winning hearts and saving souls are essential, but we also have to recognize that if we lose the vote, millions of innocents will continue to die. Americans love winners, and their hearts and minds will follow

those who consistently, visibly win. That's even truer for politicians, who must constantly weigh the risks and rewards of favoring different policies, based on the simple math of money and votes won or lost.

2. Our issue is life and death. So let's act that way. The partisans of same-sex marriage, armor-piercing bullets, and specific, debatable Israeli policies treat every attempt to push back against their cause as if it were a violent assault on innocent children. Those of us actually defending innocent children need to act that way too.
3. We must help our friends, punish our enemies, and avenge ourselves on traitors. And "friends" cannot be defined as "anyone who threw us a rhetorical bone." We shouldn't be "disappointed" when people we supported wilt under pressure and turn against us. We should be enraged and ready to impose retribution. We should work to destroy such a politician's career and send him back to practicing small-town law under an assumed name with an unlisted phone number.
4. Don't forgive petty insults. They're really test balloons, which a politician sends up to see how much he can get away with without being punished. For just the most recent example, see how Scott Walker reacted when one of his campaign aides, Liz Mair, published some Tweets that questioned the wisdom of massive, wasteful ethanol subsidies. When Iowans squawked about that, he fired Mair within twenty-four hours. Yet Walker has hired as his campaign manager the pro-choice Rick Wiley. When pro-lifers complained, he tossed us some scraps by making a pro-life speech. And we all went quiet. What that told Walker was that he could appoint Rudy Giuliani or Kay Bailey Hutchison (Rick Wiley's previous employers) to the U.S. Supreme Court if he wished to — and then he could calm pro-lifers down by … making another speech. We should not calm down or offer Walker support until Rick Wiley has found another job. We should be disciplined and thorough in vetting the key campaign hires of each putative "pro-life" candidate.

Most Americans, if left alone, might not really care about the legal contracts between homosexuals, the regulations on gun shows, or the details of land squabbles between Arabs and Jews. But three highly effective movements have taught them to care, at least when it counts.

We in the pro-life movement are fighting for something that affects every American. Our goal is simple and beautiful: full legal protection for every innocent life from conception till natural death. Like the anti-slavery and civil rights movements before us, we face entrenched selfish interests that have to cloak the evil they foster behind a cloud of double-talk — because even they know that the truth is on our side. And if abortion laws change, the culture will have to change. If we start respecting unborn children, that will also demand respect for women. And not everyone wants that — witness the loutish "pro-choice" college boys who adopted the slogan "Hoes Before Embryos." That really does say it all.

Maybe part of our failure stems from this: The truth that the unborn child deserves protection is so obvious and so important that we've been reluctant to get down in the trenches and fight like a special interest for our cause. We were confident that God would turn people's hearts and set things right. But that isn't how things work. We know from a trustworthy source that it isn't enough to be "innocent as doves." We must also be "wise as serpents." Chris Kyle, the "American Sniper," learned from his father that the world is full of wolves and sheep and that what it needs are sheepdogs. If we want to be the sheepdogs who guard a million unborn American lambs, what we need is to grow some teeth.

If any of the above sounds unreasonable to you and you're a pro-life activist, you need to find a less important cause to be tepid and timid about. If you actually work for a pro-life organization and you aren't willing to take unborn life as seriously as the gun lobby takes ammunition, you had better find another job, where the stakes aren't life and death, in the millions.

A Call for Disunity in the Pro-Life Movement

June 19, 2015

Go to a pro-life event of almost any size, or follow commentary online, and you'll hear it again and again: discussions of why the pro-life movement isn't more effective. And there's good reason to wonder why our cause hasn't yet triumphed.

But one of the causes we hear most often cited is disunity, the fact that there are hundreds of pro-life organizations out there, run by people with different priorities, strategies, and even final goals. Some would agree to politically popular exceptions to abortion laws, while others reject them. Some oppose contraception on moral grounds, while others take no position. There are those who favor returning the abortion issue to states, while others want the Fourteenth Amendment to protect life from conception. Some favor incremental whittling down of the number of abortions through laws banning "partial-birth" procedures or protecting "pain-capable" children. Other groups, it is said, seek all or nothing.

Their tactics differ too. Some lobby on Capitol Hill; others focus on statehouses. Some picket clinics with gruesome signs of butchered children, while others pray outside in silence. Some try to recruit former clinic workers to become pro-life activists, while others ferret out and trumpet the fraud and shoddy medical practice of profit-hungry abortionists like Kermit Gosnell.

Shouldn't we be disappointed that our efforts are so scattershot, our energies so spread out on hundreds of unrelated initiatives? That's what people imply when they complain of our "disunity." They imagine that we would be more successful if the pro-life movement were only more cohesive, obedient to one centrally managed plan. You know, like the old Soviet economy.

Throughout the twentieth century, intellectuals imagined that central planning and "rationalized" control over the economic choices of hundreds of millions of people would cut out the "waste" involved in capitalism. Allowing competition, as Lenin used to argue, just pointlessly squanders resources, with dozens of companies scrambling to put out shoes or vitamins, then fighting it out in the market for customers. Billions spent on advertising and marketing, and leftover, unused products that no one wanted, were the side effects of economic freedom. The market also brought unemployment, fluctuating prices, uncertainty about the future, and massive inequality. None of these things appeal to the kind of tidy-minded abstract thinker who wants life to unfold as serenely and predictably as an equation or a logic problem.

But life is not a logic problem. Life is messy, competitive, and innovative — that is, when you leave people free to make their own decisions. It wasn't the Federal Trade Commission that decided to upgrade the way we watch movies, from clunky VHS tapes to streaming videos accessed on mobile phones. It was the free competition of thousands of engineers and innovators, racing to win the loyalty of consumers.

Economic contrarian and philosophical genius Nassim Nicholas Taleb uses the free market as a prime instance of a fundamental principle he names "antifragility." A fragile system is one that works only under a narrow set of conditions, which random and unpredictable events can easily shatter. Any centrally planned economy or monolithic political movement is fragile — as we learned in 1991, when the Soviet Union collapsed under the weight of both. The opposite of fragility, says Taleb, is not simple robustness, a system that can weather the shocks brought on by new data or unexpected events. No, fragility's real opposite is antifragility, the power to actually benefit, learn from, and grow even stronger as a result of setbacks and reversals.

Nietzsche famously said, "What does not kill me makes me stronger," but you need not be an atheist to believe this. The Church calls the sin of Adam a "happy fault" because it resulted in our redemption. A penitent sinner is often a more persuasive apostle than someone who has gone through life always shielded from temptation. Some of the most powerful pro-life spokesmen are post-abortive women and former clinic workers, even penitent abortionists such as Dr. Bernard Nathanson.

The pro-life movement is wild, woolly, messy, and multifaceted — like the life it intends to protect. Activists freely take on the responsibility to work for a solemn goal, the defense of innocent lives from violence.

But as free human beings with independent wills, they choose a hundred ways to further this goal. Some of them might sound goofy to us, or even repellent. But as long as they stay within our nation's legitimate laws, we should welcome them and accept that diversity is our strength. Working differently, even separately, is not the same as working at cross-purposes. We need unity in charity, in gratitude, and in mutual respect — but the false idea that we need unity in strategy, tactics, and institutions leads to most of the ill will and infighting in pro-life circles. Accepting our need for freedom, diversity, and antifragility would go a long way toward healing the bitterness that sometimes divides our ranks.

You never know if someone else's idea, which seems to you ridiculous, might in fact have a powerful impact on hearts and minds. The pro-life initiatives that have had the greatest impact in recent years were not the fruit of committee meetings in long-standing, well-funded pro-life organizations but of entrepreneurial initiatives that seemed to come out of nowhere.

We don't want to squelch the next idea because it might be the pro-life equivalent of Twitter or the iPhone. More likely, of course, it will turn out to be a dud. Most "great" ideas are clunkers. But innovation goes on because human life itself is antifragile. The pro-life movement must be too.

The Pro-Life Art of the Deal: Can We Negotiate with Trump?

May 8, 2016

One of the things voters find most attractive about Donald Trump is his vaunted success at making deals — at outbargaining, outwitting, and outmaneuvering the people with whom he negotiates, so that he comes out on top. Whatever we think of his business ethics, it's undeniable that this is a man who knows how to come from behind, to put on a front, establish himself as a brand, and turn a truckload of rotting lemons into an Olympic pool full of lemon vodka — with supermodels swimming in it. Millions of Americans have turned to Trump in the hope that he will do the same thing for America. They are tired of all the Elmer Fudds whom the GOP likes to nominate, so they're betting on Bugs Bunny — a fast-talking, scruple-free conniver with a rough-edged New York accent.

As pro-lifers and defenders of religious liberty, and citizens sincerely worried about the direction our nation is taking, we are faced with the question of how to deal with the triumph of Donald Trump in the GOP. Should we stand fast with the #NeverTrump movement, holding to the devastating criticisms that conservatives have made of Trump's ideology, honesty, and character — and be ready to face the consequences if Hillary Clinton wins? Should we jump on the GOP bandwagon as fast as we possibly can, wagging our tails and panting for favors? Is the prospect of Hillary Clinton's winning so terrifying to us that we will take any scrap of hope that the Trump campaign might toss us?

Here's where we can learn something from Donald Trump himself. His most famous book, *The Art of the Deal,* is a kind of devil's dictionary, predicated on the idea that any negotiation is finally zero-sum: there's a winner and a loser, and you want to come out the winner. Now, in actual economics, this isn't really the case. When I pay the bill at a good restaurant, I usually feel that I've gotten my money's worth. So does the restaurant's owner. The free-market economy is based on the fact that human beings best cooperate by freely naming their price and providing goods and services to those who are willing to meet it. In the long run, everybody benefits.

But in Donald Trump's world, things don't work like that. There's a fixed, limited pie of money, privilege, and status, and their distribution depends on who can grab the power. That need not be true of business, but it is part of the essence of politics. When you hold an election, one side really loses, and the winning side wields more power. If we let politics meddle in the economy, this zero-sum logic takes over our productive lives as well. The winners of elections, the donors who grease politicians' palms, can gain a winning edge over their competitors. That's how Trump has always done business, anyway. No wonder he wants the government to reach its fingers even more deeply into business. As a practicing crony capitalist, he was always more of a politician than a businessman, anyway.

And now each of us, as conservative voters, and the movements that speak for our interests, is forced to negotiate with Donald Trump — one way or the other. That doesn't mean we endorse him or even vote for him. Walking away from the table also counts as negotiating. Some deals just aren't worth making. But if our decision to do that is to mean anything at all, we will need to make a public case for it. And that case will be stronger if we are clear about exactly what we are doing.

Or maybe there's a deal out there to be made. Like most of you, I find the prospect of a Trump presidency repugnant. Like most of you, I'm horrified by Hillary and the damage she could do, especially through the courts. Trump is counting on our horror to overwhelm our repugnance.

In other words, he thinks he holds all the cards. He is sitting in Trump Tower, sneering as longtime critics such as Gov. Rick Perry slink over to endorse him, like whipped dogs pleading for mercy. He sees social conservatives such as Mike Huckabee and Ben Carson, who endorsed him early on, as checks that he's already cashed and forgotten about. As for the rest of us, he waits for our terror of Hillary Clinton to wear us down and humble us, so we have to come to the Godfather to beg for some protection. (I recommend watching *The Godfather* and *The Godfather, Part II* as practical guides to this election.)

If we do it, we're fools. Worse than that, we're cowards. Pro-life leaders had some leverage over Trump early on in the campaign, and they managed to squeeze out of him a promise that he'd offer a list of judicial candidates vetted by the Heritage Foundation. That was to reassure us after he talked about appointing his pro-choice sister to the U.S. Supreme Court. So where's the list? Trump forgot about it, and so it seems has everyone else. He won enough Southern primaries, then moved on to the blue-state Northeast, so that promise went down the memory hole. Why on earth should he keep it now? Why offer any carrots when he wields an enormous stick — the prospect of four years of Hillary?

If we wince and cower at the sight of that stick, we have no hope of negotiating. It will mean that we are already bought and sold, at a piddling price. Then we would indeed see, as David Frum wrote in *The Atlantic*, pro-lifers and other social conservatives lose any clout we once had in national elections. If the Israel lobby, or the gun lobby, or any other organized political group behaved the way we do in elections, their causes would be lost. I saw from the inside of GOP politics how quickly, even desperately, pro-life leaders threw away their leverage and signed on with dubious leaders such as John McCain and Mitt Romney. We cannot afford to make that same mistake again.

I wrote once before, in "The Pro-Life Art of War," that we must see our movement as a special interest group, whose sole concern is preserving the unborn by force of law. It's our duty as prudent defenders of the helpless to fight hard on their behalf, and to fight smart. To do that, we must play hardball. And we still do have some leverage.

With Trump's overpowering negatives among so many demographics, he relies more than most GOP candidates on a mighty conservative turnout. He really would be crippled by a potent third-party challenge. He needs to present the front of a mostly unified party. And so, he will respond if we approach him with strength and integrity. Notice how he reacted when House Speaker Paul Ryan wouldn't endorse him: He arranged a face-to-face meeting. How much face time does Chris Christie get with Donald Trump? How much influence will Rick Perry exercise?

Trump must know — because we know — that we're *free to walk away.* If we see that a Trump presidency wouldn't really be markedly better for unborn Americans than a Hillary win but that we would have besmeared ourselves with all Trump's other negatives, then we simply shouldn't support him. We should count the presidential election as already lost — in Indiana — and pour every drop of blood, sweat, and tears into electing conservatives to Congress. We need to make Trump see that we are perfectly willing to do this. It's the only way to deal with a man who prides himself on ruthlessness.

Is the Vatican Smothering Its Pro-Life Office with a Seamless Garment?

October 11, 2017

LifeSiteNews has issued an alarming report on the official Vatican office that sets the tone for Catholic pro-life efforts worldwide. That's the Pontifical Academy for Life, whose staff Pope Francis mostly purged and replaced, in some cases with pro-choice thinkers. It now seems to have embraced the "Seamless Garment" ideology of the late Cardinal Joseph Bernardin.

The pro-life group C-Fam cited a recent statement by the head of the Pontifical Academy for Life: "Being pro-life requires the academy to 're-think the semantic value of the term life,' said the President of the academy, Monsignor Vincenzo Paglia, during a press conference on Monday." He said there were no plans to celebrate the fiftieth anniversary of the papal encyclical *Humanae Vitae* (On Human Life) next year and that the academy was instead opening "new frontiers for debate," mentioning specifically the environment, migration, and arms control.

We have warned about this before at *The Stream.* The Seamless Garment is a leftist utopian wish list with little connection to real Christian morals. Its proponents pretend that open borders, carbon divestment, and gun confiscation are all just like abortion in that:

- The correct Christian position on them is clear and unambiguous.
- The policy implications of how to act on them are obvious and unarguable.
- They are all of equal moral importance.

None of these statements is true. Not even close. The Seamless Garment is a handy political dodge for pro-choice liberals who wanted to keep on collecting Catholic votes. It falsifies Christian social teaching. It dissolves the rights of unborn children like a pinch of salt in an Olympic swimming pool of dubious progressive "reforms." They share just one thing in common: more power for the government.

Let's say we're just kidding around on the abortion issue, and we really don't care what happens to unborn children. Then that's just fine. A nihilist friend in college once quipped, "They're only babies."

But what if we were serious? What if we really thought that killing almost a million American children a year for our sexual convenience was morally . . . *problematic*? That it was just as bad as transphobic children's books? Maybe worse than white ladies making tacos?

In that case, we wouldn't cover up the death of the innocent with a moral fog machine. We would focus on it as seriously as the gun lobby and the pro-Israel lobby do on their (just) causes.

We would act like . . . William Wilberforce.

Eric Metaxas tells the story better than we can. In his powerful book *Amazing Grace*, he describes how Wilberforce and a coalition of like-minded Christian reformers changed Britain. They confronted a thoroughly rotted social elite, a fatally compromised Christian church. "Respectable" gentlemen exploited poor women as prostitutes, and society just winked. Corrupt politicians took payoffs to give special privileges from the government to cronies in private business. Anglican priests and bishops preached not the gospel but blasé Enlightenment platitudes. Some even seemed to be Deists, preaching that God is a bored absentee landlord.

But worse than all these evils was one. It stood out above all the others. Great Britain was enriching itself through the slave trade. The organized kidnapping, beating, rape, and forced labor of millions of Africans fed the country's lucrative colonies in the Caribbean. You know those wigged and powdered lords and ladies who nattered about "the rights of man" in glittering parlors? They paid for their costumed balls with blood money. Hundreds of thousands of Englishmen relied on income from sugar plantations in Jamaica and Barbados. Powerful members of Parliament defended the slave trade as vital to their constituents.

Yes, Wilberforce did lead a broad-based movement for the "reform of manners." That didn't center on etiquette. It was a cultural call for the nominal Christians of Britain to live like real Christians. To care for the poor. To be faithful to their marriages. Even to pay their workers fairly. And as Metaxas documents, that movement made a vast difference. It soon became shameful to mistreat your tenants and workers. Mass revival movements brought the gospel to rural areas where Celtic paganism still lingered. Methodist chapels helped young men stay sober and young women stay out of brothels. While France lurched from revolution to revolution, Britain pursued peaceful reforms.

But first, Wilberforce confronted the slave trade. He knew that it was different. There were no shades of gray on the question. He lived to see not just the slave trade but slavery itself outlawed in the British Empire. Britain went from being one of the main exporters of slaves from Africa to the global police force suppressing the Arab slave trade with cannons and soldiers.

How did he manage that? He wielded the pivotal virtue of prudence. Instead of grandstanding to the public and issuing utopian manifestos about all social evils, he focused his efforts on the greatest one. He separated his crusade against the slave trade from his broader Christian agenda. His campaign focused narrowly on the evils of slavery, the cruelties of plantations, and the deaths in the Middle Passage from Africa. He led a boycott of sugar, which fed the slave trade's profits. He took Englishmen on tours of former slave ships and sponsored testimonies by ransomed slaves.

Wilberforce was willing to compromise. He knew that it was a nonstarter to demand that all the slaves in Britain's colonies be liberated immediately, that their "owners" be stripped of incomes that many counted on for their livelihoods. His movement worked doggedly to make the right political bargains to ease out slavery throughout the British Empire. In 1833, the British government spent *40 percent of the nation's wealth* in payments to slave owners. That set free every slave on British soil, without a civil war such as the United States would face.

What if Wilberforce had believed in the Seamless Garment? What would he have done? For that, we can look to Cardinal Blase Cupich in Cardinal Bernardin's old Archdiocese of Chicago. He greeted the news that Planned Parenthood was selling baby parts for profit ... *seamlessly*. He wrote a column that claimed that Planned Parenthood's organ trafficking was no worse than cuts to Obamacare. Or "lax" gun laws. Or attempts to deport illegal immigrants. Or the execution of murderers.

So if Wilberforce were Seamless, he would have buried his efforts against the slave trade in a flurry of other initiatives. He would have demanded that Britain dissolve its colonial empire, establish minimum-wage laws, end child labor, grant equal rights to women, and open all its borders to unlimited immigration. If any politician didn't favor all that, he'd have refused to work with the person. Because the "anti-slavery" movement needed to address every single other issue of any possible importance. Because he wasn't that serious about ending slavery in the first place.

But, thanks be to God, Wilberforce wasn't Seamless.

What Pro-Lifers Can and CAN'T Learn from the Civil Rights Movement

January 15, 2018

Today we mark the legacy of Martin Luther King Jr. He's not just some ethnic hero but a true American one. He is even, in critical ways, a conservative paragon. We'll lay out why and draw out what the pro-life movement can — and cannot — learn from King's success.

King a "conservative"? It seems absurd at first. King sparked massive change in American life. He radically unsettled the existing social order. He rejected calls for "prudence" and "gradual change." He pointed to abstract principles to condemn concrete arrangements that had seemed to "work," after a fashion, for one hundred years since the Civil War.

His civil rights movement, however just its cause, did create a template for a long list of less worthy jihads, on behalf of disgruntled feminists, abortion mongers, and same-sex libertines. On that point, Southern conservatives proved sadly correct: overturning the racial hierarchy in America let a lot of other genies out of the bottle. Some of those spirits (e.g., abortion) are afflicting the black community worse than segregation ever did.

No surprise that when King was organizing marches and sit-ins, most of the existing conservative movement opposed him. William F. Buckley and most of the writers at the *National Review* were among them. But Buckley and *NR* came around, as did most Americans — and here's why.

More than almost any other political leader since Lincoln, King sought to polish the Golden Egg of liberty and equal opportunity, without doing violence to the Goose — that is, America as an orderly nation of laws. Both his arguments and his tactics bear that out.

Arguing for civil rights, King did not appeal to the Marxist dialectic that so many of his allies had accepted. Nor did he latch onto the bastardized and racist pseudo-Islam that Malcolm X was peddling. No, King cited St. Thomas Aquinas and pointed to "natural law," which can overrule any legislation a nation passes — be it the Nuremberg Laws in Germany or segregation in America. King pointed to the words of our nation's Founders and called them a "promissory note" to America's black citizens. And there really was no rational counter-argument to all that. He left his enemies weaponless, except for fire hoses and truncheons.

Such thuggish means backfired on white supremacists and turned the nation against them. But that need not have happened. The whole civil rights movement could have gone sidewise and sparked mass civil conflict. That happened in Northern Ireland in the early 1970s, and it could well have happened here. There were three key factors that made the difference.

King knew that one of the key psychological factors that had undergirded white supremacist laws since the days of slavery was fear of mass black violence. For centuries, some states had lived in the uneasy knowledge that in their midst were millions of strong, angry black men with grievances. The slave revolt in Haiti had terrified U.S. slaveholders. Nat Turner's rebellion led states to outlaw manumission and crack down on preachers who were teaching slaves how to read the Bible. So King insisted that every one of his activists who would violate unjust laws would not resist any violence. Not by police and not by white vigilantes. Men underwent hours of training, taking blows and abuse from civil rights organizers, to learn how not to fight back.

This tactic was both principled and brilliant. But there was no guarantee that it would work. There's nothing magical about nonviolence. It doesn't work in every situation. Gandhi famously made a fool of himself when he counseled Europe's Jews to apply his nonviolent methods against the Nazis. Such tactics can prevail only if two other factors stand in place.

In the mid-twentieth century, Britain was still largely Christian. English culture treasured a deep-seated sense of fair play and justice. Gandhi knew that when he confronted its colonial policies. His tactics would not have prevailed against the Germans. Hitler once offered Britain the unsolicited advice that it should "Hang Gandhi" and then every week hang more of his supporters until the Indian independence movement collapsed. No English government could have faced its voters if it had used tactics like that. That was true for one final reason. This factor was key to the success of both the Indian national struggle and the civil rights movement. Most of America was still Christian in some sense in the early 1960s as well.

Atrocities committed by British commanders were sure to be reported in the British national press. That gave the British public the chance to be outraged and demand a change of course. In the United States, local Southern papers might have been committed to segregation. But national papers opposed it, and so did national TV and radio networks. They would cover the violence that segregationists and police used against nonviolent demonstrators. And that would spark a moral backlash across the country.

With all these pieces in place, the moral violence of segregation would be seen in the public mind for what it was — because it was backed by physical violence. The bogeyman of black men as dangerous potential predators faded away, as dignified young black men in coats and ties patiently suffered abuse, without fighting back. Instead of new Nat Turners, they seemed like images of Christ. And a still-Christian nation began to be ashamed of itself.

What happens when not all of these crucial pieces are in place? Nonviolent witness can be blunted, or silenced. In the 1980s, thousands of courageous pro-lifers across the country tried, via Operation Rescue, to apply King's tactics to defending unborn children. They saved some babies, but as a national movement, they failed.

Pro-lifers held sit-ins in abortion mills. They went limp when the police arrested them. They chained themselves to the front doors of Planned Parenthood clinics in the ghetto and handed out leaflets about that group's racist heritage. When police used violent tactics against old women and teenagers, pro-lifers didn't resist. We know women whom burly cops subjected to "pain compliance" holds. The cops dislocated fourteen-year-old girls' wrists with nunchucks. In West Hartford, Connecticut, and Los Angeles, California, the violence was especially bad — and it was all caught on videotape.

But you would have to watch it at some pro-lifer's house on a VCR because none of that footage was aired. The media were lockstep pro-choice, just as white Southern newspapers had been rabidly segregationist. There were no outside media who could pick up the story. So an epidemic of violence, and punitive jail sentences, against pro-life nonviolent demonstrators fell into the memory hole. The movement failed.

Today, pro-lifers make extensive use of alternative, social media. The pro-life stings of James O'Keefe, Lila Rose, David Daleiden, and Sandra Merritt have been seen by millions of people. Students for Life of America, Movie to Movement, and the Susan B. Anthony List have leveraged social media to become enormous, effective movements.

But now these activists face open censorship by those social media platforms. Billion-dollar media corporations once again, as in the 1980s, could shut down a mass nonviolent movement for human rights. If these companies get away with this abuse of power, we face the same national shame we would have deserved if Martin Luther King had died, obscure, in some Alabama prison.

She Knew What to Say to Post-Abortive Women: Vicki Thorn, Rest in Peace

April 29, 2022

Imagine if in Israel people basically pretended that the Holocaust never happened. Not that they denied it, as some neo-Nazis do. Imagine instead that a keen awareness of how many people had suffered personally, or lost close family members, made the topic taboo. Imagine no programs to support the survivors, no classes in school, no movies or TV shows ever touching the subject. All with the goal of sparing people's feelings, avoiding the scabs of old traumas.

That's where America stands when it comes to abortion. We pretend that we're not a country that sacrifices almost a million children per year to the Sexual Revolution, a country that lost some 63.7 million people to this tragedy since 1973.

Last week, we lost a prophet, a woman who wouldn't accept this desperate denial. Instead, she investigated it, plunged into the dark where few researchers or academics even wanted to go. I'm speaking of my longtime friend Vicki Thorn, founder of Project Rachel. That's a Christian ministry, led by Catholics, aimed at helping abortion survivors find forgiveness and healing.

Her ministry has touched many thousands of women who were forced, pressured, misled, or (let's just admit it) successfully tempted to have abortions. Some of the most powerful pro-life leaders in America emerged from those ranks.

For fifty years, our nation's highest court, and all its laws, have been complicit in a lie — in the pretense that "science" can't tell when human life begins. It's some murky metaphysical question, or a religious article of faith, of the kind our Constitution forbids the people to decide. No surprise, then, that young women abandoned or threatened by men lurched into the darkness our Establishment had willfully cast, to obscure the obvious biological truth.

I became a pro-life activist by a very similar route. My high school girlfriend was forced by her father to abort the (third trimester) baby we both loved and wanted. When it happened, I was a naive seventeen-year-old, naive enough not to realize that such a horror was perfectly legal, that unborn babies had less legal protection than slaves did in 1860.

I was unclear about a lot of things at the beginning. In 1999, I'd been in the movement for ten years, and I was delivering a talk to a youth group at St. Philomena Church in Hawaii. I focused on the biological facts, keeping things dry. "This is a sperm, and this is an egg, and this is the moment of conception, yadda yadda." I realized that these seventh and eighth graders were bored, eager to leave.

Except for one girl. As I showed the slides of fetal development, she'd lean a little more forward with each slide. When the slide of the twenty-week-old baby in the womb appeared, her arms moved from her side to across her belly. She hugged herself and grimaced with pain, as tears formed in her eyes and slowly slid down her face.

I pretended not to notice as she wiped them dry. I was struck by the inescapable truth: this eighth-grade girl in Catholic school had already had an abortion.

And believe it or not, that shocked me. For a decade, I'd been giving talks and organizing protests, making phone calls and writing articles. Somehow, in all that time, it never occurred to me that I was regularly meeting people who'd experienced abortion. I saw it in the abstract, as a huge and monstrous evil, but not up close as a daily burden, memory, and curse — even though I'd suffered the effects of abortion myself. So that day, in that Hawaii classroom, I shared my own abortion story in public for the very first time. Painful as it is each time I do it, I've been sharing it ever since.

Vicki Thorn heard about my story and reached out to me. She told me that Project Rachel helped women heal from the trauma of abortion and ask for God's forgiveness. I wasn't yet Christian, or even a theist. But it sounded like a noble cause, I said. That wasn't what she wanted to hear. Vicki wanted to know if I'd like to attend a retreat for post-abortive men. She said, "I can help heal you and free you from your anger and rage."

I thanked her but declined. I needed that anger to propel me through all the daily hard work I had to do. As I told Vicki, "Men heal by bearing their claws, not licking their wounds."

But Vicki and I became close friends, constantly texting and talking. As it turned out, I would need her help, over and over again because my public witness for life kept opening old wounds in people I'd just met. Some would melt down in front of me, sharing with me the most painful things in their lives. I wouldn't know what to say. So I'd often call Vicki and put her on the phone with them. She talked to them.

Vicki knew what to say at two in the morning to the young woman who'd been chatting with me at a Milwaukee bar, until she saw my "Precious Feet" pro-life pin and started asking questions. I told her my story, of losing a child in high school. Her face went white, and she hugged me and started to weep uncontrollably. When she could finally talk, all she could say was, "Where were you two weeks ago?" over and over.

Vicki knew how to talk to the Navy Seal who'd confessed to me that he'd forced his wife to abort their child. This man who protected America hadn't defended his very own child.

And it was Vicki whom I put on the phone when I was hanging out with a wildly successful recording artist who'd admitted to me he was pressuring his girlfriend to abort. Vicki walked him through all the consequences it would have for the woman, for him, and for their relationship, until he relented and chose life.

I will miss talking to Vicki, and knowing that she's just a lifesaving, Christ-loving phone call away. May she rest in peace and enjoy her rich reward.

Once the Law Protects Unborn Kids, Should We Seek Legal Penalties for Women Who Abort Them?

May 11, 2022

Even Bill Maher is now realizing the truth: that America offers less protection to unborn children than all but three other countries on earth. Two of them (China and North Korea) run concentration camps. The other is brain-addled Canada, where peaceful vaccine protestors get trampled by mounted police.

If *Roe v. Wade* collapses like the cheap tent that it is, many American states will move to correct this injustice. They will impose legal penalties on doctors who kill kids for money. Some states will impose comprehensive, consistent protections for unborn children from conception forward. Others will offer limited protection, for kids who make it alive till the tenth or the fifteenth week. Still others will keep the uterus a free-fire zone and allow post-birth euthanasia for women who really want it.

States such as New York will allow infanticide, on the theory that a woman's sovereignty over her body is absolute. (*Except when we're talking about vaccines, but that's different, because of COVID. So shut up. Do you want to be a threat to public health, you anti-vax, QAnon redneck?* Ahem.)

Maternal sovereignty even reaches its deadly tentacles outside the womb. A woman has the right to have sex at will and not become a mother — period. If a child survives an abortion attempt, the mom's right *not to have a child knocking around the world to make her feel guilty* trumps the right to live of a breathing, crying baby. Mom's *ownership right* trumps everything. That's the claim of the Marquis de Sade, whose arguments got mainstreamed into Second Wave Feminism by Simone de Beauvoir and then gussied up as legal arguments by the likes of Ruth Bader Ginsburg. Female equality in society requires that women have the right to kill. This is the position of virtually every Democrat in Congress.

By any standard imaginable, this position is extreme. But that grants it certain advantages — principally, consistency. There are no "gotcha" moments in an argument with somebody who believes this. A Marquis de Sade–style pro-choicer like Nancy Pelosi simply claims that the child has no rights, period, until ... the mother grants them to him. There's no reason in principle why it couldn't extend much longer after birth. And indeed, celebrated ethicists such as Princeton's Peter Singer have proposed that the infanticide window be much longer, measured in months. That's logical consistency for you: a child, even a newborn, is chattel, with fewer rights than black slaves before 1860 or house pets, which are covered by animal cruelty laws in fifty states.

By contrast, the position most of us pro-lifers take seems somewhat inconsistent and logically unsatisfying. We want to see legal penalties for doctors, nurses, and others who perform abortions after the legal limit. (In some states, that will rightly be conception.) But we loudly deny claims by pro-choicers that we would punish women who sought such abortions.

And that seems inconsistent, even incoherent. A tiny fringe of pro-lifers have responded to this perception by imitating their enemies. If pro-choicers want to insist that an unborn baby is nothing but medical waste, we will say the opposite. We'll claim that a child in the womb is legally indistinguishable from a stranger on the street. A woman who kills her child should suffer the same penalties she would if she shot a random pedestrian. Or hired a hit man (abortionist) to commit the murder for her.

This is consistent, in the same inhuman way that de Sade's position is. Like the pro-choice position, it pretends that only one human being's claims are important in pregnancy — it simply picks the child, instead of the mother.

No laws in the United States before *Roe v. Wade* adopted this stance. Nor did laws in the nineteenth century, when medical advances made clear that life begins at conception and every U.S. state outlawed abortion. Nor did the Common Law of England, before or after the Reformation, equate abortion with simple murder and treat the guilty mother accordingly.

Pro-choice de Sade disciples pretend that this extreme position, and its logical legal outcome of prison sentences for women, is the necessary implication of protecting unborn children. They use this outrageous claim to maintain their own North Korean status quo of abortion up through birth (and in some states, after). A few pro-lifers impatient with moral complexity bang the table and agree with them — thereby giving political aid and comfort to the enemy.

Most pro-lifers have resisted this temptation, but they have done so mostly by fudging. We recognize the fact that most women who seek abortions are in some sense victims — then exaggerate it, for political purposes. We essentially pretend that all women who abort their children are hapless thirteen-year-olds who were impregnated by adults and were driven to the clinic sobbing in tears and shoved through its halls like a calf for the slaughter.

Now, make no mistake: Such horrors happen. One of us watched helplessly on Park Avenue in New York in 1992 as a sobbing woman was carried into an abortion clinic by her baby's daddy and his friend, her feet never touching the ground. The police just looked on, stoically. Many abortions in America are the fruit of coercion, desperation, and abandonment. That's a truth we must not stop telling.

But it's not the whole truth. It will happen in some pro-life states that grown, rational women will seek out illegal abortions — either surgical or chemical — for calculated reasons in the cold light of day. Indeed, groups like Planned Parenthood will find some activists and put them up to this, to produce test cases for court.

Should such women who break the law and destroy their unborn children be entirely free of consequences? To say yes might seem to undermine the entire pro-life claim, that babies have legal rights. Or else it might infantilize all women, treating half our species like helpless victims, distressed damsels without any moral agency.

But establishing legal penalties for women brings its own moral problems. It threatens the huge majority of genuinely victimized post-abortive women with punishment they don't deserve. And, of course, it's political suicide, a stance that, if insisted on, would ensure legal infanticide in fifty states forever.

Eight years ago, John Zmirak and I briefly addressed this complex question. We responded to pro-choice, de Sade–party feminist Katha Pollitt, who posed what she believed were unanswerable questions to pro-lifers. Here's how she phrased the dilemma:

> If zygotes are people, abortion is infanticide, a very serious crime.... Why should women who hire a fetal hit man get a pass?

And here's how we answered:

> For the same reasons that a doctor who attempted to assist with suicide ought to be imprisoned — instead of his unfortunate patient. Destroying

one's child is so self-destructive and unnatural that it ought to be treated more like a suicide than a murder attempt. Attempts to portray abortion as a minor surgical procedure or a lifestyle accessory have foundered on the agony of women who know the truth, from bitter experience. We wish to protect women and their children from the ultimate medical malpractice.

We think this answer still holds up and would like to unpack it a little. Along with the pre-*Roe* lawmakers all through American history and the Common Law before that, we recognize that pregnancy is a unique human situation. No other condition is comparable, not even conjoined twins. To preserve another's right to life, a mother must surrender large areas of her bodily integrity, for a long period of time. No, that doesn't give her the right to kill. But it does change how we rightly, sanely, ought to treat women who do.

We don't want to criminally prosecute women who illegally abort. Nor do we want to shrug and wink, as if women were all hapless victims or abortion weren't really a monstrous crime, as it is.

The closest our imperfect, merely human legal system can come to accommodating the absolutely special case of pregnancy is to acknowledge the unique and intimate link between a pregnant woman and her child. *We ought to treat women who illegally abort the way we treat failed suicides.*

No, that doesn't perfectly answer every moral claim and cover every case. But it comes the closest to untangling this moral Gordian knot.

Women won't go to prison. But they will face the real deterrent of a short but mandatory psychiatric custody and mandated counseling. God willing, that will prove helpful to women after the devastating destruction that is abortion. By treating abortion as legally equivalent to attempted suicide, it will recognize and honor the life of the child.

It's the best we can do in this fallen world. And it's not a political suicide pill. For those of us eager to grant increasing protection to unborn children, that is crucial.

Dancing on *Roe v. Wade*'s Grave

June 24, 2022

Ding dong, the witch is dead. Every friend of innocent life ought to be dancing a merry jig on the unhallowed earth where *Roe v. Wade* is buried. No longer does our nation's highest court pretend that the Marquis de Sade was one of our Founders. Nor that the Constitution implies that a baby is no more important than a fingernail or feces — a bodily product that may be dumped, burned, or cut up and cannibalized for parts. Nor that killing a baby is a critical part of basic "American liberty." A half century since the highest court used raw judicial power to steal from Americans their right to vote on this issue, that same court has repented.

David has taken Goliath down, Luke blown up the Death Star. A grassroots movement of housewives, blue-collar churchgoers, devoted clergy and passionate young people fought uphill for fifty years against America's elites, its law schools, its media, and most of its institutions. And it has prevailed.

Let's savor the win.

No, we won't pretend that abortion has ended in America. We agree with pro-life legal activist Josh Hammer that the struggle hasn't ended but has merely begun. Hammer is right to point out that unborn children deserve protection nationally, in each of the fifty states. And that struggle starts tomorrow.

If you think of this fight against genocide in terms of World War II, consider this moment Dunkirk. We just managed at last to rescue our forces from the Nazis. Now comes the Blitz.

Expect blue states to set up government-funded abortionists in airports. Wait for corporations like Disney to threaten states like Florida that they'll relocate if pro-life laws pass — that they'll pour the money you spend with them into lobbying Congress to press upon Mississippi and Oklahoma the same laws as California's.

Let them try. God is on our side, as is the very nature He created. For the past fifty years, the whole country has been equally blighted by abortion. The family has been undermined, young girls exploited with impunity, and minority communities disproportionately culled — as racist groups such as Planned Parenthood clustered their clinics in non-white neighborhoods. Since the whole nation was cursed, there was no chance for comparison. Now that has changed.

In dozens of states, old pro-life, pre-*Roe* laws will click back into force. In a dozen others, we'll see them pass. And then all Americans will be able to watch a side-by-side comparison of life in pro-life states versus anti-life ones. Like two patches of lawn, one fertilized and the other sprayed with weed killer, the differences will be obvious.

Pro-choicers know this on some visceral level, which is why they're panicking. They know the jig is up. While blue states race to the bottom, promoting abortion up through and even after birth, red states will calmly enact protective laws for unborn lives. No, women won't be imprisoned. No, birth control pills won't be outlawed. The Republic of Gilead in *The Handmaid's Tale* — a trashy propaganda novel — will nowhere arise on our continent.

We'll tell you what will happen, though. The pro-abort states will gradually get older, poorer, more violent, and less free. Believing that freedom begins and ends at the bedroom door, they will go on choosing top-down, socialist answers to basic economics — which will go on hurting the poor. Soft-on-crime policies and intrusive social programs will remain mere Band-Aids on gaping wounds caused by the natural side effects of the Sexual Revolution. High percentages of non-white kids will continue to be aborted. Poor communities will remain stuck in the glue trap of government dependence. By doubling down on the socially destructive legacy of the 1970s, blue cities will keep on going the way of Baltimore.

Meanwhile, pro-life red states will become younger, richer, and freer. Minority communities won't be devastated by 60 percent abortion rates, at clinics sited to target them. Most black babies will get to be born alive. But without the deadly backstop of an "easy," nearby abortion, more young girls will make wiser choices about having sex while they're still teenagers. We'll see the rate of unwed motherhood flatten, then decline — as young men feel the goad to marry girls if they really want them. A rebirth of marriage and fatherhood is the unavoidable outcome — restoring to the poor the one thing they need more than any handout: intact families to grow up in.

Meanwhile, the saner, smaller-government policies on other issues in red states will help small businesses to grow and offer better jobs to a socially healthier workforce. Citizens will enjoy their rights of self-defense and of free speech and religion and will suffer less from crime.

The difference between the blue states and the red states will quickly become as clear as the difference between East and West Germany was by the 1960s, when the Soviets had to build the Berlin Wall to keep citizens in.

And that's when we will have the political capital to act on national pro-life legislation — at the moment when a critical mass of citizens sees the poisonous fruits of the pro-choice lie and all the other reckless, destructive policies of the Left.

At that point, once unborn children have national legal protection, the pro-life movement won't vanish. Instead, it will be free to expand its focus to other life issues. That's when we can actually talk about a "Seamless Garment."

The pro-life movement, triumphant, ought to focus its energy on decoupling our economy from its dependence on China. That evil regime uses slave labor, forced abortion, and murderous organ harvesting to tyrannize a billion souls. We shouldn't be in business with it.

A final, crucial issue pro-lifers ought to champion: resisting the War Party's domination of U.S. foreign policy. Right now, a bipartisan coalition of reckless interventionists are pouring U.S. billions into escalating the war in Ukraine. They're killing any chance at a negotiated settlement and risking nuclear war, just to weaken a U.S. rival, Russia. These same empire builders steered the United States into useless interventions in Yugoslavia, Iraq, Afghanistan, and Libya, costing hundreds of thousands of innocent civilian lives.

We must throw the warmongers out of power and seek peace in the world that mirrors the peace in the womb.

The Pro-Life Movement Is an Unstoppable Juggernaut of the Young

January 18, 2023

This year I'm attending the National March for Life in Washington, D.C., in a different spirit than in previous years — because the battle has changed. The *Dobbs* decision overturning *Roe v. Wade* was a massive achievement, the fruit of fifty years of dogged, thankless toil.

Like the rescue of the British Army at Dunkirk, *Dobbs* wasn't the beginning of the end. But it was the end of the beginning. We already see strong protections for unborn life in several states, which the Biden administration seeks to undermine by slipping chemical abortion pills across the counter at CVS and Walgreens. Stuka bombers and U-boats still menace us from Berlin.

We need to understand the history of our movement, to thank its lonely pioneers and learn from their achievements — and then to welcome its newest recruits, who will carry the cause to triumph.

The first generation of the pro-life movement were Good Samaritans who saw an innocent traveler robbed and left for dead on the road by black-clad assailants. Without professional training or resources, they dropped to their knees on the pavement. They ripped the sleeves off their shirts to make a tourniquet. These pro-lifers weren't political activists by trade. They were cops, wives of firemen, and little old ladies carrying rosaries and Bibles. On shoestring budgets, with little support from churches, they founded things such as the New York State Right to Life Party and the National March for Life.

We ought to remember the names of the people who created the largest reform movement in our nation's history. Just a few include Ellen McCormack, who ran for the Democratic Party nomination for president on a pro-life platform. And Nellie Gray, founder of the March for Life. And Dr. Mildred Jefferson, the first black woman to graduate from Harvard Medical School, an eloquent pro-life spokeswoman. And Fr. Paul Marx, a dogged missionary on behalf of a Culture of Life. And Joe Scheidler, who spent decades on sidewalks with a bullhorn outside abortion mills, undaunted in his fedora. These are giants, whose shoulders we stand on.

I am most familiar with the second generation of the pro-life movement because I was part of it. We arrived on the crime scene like paramedics, learning what we could from the Good Samaritans who were still kneeling on the sidewalk. We tried a variety of strategies, from Operation Rescue, pioneered by the hero Joan Andrews, to pro-life amendments championed in Congress by men like Rep. Chris Smith. We produced the first instructional videos and held the first pro-life conferences.

After I lost a daughter to a forced abortion, I devoted my own life to honoring hers by protecting other unborn children like her. Inspired by an open letter from the prophetic Paul Weyrich about the urgency of changing the culture, I decided to skip law school. Instead, I studied political science, communications theory, and rhetoric — to learn how to persuade my fellow citizens to hold innocent life as sacred. Part of that effort included being the executive producer of the movie *Bella*. Countless other pro-life films helped inspire and convert people: The truth is on our side, so beauty should be too.

The third generation of the pro-life movement were the skilled doctors in the trauma ward, who welcomed the patient and struggled to stabilize his vital signs. These people had come of age in pro-life activism, often thanks to parents who'd carefully formed them in the art of cultural resistance. Kristan Hawkins built Students for Life of America into the largest and most effective student group of any kind in the country.

Mark Crutcher of Life Dynamics pioneered journalistic tactics that Lila Rose used to expose Planned Parenthood. David Daleiden and James O'Keefe took such exposés to a whole new level and put the sordid abortion industry permanently on the defensive. Abby Johnson went from working inside a Planned Parenthood to founding a group convincing abortion employees to quit.

Now we welcome the fourth generation of pro-life apostles, the specialists and surgeons who will deliver the patient from danger. They are too numerous to count and too diverse to describe. They come from every social and religious group and ethnic background, and even from every sector of today's political spectrum. This year at the March for Life, I will rub shoulders with students who grew up attending the Traditional Latin Mass, and tattooed LGBT pro-lifers, along with everyone in between. Savvy new voices like Autumn Higashi are echoing across social media and cannot be silenced.

The abortion industry doesn't know how to answer people like Terrisa Bukovinac, founder of Progressive Anti-Abortion Uprising, who uses liberal and animal rights arguments to shred pro-choice excuses. Or Ayala, who was raped from the age of eleven and got pregnant at fifteen. She chose to keep her child and is now a passionate pro-life advocate. Or Treneé McGee, a progressive, black, pro-life Democrat legislator in deep-blue Connecticut. Or Destiny Herndon-De La Rosa and her New Wave Feminists.

This generation is clever, creative, and absolutely relentless. They are giants, standing on the shoulders of the giants who came before them. By the time these people are finished, innocent unborn life will be protected from conception on every square inch of U.S. soil, from Maine to Maui.

To make that victory possible, we must learn the real lessons of fifty years of struggle. What did we learn in that time? That in this case, our diversity really is our strength. The power of the pro-life movement is in its sheer multiplicity, in the thousands of flowers that bloom across the country, growing from awakened consciences. There is no single formula, list of arguments, or set of "official" tactics. This is a movement first of the heart, which realizes the inviolable dignity of the human person at his most vulnerable — in his mother's womb. And you can't dictate that in a memo.

We also need to do one other, crucial thing. Before *Dobbs*, the pro-life struggle was focused on Washington, D.C., on urging our highest court to correct a historic lie. Now the front has shifted to each of the fifty states. We need to update, support, and massively get behind the pro-life organizations in each of our states — especially blue states. These are the groups that fight now in the trenches to save thousands of lives. They're also the groups getting targeted by Jane's Revenge and Biden's Department of Justice.

The war is inside the states. And that's why I think this will be my last year at the National March for Life in D.C. I think in future years I will be attending local marches at the capitals of blue states. But this one last time I wanted to meet with those still standing from the first three generations of the pro-life movement and tell them what an honor and a privilege it has been to spend my life alongside them.

We Shall Go On to the End of the Long March for Life

January 19, 2024

Fans of history will remember the following crucial turning points in world-changing conflicts:

- When George Washington defeated the Hessians at Trenton in 1776, and the Patriots declared victory and then went home to their farms.
- When Abraham Lincoln issued the Emancipation Proclamation in 1863, so the Union decided the war was finally over.
- When the British ferried home their battered, beaten troops from Dunkirk in 1940 and promptly laid down their arms.

Wait, that isn't what you learned in school? Seriously? Perhaps you learned instead that the authors of these achievements realized their wars were far from over. Maybe (if your teacher was really good) you learned that these partial victories made life even harder for a while because they outraged the enemy and stiffened their resistance. If so, then you'd know about later, bitter events such as the Patriots' winter at Valley Forge, the brutal Battle of Gettysburg, and the blood-soaked Normandy landing.

The Patriots weren't fighting for control over northern New Jersey but for full independence for all thirteen American colonies. The Union wasn't fighting to declare slavery null and void in the states it hadn't yet conquered but to prevent Southern independence — and after this declaration, to obliterate slavery nationwide. And the British weren't fighting Hitler just to get their Expeditionary Force back home alive but to stop the German conquest of Europe.

Likewise, we in the pro-life movement after 1973 were in no way fighting merely to expunge a few intellectually disgraceful Supreme Court decisions, as if to vindicate the honor of the U.S. legal system. This last point might not be obvious to some conservative legal types who, for decades, have seemed more outraged at *Roe v. Wade*'s faulty logic and dishonest scholarship than the deaths of some one million preborn Americans every single year.

As defenders of the innocent, we need to remember how bad the impact of those decisions was: It was as complete and appalling a catastrophe as the fall of France in 1940. Suddenly, abortion was de facto legal for all nine months of pregnancy for any reason in each of the fifty states. The preborn were as besieged and abandoned as Churchill's United Kingdom was in 1940. Overturning *Roe* was a historic achievement, but only in the same way that Dunkirk was. As Winston Churchill reminded the desperately relieved British public who welcomed home their soldiers: "Wars are not won by evacuations."

Overturning *Roe* was, of course, the right thing to do. But we must be clear-eyed and honest about what it accomplished: It slowed down and frustrated our powerful, relentless enemies and pulled us back from the brink of surrender. That's a lot, but that is all.

And what came next was ugly: the Blitz, the Battle of Britain, the grinding submarine war that saw thousands of Britons drown in the icy North Atlantic. The enemy didn't take its failure at Normandy as a signal to negotiate in good faith, or as some demoralizing defeat that sapped its strength. Instead, they were emboldened to new and fanatical efforts, like sharks that taste blood in the water but can't quite reach their victims.

And that's how the pro-choice movement reacted to the fall of its phony Supreme Court decisions. We saw massive spending and dazzlingly dishonest ad campaigns bamboozle the voters of Ohio to amend their state constitution, enshrining abortion through birth. We witnessed politicians whom we had trusted suddenly lose their nerve. How else to describe Donald Trump dubbing as "extreme" the logical and nationally popular "heartbeat" bill Ron DeSantis signed in Florida? Yes, that's right, I said "popular," because nationwide there's strong support for choosing that seemingly logical starting point for protecting human life.

Why doesn't Donald Trump know this? Probably because he's listening to advisers. The last time he did that, he appointed people like Gen. Milley, Anthony Fauci, Christopher Wray, Bill Barr, and Nikki Haley — who backstabbed not just Trump but all his voters and our country.

We know that Winston Churchill's colleagues, almost the whole of his cabinet, pressured him to negotiate with a seemingly unbeatable Adolf Hitler. It was the "rational," "prudent," "sensible" thing to do. Committing the nation instead to years of "blood and sweat, toil and tears" was indeed extreme. It was also the only hope.

There are two powerful movies that depict the bleak world Churchill faced: *Darkest Hour* and *Dunkirk*. Watching them would remind pro-life Americans where we stand on the wartime timeline. The Nazis are still at the gates. The Luftwaffe is still flying. And we still will never surrender.

Chapter 2

PEACE

International Terrorists Target Civilians

Date unknown

An international terrorist organization is running amuck. These vicious terrorists have the ability to destabilize any nation and the will to attack any target on the planet. This organization possesses nuclear, biological, and chemical weapons. It has targeted civilians.

Recently this organization bombed railroads, bridges, power plants, a cigarette factory, water pumping stations, civilian airports, oil refineries, ski resorts, and even residential apartments. It appears to lack any sort of ideology. Its motives are hidden behind a fog of lies and propaganda.

What it gained by its barbaric actions is unclear. What is most perplexing is that the organization becomes more popular with the American public with each atrocity it commits.

Who is the group? The Russian Mafia? Muslim fundamentalists? The Irish Republican Army?

This group of madmen is known by its acronym NATO. The aggression of the North Atlantic Treaty Organization has violated not only the United Nations Charter but also its own charter and the Geneva Convention — which outlaws the bombing of civilians.

The mainstream press has not remained silent. In fact, the media enthusiastically supported the recent NATO terror campaign in Yugoslavia. The only atrocity that bothered the press was — you guessed it — the bombing of a television station. Civilians are apparently acceptable targets unless they have a valid press pass. When depleted uranium bombs fell from American planes and slammed into residential neighborhoods, killing civilians by the hundreds, the press reported it as "collateral damage." When the Yugoslav military gunned down KLA guerrillas with small arms, the press called it an "atrocity."

NATO just turned fifty. It promises to continue to grow larger and more powerful in the future. Martin Walker told us in *Europe* magazine, "Don't be surprised to see a 100th anniversary celebration of NATO 50 years from now. Of course, with NATO this powerful, how many of us will make it to 50?"

Let's blow the candles out on NATO before it blows up any more children!

From a Clear Blue Sky

September 11, 2011

It was a brilliant summer day in a world at peace. The world's superpowers, once locked in conflict by irreconcilable ideologies, were now alike committed to stable, prosperous coexistence. Their vast military establishments, they said, existed solely for self-defense. Except in a few backward lands, horse trading had replaced brinkmanship.

New industrial and information technologies were annihilating distance, uniting mankind, and globalizing the world economy. The English language had leaped far beyond its island home and now knit together hundreds of millions of people on four continents. Medical advances were rapidly stretching the human lifespan, while new agricultural methods offered hope of eradicating hunger. Research, science, and philosophies of progress had weakened the hold of religion in countries that once had fought bloody doctrinal conflicts and persecuted dissenters. Transnational organizations in defense of human rights were striving with rising success to eliminate evils such as forced labor and torture, and reform movements in once-tyrannical countries promised to gradually introduce democracy. Man had become, more than ever before, the measure of all things, and political philosophers predicted with confidence that mankind's self-destructive history was drawing to an end; we had entered a new and perhaps the final phase of human development, an age of reason. The sun that dawned that morning shone as bright as all our hopes in a sky almost clear of clouds.

So it was on June 28, 1914, in Sarajevo when Archduke Franz Ferdinand came to visit. So also on September 11, 2001, in Manhattan as millions of New Yorkers made their way to work. Those of us who remember what occurred just ten years ago should know that all of it happened once before: An act of political terror committed by a small band of conspirators plunged the world into a conflict that would take on a life and logic of its own — claiming countless lives, causing undreamt-of destruction, consuming vast resources, making mincemeat of ancient liberties, reviving bloodthirsty fanaticisms that enlightened people had thought long dead, toppling governments, causing ethnic cleansing that displaced millions of civilians, and plunging the wealthiest part of the world into economic stagnation and crippling debt. The fact that history grimly repeats itself should surprise only those who do not believe in Original Sin — which means that it surprises almost everybody.

What can we learn from reading these two great signposts of disillusion? Perhaps there is no useful lesson we may draw beyond a bitter irony, a grim smile of agreement with Rudyard Kipling:

> As it will be in the future, it was at the birth of Man
> There are only four things certain since Social Progress began.
> That the Dog returns to his Vomit and the Sow returns to her Mire,
> And the burnt Fool's bandaged finger goes wabbling back to the Fire;
>
> And that after this is accomplished, and the brave new world begins
> When all men are paid for existing and no man must pay for his sins,
> As surely as Water will wet us, as surely as Fire will burn,
> The Gods of the Copybook Headings with terror and slaughter return!

But that is too easy, isn't it?

It might do, for those who plan to have no children, to leave behind no hostages to fortune. For anyone else, what is needed is more than cynicism, or stoic acceptance of what Freud called the "Thanatos principle," man's inborn compulsion to build, tear down, then rebuild the Tower of Babel. We want more than insight. What we crave, more than bread, is hope.

Hope is radically different from optimism. Stock analysts and campaign managers are optimistic — even when caution is called for. Optimism is the fragile dream that pervaded the West in 1914 and 2001. It was shattered by just one attack. Hope can survive in cancer wards and even concentration camps — as Aleksandr Solzhenitsyn and Viktor Frankl have testified. Hope exists, if you will, in a fourth dimension that cuts across the world we can see at an angle we cannot imagine. It rises from secret places in the heart where the torturers cannot find it and spreads through quiet gestures or silent prayers they cannot quash. Hope is what Winston Smith hungered for in Orwell's *1984*, but all he knew how to look for was optimism — a plausible prospect for social change. And so he cursed God and died.

If we, in our darkening times, would not learn to love Big Brother, we need a higher, indestructible Love. To find it, we must claw our way through the detritus that blocks our path. Much of the rubbish consists of the empty boxes that held our optimism, the wrapping paper from the gifts we gave ourselves. We must realize, deep in the bone, that there is no salvation in a cargo cult, that we can place no faith in princes or in whispered, promised knowledge that will help us be "as gods."

The centuries-long effort to place man at creation's apex, which our ancestors hailed as "humanism," ended by goading men to sterilize, butcher, and bomb their brothers. The adventure of secular science led by a straight, steady path from Galileo's ebullient "*Eppur si muove!*" to Robert Oppenheimer's epiphany: "Now I am become Death, the destroyer of worlds." Without renouncing the wondrous powers to improve man's life that come with scientific discipline, we urgently need to rediscover what too many humanists and scientists impatiently set aside. We must rummage through their libraries and labs to find the questions they suppressed, the data they fudged. We have spent five centuries asking only "How?" We must step back and ask again, "Why?" The answer will help us resist many temptations, of the sort our race falls into so very easily — to use the superhuman powers we gain in inhuman ways to treat the weak, the "other," the enemy, as subhuman, as flies we can kill for sport — as Gloucester muses in *King Lear*.

To restrain ourselves and each other, to prepare a livable future, there are certain fundamental axioms we need to accept as the bedrock of human rights and lasting peace. We do not need an infallible authority to reveal them; any honest student of twentieth-century history could piece them together by looking at which perennial truths totalitarian movements systematically sought to deny:

1. The unique and absolute value of every human person, at each stage of life, who must be treated not as a means but an end in him or herself
2. The transcendent moral order against which every law, custom, or policy must be judged, regardless of culture or government
3. The duty of governments to serve the governed and defend — not replace or control — the free institutions of civil society
4. The priority of certain core humane values over economic or political expediency

By slowing or even stopping us short of choosing "easy" shortcuts that render us less human, these "Gods of the Copybook Headings" may well be thought of as commandments — or if you prefer, the wisdom of history, for which our parents and grandparents paid such a very high price in the past hundred bloody years.

Flying into the Abyss on John Brennan's Drone

February 8, 2013

Beware that, when fighting monsters, you yourself do not become a monster ... for when you gaze long into the abyss, the abyss gazes also into you.

— Friedrich Nietzsche

It is not the American way to disregard the sanctity of human life. When our Republican officials tried to hide and then justify the use of "waterboarding," the media was all over it. When U.S. soldiers desecrated the bodies of fallen Afghan troops, the media again roared to life even in defense of the dead. And when, during the bloodiest war of the last century, American troops wished their German POWs a "merry Christmas" at the Battle of the Bulge, our media immortalized this great inspiring story, letting all the world know that, as Americans, we recognize the dignity of even our bitterest enemies.

Our sensitivity to violence and our abhorrence of cruelty have led us to put our trust in the most advanced techniques when it comes to war. We favor intelligence over brute force, and careful precision over ballistic attacks. If there must be war, the American people want to see their country succeed with clean proficiency and with minimal loss of life. For these reasons, we have placed high hopes in the U.S. drone program. John O. Brennan, the mind behind the drone program since 2002, has assured the American public that "never before has there been a weapon that allows us to distinguish more effectively between an al Qaeda terrorist and innocent civilians," and promises that drones are equipped "to precisely target" our country's most dangerous enemies "while minimizing collateral damage."

In light of the many shocks that continue to plague us in the news, the public is more and more eager to hold on to the idea of a clean and clement kind of warfare. We were all appalled at the recent shootings at Sandy Hook. The media showed due reverence in bowing their heads and hosting moments of silence on the air across the nation after the deaths of those twenty innocent American children. We do not mourn them because they were American but because they were human beings. And we reel in disbelief at the violent manner in which they were killed — how they were so senselessly struck down by a stunted, juvenile villain.

But if it took such a person to commit the kind of slaughter we saw at Sandy Hook, what will we say of John Brennan, a middle-aged man who enjoys being praised as priest-like and exceptionally ethical in his approach to warfare?

U.S. drone pilots have struck down no fewer than 178 innocent civilian children in Pakistan and Yemen. These killings were all committed via remote control, and those who pulled the triggers were always safe inside control rooms on U.S. turf.

This kind of violence is enough to shock anyone into silence. It's perfectly understandable to be momentarily at a loss for words when faced with bloody murder. But it is difficult to understand why anybody, let alone virtually all of the American mass media, would refrain from screaming bloody murder while these attacks continue. After all, isn't that what the media did for the children of Sandy Hook Elementary?

Unlike Adam Lanza, John Brennan is no disheveled, frustrated twenty-year-old. No fit of emotional frenzy surrounds Brennan's drone strikes. Rather, more like the comic-book villain he resembles, his acts of cruelty are calculated — and the fruit of a long and deliberate career.

And yet the media remain silent. Why? Are they perhaps ashamed? After all, it is the media's president who allows for these murders. The president who was named "Person of the Year" by *Time* magazine. The president who has been a guest on *The Late Night Show* and *The View*. The president whom *The New York Times* so "enthusiastically" endorsed during his campaign for reelection. This is the president who turns to John O. Brennan and says, "You have been one of my closest advisers." This is the president who nominates Brennan to be the new head of the CIA. President Obama has even called Brennan a "great friend." Can it be any surprise that the American media are shamed into silence?

But what of the many who read silence as assent? Busy Americans in other lines of work than news coverage find it difficult to believe what they don't see covered in the news. While we all keep busy doing our jobs, we rely on those in the media to do their job as well.

What will our media say in five years if America's enemies, whose innocent children we have left dead with no memorial, develop the technological capacity to pilot drones into our country? What will be the tone of our reports when innocent children are struck down in the streets of New York or Washington, D.C.? What moral grounds could we pretend to have against such a retaliation?

At Whole Life, it is our mission to assert the intrinsic dignity of every human person, especially of children, even the children of our enemies. It is also our job to remind policymakers that, even in war, positive law must always strive to conform to the supra-positive law, as acknowledged at Nuremberg. This is especially important when it comes to the state's use of lethal violence.

We are not all-powerful. We cannot play God by denying these children their dignity. Far from having that kind of power, we are showing ourselves to be moral weaklings. The American media should take this as a call to return to their duty. They must return to their posts and do what little their humble institution can do: report the truth.

The American people have the moral fiber to at least avert their eyes when it comes to the atrocities that John Brennan commits against the innocent civilians of Pakistan and Yemen. In fact, Brennan may be the only man perverse enough to look on dry-eyed at the hours and hours of drone-captured footage of unarmed men, women, and children running for their lives, hiding beneath cars, against the walls of shops, and even in their own homes before being gunned and bombed to pieces — and still call the drone program "ethical." But the rest of the country would never stand for it, if only they were given the chance to see for themselves what their country is doing to the innocent.

Brennan may think he's a big man, but he's got as tiny and shriveled a conscience as the worst of America's enemies. Here I would like to present the names of just a few of the 178 children who have been slaughtered *so far* by U.S. combat drones in Pakistan and Yemen. These are not American citizens, but they are human beings, each with an incomparable worth and dignity:

Pakistan
Name | Age | Gender

Noor Aziz | 8 | male
Abdul Wasit | 17 | male
Noor Syed | 8 | male
Wajid Noor | 9 | male

Syed Wali Shah | 7 | male
Ayeesha | 3 | female
Shoaib | 8 | male
Hayatullah Kha Mohammad | 16 | male
Tariq Aziz | 16 | male
Sanaullah Jan | 17 | male
Maezol Khan | 8 | female
Nasir Khan | male
Naeem Khan | male
Mohammad Tahir | 16 | male
Azizul Wahab | 15 | male
Fazal Wahab | 16 | male
Ziauddin | 16 | male
Mohammad Yunus | 16 | male
Fazal Hakim | 19 | male
Ilyas | 13 | male
Sohail | 7 | male
Asadullah | 9 | male
Khalilullah | 9 | male
Noor Mohammad | 8 | male
Khalid | 12 | male
Saifullah | 9 | male
Mashooq Jan | 15 | male
Nawab | 17 | male
Sultanat Khan | 16 | male
Ziaur Rahman | 13 | male
Noor Mohammad | 15 | male
Mohammad Yaas Khan | 16 | male
Qari Alamzeb | 14 | male
Ziaur Rahman | 17 | male
Abdullah | 18 | male
Ikramullah Zada | 17 | male
Inayatur Rehman | 16 | male
Shahbuddin | 15 | male

Yahya Khan | 16 | male
Rahatullah |17 | male
Mohammad Salim | 11 | male
Shahjehan | 15 | male
Gul Sher Khan | 15 | male
Bakht Muneer | 14 | male
Numair | 14 | male
Taseel Khan | 18 | male
Zaheeruddin | 16 | male
Qari Ishaq | 19 | male
Jamshed Khan | 14 | male
Alam Nabi | 11 | male
Qari Abdul Karim | 19 | male
Rahmatullah | 14 | male
Abdus Samad | 17 | male
Siraj | 16 | male
Saeedullah | 17 | male
Abdul Waris | 16 | male
Darvesh | 13 | male
Ameer Said | 15 | male
Shaukat | 14 | male
Inayatur Rahman | 17 | male
Salman | 12 | male
Fazal Wahab | 18 | male
Baacha Rahman | 13 | male
Wali-ur-Rahman | 17 | male
Iftikhar | 17 | male
Inayatullah | 15 | male
Mashooq Khan | 16 | male
Ihsanullah | 16 | male
Luqman | 12 | male
Jannatullah | 13 | male
Ismail | 12 | male
Adnan | 16 | male

Najibullah | 13 | male
Naeemullah | 17 | male
Hizbullah | 10 | male
Kitab Gul | 12 | male
Wilayat Khan | 11 | male
Zabihullah | 16 | male
Shehzad Gul | 11 | male
Shabir | 15 | male
Qari Sharifullah | 17 | male
Shafiullah | 16 | male
Nimatullah | 14 | male
Shakirullah | 16 | male
Talha | 8 | male

Yemen

Afrah Ali Mohammed Nasser | 9 | female
Zayda Ali Mohammed Nasser | 7 | female
Hoda Ali Mohammed Nasser | 5 | female
Sheikha Ali Mohammed Nasser | 4 | female
Ibrahim Abdullah Mokbel Salem Louqye | 13 | male
Asmaa Abdullah Mokbel Salem Louqye | 9 | male
Salma Abdullah Mokbel Salem Louqye | 4 | female
Fatima Abdullah Mokbel Salem Louqye | 3 | female
Khadije Ali Mokbel Louqye | 1 | female
Hanaa Ali Mokbel Louqye | 6 | female
Mohammed Ali Mokbel Salem Louqye | 4 | male
Jawass Mokbel Salem Louqye | 15 | female
Maryam Hussein Abdullah Awad | 2 | female
Shafiq Hussein Abdullah Awad | 1 | female
Sheikha Nasser Mahdi Ahmad Bouh | 3 | female
Maha Mohammed Saleh Mohammed | 12 | male
Soumaya Mohammed Saleh Mohammed | 9 | female
Shafika Mohammed Saleh Mohammed | 4 | female
Shafiq Mohammed Saleh Mohammed | 2 | male

Mabrook Mouqbal Al Qadari | 13 | male
Daolah Nasser | 10 | female
Abedal Ghani Mohammed Mabkhout | 12 | male
Abdel-Rahman Anwar al-Awlaki | 16 | male
Abdel-Rahman al-Awlaki | 17 | male
Nasser Salim | 19 | male

Each name on this list represents a family, a circle of friends, or an entire community whose rage against our country may never be checked until they do to us what John Brennan has done to them. God help us. And God protect our children.

Redeeming Night Terrors

August 30, 2013

My daughter woke up screaming as if a bear had crawled through her window. I raced into the room, seized her, held her, and waited it out. I'd learned firsthand that nothing I could do would wake her up, console her, or comfort her in the least. What she was suffering wasn't a nightmare, doctors assured me; in fact, when she goes through these fits, she's so deeply asleep that her mind is blank, and she wakes up in the morning remembering nothing. So all I could do was hold her, keep her safe, and suffer with her. Welcome to "night terrors," my friends.

In Eva's case, she doesn't have them every night, but sometimes they will come in clusters so that three or four nights in a row, I must rush to the rescue at three or four in the morning and hope that the rest of my kids can get back to sleep when it's all over. When the night terrors first started happening, I couldn't sleep — I'd lie there and stare at the ceiling. First of all, it was the relief that nothing serious was happening (it always takes a second or two for my sleepy rational brain to reassure my twisting gut that my daughter is howling with fear not because a wolf or a prowler has attacked her but thanks to some random brain static generated by the transition into REM sleep).

I feel relief. Then compassion, concern, and tenderness.

After a few weeks of this, I knew there had to be a better way to handle all this — and by "better" I don't mean something like getting some earplugs and leaving this mess to my wife. The doctors told me that this condition would pass as her brain developed and grew. So I needed a way to cope — or better yet, to transform this patch of nighttime shock and awe into something useful and good. This is where Jesus comes in: Christianity, at its heart, transforms suffering into holiness. It takes that ugly toxin and turns it into a whole family of medicines, such as empathy, patience, humility, and love. But you have to work the chemistry right, and to learn the formula, I turned to a favorite saint: Ignatius of Loyola.

It's hard for someone like me to resist a saint like Ignatius: He started off a vain soldier, a triumphalist, renowned alike for bravery and braggadocio. He pursued the ladies of the court and chased after glory and wealth. In other words, he was a guy. If he were alive (and unconverted) today, I think that Dana White would sign Ignatius onto a UFC contract. But after a battlefield injury ruined his leg — and hence, in his eyes, his looks — he spent long months in bed reading the only books on hand: one about the life of Christ and another about the lives of the saints. And Ignatius was converted. He took his own raw materials and turned them on the pivot of the Cross: The militarist became a militant preacher; the soldier became a pauper; the womanizer pledged his faith to the Virgin Mary. You know what happened next: He started an army that would conquer the earth's four corners for Christ, or willingly die trying.

What I learned from Ignatius was his technique called the "composition of place."

It's the method he used to teach lay Christians to read the Scriptures — not as amateur scholars or proof-texters but, rather, as participants. Since the goal of the Christian life is closeness to Christ, why not use His own words and story to train your imagination and heart by His example? So Ignatius takes a scene from the New Testament and teaches us how to "be" there in our minds: to taste the olive oil, smell the sweat, hear the crowds, feel the heat, and see the beards. Once we've tried to register in every sense what it might have been like to be present alongside Our Lord, we tap into the emotions that Christ or the apostles might have felt: the fear, the joy, the confusion, the hope. A few months of this sort of thing, and Christianity ceases to be an abstraction — as it too often is, even for solid believers — and becomes a part of your lived reality.

We Shall Return: The Six Core Principles of American World Leadership

April 20, 2015

When Gen. Douglas MacArthur was finally ordered to evacuate the Philippines in 1942 after a bitter defensive fight against overwhelming Japanese firepower, he vowed to those islands' residents: "I shall return." America needs to offer the world a similar promise, that after the eight years of Barack Obama's rudderless leadership, which somehow managed to be neither principled nor pragmatic, we shall return. Yes, many Americans welcomed the election of Obama as an exciting, fresh start. So did much of the world, which greeted him with messianic fervor and granted him the Nobel Peace Prize simply for showing up. We have learned a grim lesson together.

Especially over the past two years, as we marked the somber centennial of the outbreak of World War I, we have seen the explosion of violent ethnic conflicts, the implosions of sovereign states, and a vast increase in religious terrorism. On the bitter anniversary of the Armenian Genocide, commemorated this month, religious zealots threaten the lives of other minorities, from the Assyrians and Yazidis of Iraq to the Christians of Kenya, Nigeria, and Pakistan, the Nuba of Sudan, even Ethiopians in Libya. The world's quotient of ugliness and intolerance has not diminished in one hundred years.

Unlike the often-dilettantish politicians of August 1914, we know precisely how costly in human lives the collapse of international order can be. Some one hundred million murdered civilians perished in the past century because of feckless or reckless decisions. Now that weapons are even deadlier, and hatreds even sharper, the duty to hold peace together is more solemn than ever before.

Let's hope that whoever wins the next presidential election pledges to repair the international damage left behind by the current administration. Let's pray that the candidate can admit past mistakes but remain deeply committed to these ideals that governed American foreign policy for most of its history:

1. **We are friends of freedom.** The basic human rights to life, liberty, property, and the free exercise of religion are the logical extensions of the

Judeo-Christian tradition, which views the human person as an image of God, with all the dignity that implies. Regimes that treat such rights as less than sacred may join us at times to fight greater evils, but our true and lasting partners will always be governments that treat their people with respect. Such regimes are often liberal democracies, but not always; in some countries with fragile protections for minority rights, majority rule would lead to less freedom, not more. Much more important is the protection and growth of a free civil society, which can lay the groundwork for a democratic society in the future.

2. **We pursue and protect our legitimate national interests** and project force primarily to further that end — not to transform the world in our own self-image. We lack both the power and the godlike knowledge to accomplish such a task, even if we thought that it was desirable.
3. **We also will use force to defend our allies from harm** and to blunt the assaults of tyrants or terrorists against the helpless. We are the natural friends of embattled minority groups whose human dignity is threatened by hostile governments. We are especially committed to aiding religious minorities, since their struggle for freedom so closely mirrors the reasons our country was founded. Our policies in the Middle East, for instance, will be guided by this principle.
4. **We believe in free trade, free markets, the protection of private property, and economic growth** as the answers to poverty — not redistribution of wealth, state seizure of private businesses, government monopolies, or economic nationalism. But freedom is a two-way street. We expect our trading partners to play by the same rules that we do.
5. **We will work with and through international institutions** when doing so accords with each of the aforementioned principles. Cooperation with honest partners is key to exercising leadership. **But we will not violate those principles or leave our allies hanging** because of decrees by transnational organizations or entities. Like military force, they are a means, not an end in themselves.
6. **America will be true to its word**, consistent in its principles, loyal to its friends, and steadfast before its enemies. It will not seek quarrels lightly or retire from them without victory.

These are the maxims that made America great, that allowed her to grow from a marginal string of settlements on the edge of a howling wilderness to the champion of freedom against totalitarian empires. If we return to this creed with fortitude and humility, we can again serve the world as a solid bulwark of justice in increasingly desperate times.

Hiroshima Seventy Years Ago Today: Right or Wrong?

August 6, 2015

By August 1945, with most of its major cities already in ashes from Allied firebombing, Imperial Japan was militarily helpless to do anything but resist a ground invasion of its home islands. Its fleet had been sunk, its air force shot from the sky, its armies evicted from their vast conquests. A nation that could not feed itself was cut off from all trade and entirely surrounded by enemies. American strategists, still smarting from the furious struggle of doomed Japanese on Okinawa, warned of the cost in American soldiers — some put estimates in the high six figures — should the Allies attempt to take the islands. Others wondered if such an invasion was even necessary, since their foe had neither fuel nor food. Still others — perhaps those with the ear of President Truman — thought it wise to showcase the new American weapon, developed at such great cost and in utter secrecy, to send a warning shot to a grasping, ambitious Stalin.

On August 6, 1945, a lone American plane entered the skies over Hiroshima — an industrial town of small military worth — and dropped a single bomb named "Little Boy" from a height of about thirty-one thousand feet. The atomic blast that resulted killed some eighty thousand people almost instantly and caused the deaths of some sixty thousand by radiation poisoning and other causes before the year's end. Lingering illnesses would claim many more; according to the city of Hiroshima, the final death toll of the bombing was 237,062.

When the first bombing failed to provoke a Japanese surrender, a second was planned for August 9. After weather conditions forced pilots to avoid the initial target city of Kokura, another American plane descended on the ancient capital of Japanese Christianity, Nagasaki, and again dropped one bomb — this one named "Fat Man." The military targets in the town — major factories — were destroyed that day. So were seventy-five thousand civilians; at least an equal number would die within the year.

Were such Allied air attacks war crimes? Before we decide that question, let us first be fair to the men who made the decisions to launch those attacks in a desperate attempt to end a war that had threatened their nations' existence.

The West was engaged in a total war, one launched by enemies that scoffed at "outmoded" standards of civilized behavior. One of the key factors that drove American leaders such as Franklin Roosevelt toward a confrontation with Japan was their real moral outrage at the sickening cruelty Japan practiced in China — routinely raping and slaughtering civilians by the thousands, using Chinese (and later, Allied) prisoners as targets for bayonet practice and as guinea pigs on whom to test viruses for biological warfare. The barbarism of Nazi conquests, accompanied by terror bombing, genocides, and the mass execution of hostages, proved a similar goad to our fitful alliance with an embattled and isolated Britain.

With these atrocities in mind, we can begin to understand why Allied leaders insisted on unconditional surrender — a policy that prolonged the war into 1945, by far its bloodiest year, and guaranteed that the Axis governments would resist to their last iota of strength — arming twelve-year-old boys in Germany with rifles they couldn't lift and preparing old men and peasant mothers in Japan to fight with rocks and sticks. Our two most dangerous enemies fought to the very bitter end before submitting.

It is true that Americans were subject, as all men are subject, to the blind ferocity of war and tempted to answer enemy ruthlessness tit for tat. Niall Ferguson, in *The War of the World*, documents the fact that frequently Allied soldiers simply shot German or Japanese soldiers attempting to surrender. Other soldiers collected the severed ears or boiled skulls of their enemies; a chilling photo in Ferguson's book shows a wartime photo of an American girl reading her soldier boyfriend's letter from the front, perched beside the "Jap skull" he proudly sent her. Such ugly facts, along with the savagery of our bombing campaigns, led the great Catholic philosopher Elizabeth Anscombe to describe the insistence on unconditional surrender, instead of a negotiated peace with the Axis governments, as "visibly wicked" and driven by "villainous hatred."

But that is unfair, for several important reasons. The atrocities committed by the German and Japanese regimes against civilians outside the course of combat had genuinely shocked and disgusted the leaders of Great Britain and America. The vicious irrationalism espoused by the leaders of both enemy countries; the proudly Machiavellian dishonesty of their diplomacy leading up to the war; the blatant immorality of their war aims; all these factors made it unthinkable for Allied leaders to negotiate with the existing governments of Germany and Japan and to work out peace arrangements that would leave those nations' ruling elites in power.

Neither the Germans nor the Japanese had shown the slightest inclination to bargain in good faith or to respect the rights of the peoples they had conquered. Why should the nations they had tried and failed to conquer offer these nations' leaders any quarter? A negotiated peace, it should be obvious, would have made trials such as were held at Nuremberg impossible. Indeed, any truce that avoided Allied occupation would have permitted the guilty powers to erase most of the evidence of their war crimes.

But the starkest goad that drove the Allies to demand unconditional surrender in the Second World War was the vivid memory of how the First World War had ended. At the moment the kaiser's government gave up the fight on November 11, 1918, not a single foreign soldier stood on German soil; in fact, German armies still held large swaths of Belgium and France in the west and vast chunks of former Russian territory that had been captured during the war. The harshly punitive victors' peace imposed on Germany, which helped guarantee future conflicts over territory and reparations, could be blamed on the Social Democratic politicians who had come to power just in time to sign the one-sided Treaty of Versailles.

What is more, the military that really had lost the war could foster the myth that Germany had been "stabbed in the back" on the verge of final victory. That blatantly baseless narrative was deliberately fostered by German officers after the war — for instance, by hiring propagandists to spread it among the ranks of unemployed army veterans. One of the most gifted speakers they employed was a failed Austrian art student named Adolf Hitler.

Allied leaders were not about to make that same mistake again. They could not negotiate a peace while German armies still held France and other conquered nations and still operated extermination camps such as Auschwitz — a peace that would leave in power some slightly watered-down version of Nazi militarism, and that might in ten or twenty years in turn be denounced as yet another "stab in the back." Germany would have to be conquered, occupied, and purged. So would the murderous, almost psychotically militaristic Japan. It is impossible to blame Franklin Roosevelt, Harry Truman, or Winston Churchill for insisting on this point. Anything less would have seemed like masochistic appeasement.

With all that said, there were real opportunities the Allies missed that could have shortened the war, or at least spared civilian lives, and kept our own code of making war more distinct from that of our murderous enemies. In 1944, when German officers were conspiring (with the aid of Pope Pius XII, who used Vatican couriers to transmit their messages) to kill Adolf Hitler, seize power from the Nazis, and seek a separate peace with the Western Allies, they contacted British intelligence and were spurned. An internal revolt against the Nazi regime such as Claus von Stauffenberg bravely attempted really would have offered a chance at a peace with honor — and limited the westward march of Stalin's conquering armies.

Likewise, in the Pacific, the Americans could have made it clear much earlier that they were open to leaving the Japanese emperor in power — albeit in a truncated and purely symbolic role, ruling a demilitarized Japan. The failure to communicate to Japan this willingness helped push the United States toward the ugly choice of either using the atomic bomb on cities or mounting a full-scale invasion against fanatical, desperate troops who had been trained to die or commit suicide before surrendering.

Were there other choices? Were they practical? Could we have used the atomic weapons we had developed in a less inhuman way, one that better respected Western moral norms — for instance, by preparing for an invasion of Japan and "telegraphing" where it would occur, then using our atomic bombs primarily on Japanese soldiers instead of civilians? This is not alternative history, nor are we qualified to play armchair general at the safe distance of seventy years. There may have been practical difficulties with any such alternative scenario that would have rendered it far too ineffective. What we can say with certainty is that alternative scenarios should have been seriously considered and never passed over lightly.

Limiting civilian casualties should have been at least one of the factors in choosing bomb targets, yet there is little evidence that Allied leaders even worried about the ethics of liquidating enemy citizens from the air; indeed, it appears that on this point, the Allies permitted their enemies to drag them down to their level.

A decent regard for civilian lives does not imply that we should be willing to sacrifice indefinite numbers of our soldiers to avoid any and every innocent death. Commanders must balance their first concern — winning the war with minimal losses — against the solemn duty to spare civilians wherever possible. We can never target civilians directly or intentionally or totally disregard the cost in civilian lives of a military victory. To do so is to let our enemies' worst instincts infect our own morality — with consequences that may well outlive the peace.

Our conduct of the Second World War was not determined entirely by the desire to spare our soldiers' lives. Had that been our main concern, we could have refused to invade continental Europe at all and spared our men such slaughters as happened at Anzio and Normandy — leaving the conquest of Hitler to Stalin's advancing armies. Our leaders knew that a Communist-occupied Western Europe was not in America's interests, and so they were willing to spend the lives of hundreds of thousands of men to avoid it. Restricting our use of massive urban bombing in the war would also have cost soldiers' lives. Our statesmen could have decided that such a grim sacrifice was worthwhile, both to spare the lives of noncombatants and to avoid the degrading moral effects of ruthlessly destroying civilian populations.

Abolition of Strategic Nuclear Weapons: A Just War Analysis of Total War

August 6, 2016

The continued possession of nuclear weapons by the United States and other nations must be tempered by a comprehensive understanding of Just War Theory. Despite being reduced from their Cold War–era peak, nuclear-weapon arsenals still have such sheer destructive power as to threaten humanity's future while also violating basic principles of military ethics. The tradition of military ethics known as Just War Theory holds that uses of military force (1) must discriminate between military personnel and civilians and (2) must not cause so much harm as to outweigh whatever good the use of military force is intended to achieve. Nearly all conceivable uses of nuclear weapons fail to meet either of these Just War requirements. To remedy this situation, strategic nuclear doctrine needs to be radically changed, and the sizes of nuclear stockpiles need to be dramatically reduced. Nuclear nonproliferation also needs to be given top priority. The United States has an important role to play in all these efforts and can benefit from their success.

Stockpiles of nuclear weapons, both deployed and non-deployed, held by the nine known nuclear powers stand at roughly 10,300 warheads. Many existing nuclear warheads — including a large number of warheads in the arsenals of the United States and Russia, the two largest nuclear powers — have yields in the hundreds of kilotons. Of the United States' deployed nuclear warheads, more than three-quarters have explosive yields of one hundred kilotons or more. Given that the bombs that devastated Hiroshima and Nagasaki had yields in the range of fifteen to twenty kilotons, using almost any warhead in current nuclear arsenals against a populated area would cause massive indiscriminate death and destruction.

Even if the target were a purely military one, the bomb's effects would take a staggering toll on surrounding civilian populations. This kind of indiscriminate destruction violates the principles of discrimination and proportionality, as understood in Just War Theory. Just War Theory is a venerable school of ethical philosophy meant to regulate the circumstances under which and the means by which war can legitimately be waged. Just War Theory tends to be associated with Christian tradition — versions of the theory have been articulated by Christian thinkers such as Augustine, Thomas Aquinas, Martin Luther, and John Calvin — but it also has points in common with other religious and philosophical traditions.

In particular, the notion that even in wartime limits or restraints need to be put on the use of military force is one that can be found not only in Christianity but also in faiths such as Hinduism and Islam. This requirement of restraining military force's use is reflected in contemporary Just War Theory in the principles of (1) discrimination, which dictates that military force should be directly and intentionally used only against opposing military personnel and not civilians of the opponent nation; and (2) proportionality, which dictates that military force should not cause more harm than good — killing enormous numbers of civilians unintentionally (what is euphemistically called "collateral damage") is a prime example of the disproportionate use of force.

The Just War principle of discrimination has been expressed in contemporary international law through the Geneva Convention governing treatment of civilians in wartime. Nuclear weapons make a mockery of these ethical and legal principles, however.

As long as the United States and other nations maintain their current nuclear weapons arsenals, they are guilty of planning and preparing for indiscriminate and disproportionate uses of force — in effect, for committing war crimes. Such military postures are an injustice not only against the millions of civilians targeted by nuclear weapons but against members of nuclear nations' armed forces: Maintaining current nuclear arsenals implicates thousands of military personnel in unethical and criminal behavior. Maintaining such arsenals also undermines any moral high ground the United States or other nations might wish to hold in the eyes of the world. Terrorist groups such as Al Qaeda and ISIS and various tyrannical regimes kill or threaten civilians and are rightly condemned.

Such condemnations ring hollow, however, coming from nations whose own defense posture rests on threats of killing millions of civilians. If nations wish to be convincing in their condemnation of terrorist groups and tyrannical regimes and to use public diplomacy effectively to undermine such groups' and regimes' legitimacy, then the injustice of current nuclear arsenals must be ended. In the same way, continued maintenance of current nuclear arsenals undermines efforts to prevent additional nations from trying to acquire nuclear arsenals of their own. Efforts to prevent new nations from becoming nuclear powers appear hypocritical when coming from nuclear-armed nations that plan to keep the full range of their own nuclear weapons indefinitely.

Moreover, continued maintenance of existing arsenals is a provocation to non-nuclear powers, some of whom might feel they must acquire nuclear weapons simply to protect themselves from current nuclear powers. Even if all these ethical and political considerations are set aside, however, nuclear weapons still pose a larger threat to humanity. Use of most or all of the weapons in current global stockpiles in a major nuclear conflict would cause death on an unprecedented scale and devastate the global environment. This alone is reason for trying to dramatically reduce, and end the strategic use of, nuclear weapons. When this and the other reasons given above are taken together, our task becomes imperative.

To pursue nuclear reduction and nonstrategic use does not mean world leaders must embrace outright pacifism or refrain from protecting their nations and national interests. Nations' interests and policies will almost inevitably come into conflict — although one always hopes violent conflict can be avoided — and leaders can legitimately and reasonably adopt various national security policies to deal with such conflicts. Nevertheless, defending national interests or even national survival must be kept within ethical limits, such as discriminating between combatants and civilians in wartime. Nuclear weapons render such discrimination nearly impossible. Reducing these weapons and restricting their usage to tactical maneuvers will enable world leaders to bring national defense within the limits of discrimination and proportionality defined by Just War Theory.

Reversing the nuclear arms race as it has unfolded over the past seventy years is an enormous undertaking that will involve careful and intensive diplomacy that adapts as necessary to different circumstances. Nevertheless, the broad outlines of how the nine current nuclear powers, and other nations, can gradually reduce the number of nuclear weapons to zero can be defined:

1. The first goal to be sought should be an across-the-board reduction of current nuclear-weapons arsenals by 50 percent. For all nine nuclear powers to cut in half the number of nuclear warheads in their possession will send a clear message about the nuclear powers' commitment to reducing their arsenals significantly. At the same time, it would still

leave nuclear powers with sufficient deterrent capabilities while they build trust and refine verification and monitoring procedures. Such trust and procedures will build confidence for making additional arms cuts.

2. Once the initial 50 percent reduction has been made, the nuclear powers can proceed with negotiating further reductions, with a possible next goal being cutting the newly reduced arsenals by one-third. As nations cut their arsenals, they should emphasize not only reducing the absolute number of warheads but also eliminating warheads with the greatest destructive powers: warheads with megaton yields, followed by those in the higher kilotons, and so on. The ultimate goal should be elimination of the nuclear arsenals or at least their reduction to a tiny number (perhaps ten or fewer) of very low-yield warheads (perhaps 0.3 kilotons) to be used only in tactical defensive maneuvers and never on civilian population centers. Such minimal nuclear arsenals could theoretically be used within the restraints of the discrimination and proportionality principles — if they were used against an opposing naval group in the open ocean, for example.
3. Other steps to lower the risks of nuclear conflict and violations of Just War principles can be taken in tandem with the reductions outlined above. One important step is to lower nuclear weapons' readiness for use: take them off alert status; decouple warheads from delivery vehicles; put warheads and delivery vehicles in storage; and otherwise gradually increase the time and number of procedures necessary to make the weapons operational. These steps would decrease tensions among nuclear powers and lessen the risk that nuclear weapons would be used by accident or because of misunderstanding.
4. Nuclear doctrine should be revised according to the principles of discrimination and proportionality. Nuclear powers — ideally in concert but individually if necessary — should make official declarations that they will never use nuclear weapons against cities or other civilian population centers or against military forces whose targeting could indirectly kill civilians. Targeting of existing weapons should be changed accordingly, and military law should be revised to require military personnel to refuse to obey any order to use nuclear weapons against such targets. (This final

step will relieve the men and women of the armed forces from the current shameful situation in which they are effectively expected to commit war crimes.)

5. All these steps should be linked to nonproliferation efforts. As existing nuclear powers gradually eliminate their arsenals, non-nuclear powers should be encouraged to reaffirm their rejection of nuclear weapons in all relevant treaties and conventions. The monitoring and verification procedures adopted as part of the nuclear powers' negotiations can be used for checking the compliance of non-nuclear powers as well.

For too long, humanity has been threatened by the catastrophe of nuclear war, and for too long, the existing nuclear powers have been ethically compromised by maintaining nuclear arsenals that can be used only in indiscriminate and disproportionate ways. We must begin the work of removing the nuclear threat and bringing national military policies into accord with Just War principles.

I'm an Old Soldier. Now My Son Might Deploy to Syria, and I'm Worried

April 8, 2017

I was an infantryman. My brother was an infantryman. My father was an infantryman. My grandfather was an infantryman in both World War II and the Korean War. And so on, up through my family tree. I've been a soldier in a family of soldiers that has served this country in most of the wars it has fought since its founding.

This week, my son deploys to the Middle East. And Donald Trump appears to be changing before our eyes into something none of us voted for. Before long, my son could be on the ground in Syria, part of a new American campaign that's no more likely to produce any good than anything else we've done in that troubled part of the world.

Beyond scaring me down on my knees, these facts have forced me to think about America's legacy in the region. Things are not always as they seem. Remember all the warnings we heard about how Iraq was building weapons of mass destruction? About its ties to the attacks on 9/11? Remember Colin Powell at the United Nations, putting all his credibility, and America's, on the line to urge the world to join us? It was based on bad intelligence. Dust in our eyes. Dust in the wind.

The real question now is not whether Assad is a bad guy. Of course he is. But look at the real alternatives. They're all much worse for religious minorities in the area, including Christians.

More important than bad intel from past conflicts, remember the promises we made to Iraq and its people. We swore that we would bring freedom, order, and prosperity. Do we even remember that now?

Iraqis do. With bitterness.

In January, I traveled to Iraq and Kurdistan, researching a film I'm making. Its heroes? The one million Christians who were purged from their ancient homeland, right under our soldiers' noses. (Our men were following orders, and the Bush administration never ordered them to prevent it.) I'm documenting these and other religious refugees as they fight for their faith and their families — as they cling to their human dignity in the wasteland we left behind.

As I made my way toward Mosul, I passed through the legacy of our last "humanitarian" intervention. Our last war against a war criminal. Our proud patriots' achievement stretched out before me as I snaked down the dusty roads: one abandoned settlement after another. Some places with noble and ancient names were now neatly organized piles of rubble.

Here's what the locals told me: After the United States invaded, dissolved their army, fitfully tried to keep order, and then finally — under Obama — cut and ran, those towns were captured by ISIS. The men and boys were hunted, the girls kidnapped and raped. The survivors hid out in the hills. Then U.S. airstrikes flattened all the buildings. Then ISIS booby-trapped the rubble and burned whatever was left. And that's what is left of much of Iraq.

While I was still in Kurdistan, I finally got overwhelmed. I met with local imams, whose people had suffered alongside the Christians. As *The Stream* has reported, those groups now fight together against ISIS. They also fight Al Qaeda and its Turkish sponsors and allies. After I heard their stories, I blurted out an apology. "I'm sorry. Americans are sorry that we invaded and then abandoned you."

The imam nodded solemnly and addressed me with great dignity. "We know that Americans think they are responsible for the actions of their government. We are not so naive. Americans are good people. Your elite must play on your goodness even to do evil."

It's our duty as responsible citizens to listen skeptically when men with power call us to war. We owe at least that much to the victims of past mistakes. It has become standard practice in American war making to take some atrocity, inflate it or invent it, and use it to sell a war to the general public. The spurious "Gulf of Tonkin incident" sold us the whole Vietnam War.

We were sold the first Gulf War in part by the fiction that Iraqi soldiers were yanking premature babies out of incubators in Kuwait. (The "witness" who spoke before Congress was a relative of Kuwait's ambassador, coached by a PR firm.) There were good reasons for liberating Kuwait. So why did our leaders decide to lie to us? Do they think we can't be trusted with the truth?

In the three months since I've returned to our peaceful shores, I've been haunted by what I saw: by the fathers who choked up as they told me what happened to their daughters; by the pastors who were still picking through the ruins of ancient churches; by the ruin left behind by irresponsible politicians. Now I wonder whether my son will risk his life to pile up rubble in yet another country.

President Trump: Find Peace in Syria by Looking to Switzerland

April 10, 2017

We're all Syria buffs now. We're barraged with conflicting reports, atrocity stories, and carefully nurtured narratives. They all seem to goad us to back a major U.S. involvement in that country. (Can you spell "q-u-a-g-m-i-r-e"?) So let's step back and think for a minute.

How much hope is there for a country where citizens speak three quite different languages? Where they adhere to starkly opposed religions — each of which damns the members of the other as heretics or infidels? Where religious or ethnic atrocities on each side feed into a history of bitterness?

We are speaking now not of Syria but of Switzerland.

That's right, one of the richest, most peaceful countries on earth. The Swiss have low taxes, minimal government, and the most democratic constitution in human history. Citizens' religious freedom, property rights, gun rights, and freedom of speech are protected even better than in America. Most of a Swiss person's taxes go to his town, not the federal government. Any citizen can collect signatures to force a national referendum to change the laws.

But Switzerland was once a lot like Syria. Its ethnic factions engaged in vicious attacks and bloody vengeance. Its churches used to whip their members into mutual holy war. Catholics would march with the Eucharist in elaborate processions through Protestant towns. This risked armed attacks by Calvinists. So young Catholics formed shooting clubs. They would march alongside their priests, brandishing rifles. As recently as 1847, the Catholics and Protestants fought a brief civil war that ended with the Jesuits expelled and banned from the country.

So what was it that rescued Switzerland from turning out like Syria? What could President Trump learn from the Swiss success story? The answer is simple. Localism and decentralization saved Switzerland. They could save Syria. In fact, a peace plan based on these principles is currently on the table at the Russian-sponsored Astana talks — which the United States so far is boycotting.

True American "federalism" is a fine example of localism in action. Let Maine and Mississippi, California and Colorado, make most of their own laws. Suit laws to the values and habits of their citizens. In the teachings of the popes, this idea is called "subsidiarity." It is designed to keep political power as close as possible to the citizens whom it impacts. You can debate most of your tax burden at your local town meeting.

For more on subsidiarity, see the chapter John Zmirak and I wrote about it in *The Race to Save Our Century*.

Rebuilding after the 1847 civil war, the Swiss did not look to the rigidly centralized government of France. Instead, they modeled themselves on the still quite loosely knit United States. They embedded in their new constitution protections for the rights of every region and left most of the political power in each region's hands.

There were some, of course, who wanted a powerful central government that could impose one faction's wishes on everyone. The Swiss who thought like this had welcomed Napoleon's invasion. But the country's deep divisions made such a scheme impossible — at least without a tyrannical government willing to batter the Catholics and Calvinists, French and German speakers, city folk and farmers into sullen, begrudged submission.

Of course, that is what Bashir Assad's harsh secular government has done in Syria. He repressed the Sunni majority while protecting his own embattled (Alawite) minority, along with Christians and other smaller groups. Brutal coercion is likewise the program of Islamist rebels backed by Turkey and Saudi Arabia. Forcibly homogenizing peoples and regions is the model of twentieth-century statehood: A powerful central government, dedicated to "national greatness," crams one ideology down the throat of every hamlet and village.

That's the model Western powers imposed on the Middle East, along with crackpot borders that took no account of ethnic or religious differences, in the Sykes-Picot Agreement in 1916.

Up till now, the only alternative to thuggish, centralized nationalism of the sort practiced by Assad (and before him, Saddam Hussein) has been Islamist theocracy. Islamists like the Al Qaeda factions now covet power in Syria. They also wish to impose a single creed and way of life on vibrant, diverse regions. The difference is that Islamists look to sharia as the source of all law and order. That's bad news for religious minorities. That's why millions of Alawites and Christians now look for protection either to Assad or to Kurdish militias.

If Assad were to reconquer Syria, he would brutally crush Islamists and make life hell for religious Sunnis.

If the United States topples Assad and lets "nature" take its course, murderous theocrats linked to Al Qaeda would do the same to Alawites, Shiites, and Christians.

If Turkey has a strong hand in the settlement, the government it sponsors will crush the Kurdish militias, who seek autonomy for their distinct and long-suffering nation.

There is no prospect of a strong centralized government that would honor human rights and democracy. That's not an option in a nation this religiously and culturally fractured. Whoever holds the whip hand of a powerful national government will crush and subdue the others. That is why each side fights so brutally. It's why most of the factions, including Assad, but not the Christians and Kurds, have resorted to chemical weapons.

There is a better way. The peace talks at Astana, stalled for now, envisioned a Swiss-style solution for Syria. Each of the regions now controlled by one faction or another would form a kind of "canton," with most of the powers that normally go to a central state. These cantons would be linked by a loose confederation, designed to keep peace among them. (Some other Alawite, not Assad, should be its figurehead.) People unhappy in the canton where they ended up would likely vote with their feet and move to a friendlier region.

The Swiss model is already present in Syria. The Federation of Northern Syria, led by Kurds allied with Christians and tolerant Arabs, is composed of self-governed cantons in voluntary association. It's the one part of Syria where women take part in politics, all religious groups are free, and power stays close to the people. *The Stream*'s Johannes de Jong has written in depth on how federalism works now in this part of Syria.

Such a plan isn't perfect. It will frustrate the ambitions of every group. And that's the point — because in Syria today, such ambitions often include erasing minority rights, forcing people to change religions, or simply wiping them out.

In Iraq we tried another plan: Seize power from brutal, secular nationalists; then spend trillions to set up a fragile central democracy and leave. That's what gave us ISIS and left most of Iraq either in ruins and cleansed of Christians or ruled by intolerant Shiites who obey the Islamic Republic of Iran. There is no constituency for tolerant, democratic central government in the Arab world. That is why such a government does not exist. Anywhere.

We could deny that fact, for ten or twenty years, and have another Afghanistan on our hands. Or we could admit it and leave behind a howling wasteland like Iraq.

How about this: Instead of trying this brutal, foolish plan yet again with yet another country, why don't we look to a model that actually works? Maybe Switzerland, instead of the United States or Russia, should lead the Syrian peace talks.

Thirty-Eight Minutes in Hawaii: My Family and the False Missile Alarm

January 6, 2018

I woke up abruptly. Overzealous JROTC cadets ran and yelled on the high school track across the street. I rolled over and grabbed my reading glasses. Time to return to the book that I'd fallen asleep reading: *Leo Strauss and the Politics of Exile* by Eugene Sheppard. Thirty minutes later, I faced a tough choice. Should I go down and check on my children? Or watch an old Lomachenko fight on YouTube?

Then my wife called up, "Babe, it's garbage day. Take out the trash!" So I rushed downstairs. My typical Saturday ritual. As I dragged the trash out, a bizarre sound boomed from my phone. I read the message:

Ballistic missile threat inbound. Seek immediate shelter. This is not a drill.

"So it's today," I thought. I'm a student of the bloody twentieth century, a hundred years of genocide, democide, and total war. I've lived on Oahu for almost thirty years, in sight of Pearl Harbor. It's still a key target for a surprise attack. I've long thought that Oahu could be the spot where the next great tragic war begins — though not where it ends. Decades of thinking on this inspired me to write a book on the subject with John Zmirak: *The Race to Save Our Century*. I also recently co-authored a white paper outlining a path to abolish city-busting strategic nuclear weapons.

Whenever someone suggests that I'm some do-gooding humanitarian, I correct them: "No, I'm just trying to save my children." Oahu is a small island. But it's one of the most important strategic locations for the projection of U.S. power to the East, confronting both North Korea and China. Knowing that, you come to accept a grim reality: Oahu is one of the most likely flash points for the start of World War III.

So when I saw the alert on my iPhone, I faced it with the same realism with which wise Midwesterners greet tornado warnings. And like them, I had a plan.

I rushed into the house. "Kids, get in the car. Babe, grab the case of water bottles." They knew the drill, and soon the minivan was fully loaded. I filled water jugs and two mugs of coffee and grabbed my 9mm.

I was rushing to shelter my family behind the Waianae Mountain Range. That might shield us from whatever was about to hit Pearl Harbor. We had ten minutes, I calculated, to get there and hide in the Makua Cave.

Ignoring signs, police, and the rules of the road, I gunned the minivan. We raced for the shade of the mountain.

My thoughts were far away, with my daughter and my wife's mother. They both live in Waikiki. Surely I should call them. But tell them ... what? I knew there was no place for them to go. Was that worth calling to tell them? Then the phone rang. That amazed me. Why were they working? They hadn't in Washington, D.C., on September 11, 2001. I knew because I'd been there.

It was my mother-in-law. She wanted to know what to do. She lives five minutes from Diamond Head Crater. So I told her to drive down into it and hide in its abandoned fallout shelter. Then my daughter called on my son's phone and asked the same question. I gave the same inadequate answer. As I talked to her, I knew that this might be the last time I heard my daughter's voice. My wife marked the tears in my eyes.

As we made the turn into the shadow of the mountain, I felt we'd won a small victory. The first missile must have been intercepted. Or else the inept North Koreans had dropped a rocket in the middle of the Pacific. Before the next wave of missiles hit, we would make it to Makua Cave.

My hopes that this was a false alarm were fading. "If this were a hack or a hoax, the government would have texted us already." This thought pressed my foot even heavier on the gas pedal. I turned into the empty oncoming lane and passed some twenty cars. A man in a pickup gunned his truck and started to follow me. He was honking his horn and trying to get my attention.

My first instinct was anger. "This dude wants to fight me for driving like an idiot. He must have his phone off," I thought. He was a big Hawaiian dude, waving at me with animated gestures. So I slowed down and let him pull up next to me. I rolled down the window.

But he wasn't trying to rebuke me for my crazy driving. He wanted help. "Bro, what should I do? You seem like you have a plan. Where should I go?"

I took a deep breath and then shouted, "Get to Makua Cave! Put as much mountain as you can between yourself and Pearl Harbor."

The man held up his phone, despair on his face. "I can't reach my wife! What should I do?"

Oh, man. My wife was right next to me. And most of my kids. I shook my head and told this poor guy: "*There is no time*, bro. Drive to Makua Cave!"

He looked at me and then looked at his phone. I watched as he did a U-turn and drove his truck back toward what would probably be Ground Zero. Back toward his wife.

Just as we pulled up to Makua Cave, my cell phone rang, and the State of Hawaii finally let us know that this had all been a big mistake.

In thirty-eight minutes, I'd gone from rolling out my trash can to loading five of my seven children into our minivan in a desperate attempt to outrun a nuclear missile. I'd heard my oldest daughter's voice for what I thought was the last time. I'd given her and my mother-in-law a destination I knew offered nothing but hope. And I'd watched a total stranger turn away from safety to go and try to save his wife.

So there we were at this … cave. There was only one thing left to do. Unload the kids and take a photo on Instagram. As we entered, a tourist was there with a walking stick and a backpack. "I guess we won't die today," I said. He gave me a look of fear and confusion. He hadn't gotten the alert. And he saw a 9mm gun stuck in my waist. So I told him what had just happened to the whole state of Hawaii. He looked … relieved.

On the drive home, my ten-year-old son asked me this question: "Dad, why don't we just nuke North Korea off the face of the earth so we don't have to worry about this anymore."

I breathed deep and posed him another question. "Are there children in North Korea?"

"Yes."

"Are they as precious as you?"

"I don't know."

"Of course they are. Are there fathers in North Korea?"

"Yes."

"Are their lives as precious as your father's?" He didn't answer. So I concluded, "It is better to suffer injustice than to inflict it."

It will be hard for people outside Hawaii to understand the profound impact of this false alarm. A neighbor child told us how her family hid in the closest, and her mother cried for an hour. Another family prayed the Rosary and "waited to meet Jesus." Another friend told me, "I watched TV and hoped it was a mistake."

As a filmmaker, writer, and activist, I have reflected on democide and total war for almost three decades. I've traveled the world from Sudan to Iraq. A year ago this week, I was in eyeshot of ISIS, as I traveled with Yazidi and Kurdish soldiers who fought to defend their families. Those families often fled for safety to . . . caves.

And today, I had walked in their shoes.

Tulsi Gabbard: Patriot and Peacemaker

August 4, 2019

If you've been morbidly curious enough to watch the Democratic primaries, you've probably noticed the only interesting candidate. I mean Tulsi Gabbard, with her sane foreign-policy views.

Apart from her, the field of contenders seems to be reading from one shabby script. They "know" that President Trump cannot possibly win reelection. So they're treating the presidential race like a Democratic primary in Boston — that is, as de facto, the genuine election.

We've had so many crushingly costly wars since 2001, you'd think that the candidates would address foreign policy. But few of them seem interested. Several of them supported disastrous American interventions, such as in Iraq and Libya. But now that it's way too late, they assure us that they wouldn't make such mistakes again. Are you impressed? Neither am I.

Tulsi Gabbard is the exception. She played no role in promoting those conflicts. But she did serve bravely in combat in Iraq. And she has returned to speak for the soldiers we've squandered overseas, chasing goalposts that never stop moving; and also for the civilians who suffered brutal ethnic cleansings, when we promised "liberation"; and even for taxpayers, whose money got poured out by the trillions in the desert, profiting only military contractors with good connections.

The high point of the most recent debate? When Gabbard challenged Sen. Kamala Harris for her hypocrisy and authoritarian instincts. She noted how Harris was a ruthless and merciless prosecutor of drug offenders and then joked about smoking marijuana herself. Gabbard noted how hollow Harris's rejection of capital punishment rings. You know, since she deep-sixed evidence that would have freed an innocent man from death row.

And Harris was wounded. There was political blood in the water. So what happened next? Big Tech's censors went after Gabbard again. She was already suing Google for suspending her ads (and no other candidates'). Now, in the wake of her big moment at the debate? As *Reclaim the Net* reports, her duel with Harris "briefly propelled Gabbard to the top of Twitter's trends, albeit with an accompanying article that didn't mention Gabbard or the moment in question."

So some functionary at Twitter quickly stepped in.

Then mysteriously, Gabbard was scrubbed from Twitter's trending list while mentions of the nine other candidates remained. The description for #Harris even acknowledged the interaction and said that Harris was trending with Tulsi. However, no trending hashtags for Gabbard appeared on Twitter's list of trending hashtags.

And the official talking points of the chattering class went flying to network offices.

After the debate, CNN anchor Anderson Cooper asked Gabbard about the Syrian dictator Bashar al-Assad, and people started to use a section of the interview to suggest that Gabbard refuses to criticize Assad's actions, even though the full interview shows her addressing this.

Right after that, as if on cue, the hashtag #Gabbardrussian was suddenly everywhere. Tweets started appearing that accused Tulsi Gabbard, instead of Donald Trump, of being a Russian agent.

What on earth is that about? On what basis do people level the shocking charge of dual loyalty, even treason, against a U.S. member of Congress and combat veteran? It reminds me of old, anti-Semitic canards about Jewish Americans and Israel. And here's where Christians ought to get very, very suspicious. And where I get angry.

I remember when the War Party — including the whole political spectrum from George W. Bush to Joseph Biden — promised that an invasion of Iraq would yield peace and prosperity. That the oil from the invasion would pay for the whole operation. That we'd build a fresh democracy in Iraq, whose grateful citizens would promptly respect the rights of religious minorities. Especially the almost one million Christians whose churches have been there since St. Paul went to Damascus, while most of our ancestors were worshipping rocks and trees.

It didn't pan out that way. Most of those one million Christians were driven out by Islamists, if they weren't killed by ISIS or herded into rape camps. The U.S. intervention in Iraq was a catastrophe for Christians, Yazidis, and other religious minorities. I know because I've met them. I've toured the miserable settlements where Iraqi Christians still live, because Islamists won't even let them enter refugee camps. I've listened to fathers tell me what it's like to see ISIS steal their wives and daughters.

But that didn't satisfy the America-last war jockeys. They wanted to repeat the Iraq War, only this time targeting Syria. As in Iraq, a secular dictator who didn't target Christians but did cozy up to Russia faced off against his enemies. In Syria, the only powerful forces trying to overthrow Assad were radical jihadists — men linked to Al Qaeda and some of them veterans of ISIS. Still, Sen. John McCain and other neoconservatives wanted the United States to arm them and fund them.

During the foreign-policy debate in the GOP primaries, several candidates even demanded that the United States risk war with nuclear-armed Russia by shooting down Russian planes. All to help … Al Qaeda, the folks who bombed the World Trade Center and the Pentagon. Among the GOP candidates, only Rand Paul, Ted Cruz, and Donald Trump rejected this madness. As Jack Hunter writes:

> There have been multiple reports that the US was aiding al-Qaeda with its Syrian rebel support. Even President Trump acknowledged this, thus ending Obama's policy in 2017.
>
> Among the Democrats, Tulsi Gabbard stood almost alone in speaking up. She went further, and flew to Damascus, to meet with that country's leader, and try to avoid a U.S. war on behalf of al Qaeda.

With Trump's election, the United States pivoted, and instead of backing jihadis, it allied with Kurds and Christians. *The Stream* has been one of the few venues reporting on the oasis of religious freedom that emerged in northeastern Syria. The Syrian Democratic Forces based in that oasis fought ISIS on our behalf, losing tens of thousands of soldiers and finally winning. American deaths? We lost seventy-three brave servicepeople.

Yes, Bashar Assad is still in power. He's still a dictator. But you know what didn't happen? A massive, expensive U.S. intervention that lost thousands of American lives. Nor did we shoot down Russian planes, risking World War III. Nor did Al Qaeda march into Damascus and slaughter the Christian men and boys, then march women and girls into rape camps. That is what happened when Turkey helped jihadis invade the Afrin region in January. If it had been up to the War Party, none of that would be true.

So yes, Rep. Tulsi Gabbard helped stop a useless war that would have meant genocide for Christians. Does that make her a "Russian asset"? That's what some people with a lot of cash to throw around want you to think. But whoever said that military contractors don't know how to exert influence?

I'm proud that a congresswoman from my home state of Hawaii helped guarantee peace and religious freedom. I wish more Democrats, and more Republicans, had her solid, patriotic priorities.

Our Thirty-Year Victory Dance on Top of Russia Planted the Seeds of War in Ukraine

February 25, 2022

I was reading a book by *The Stream* contributor Prof. Paul Kengor on Ronald Reagan and the Cold War, and I had a kind of epiphany. Suddenly I understood why Russia's troops are even now invading neighboring Ukraine:

Vladimir Putin is a monster. But he's a monster we created. Don't worry; I will explain. But first, a short history lesson.

When German soldiers marched into the Soviet Union in 1941, at first many greeted them as liberators from Stalin. Russians quickly learned better, of course. Hitler's regime was built on radical Darwinism applied not to species but to races: he saw all Slavs as "subhumans," fit only to serve Aryan masters as serfs and menial laborers.

The Nazi hierarchy specifically ordered the Wehrmacht to suspend the old rules of war: make no distinctions between enemy soldiers and civilians; take no account of the well-being of conquered territories, except insofar as it served the German war effort; don't worry if Russian POWs die of malnutrition, unless they're needed for slave labor in factories; and organize killing units to wipe out local Jews and "commissars."

Within months, Russians who might have welcomed a regime other than Stalin's were forming partisan units to fight for him against the Germans. They sabotaged rail lines, murdered officers, poisoned wells, and forced the Nazis to commit many thousands of troops to subduing already conquered regions. A big part of Nazi defeat in Operation Barbarossa can be traced to their brutal policies.

By contrast, when Americans and Britons stormed into Germany, no partisan units formed. Generally, Germans were relieved that Western forces, and not the Russians, were the ones moving in on them — even though the Allies had bombed whole cities into rubble.

While Germans might still have been infected with Nazi ideas, they knew that Western soldiers had not come to wipe them out — or to subject them as slaves or colonize their country. We said that we came to liberate even the German people from a totalitarian government. And our actions showed that we meant it.

Likewise, Ronald Reagan in his speeches assured the world, including those listening in Russia, that his quarrel was with Communism — not Russians. He denounced the godless system that had starved and tortured Russians for seven long decades. But he never demonized Russians as a nation or a race. He didn't speak of making the United States the single hegemon of a "unipolar" world. Nor did he show any sign of wishing a perpetual quarrel with Russia.

Reagan's honest rhetoric, both in public and in private talks with Mikhail Gorbachev, doubtless played a role in the almost bloodless collapse of first the Soviet Empire, then the Soviet Union. Russians knew that they weren't surrendering to America; they were just shaking off a deadly, toxic regime.

Too bad that American policymakers didn't get Ronald Reagan's memo. Too many conservatives clung to a Cold War stance, pretending that Russia posed a permanent threat to Europe. Too many liberals weaponized human rights concerns as pretexts for advancing American power. Both factions of our foreign-policy elite — the neocons and the globalists — agreed that the United States should treat the Soviet implosion as a power vacuum that we must fill.

Exploiting the erratic leadership of Boris Yeltsin, neoliberal economists such as Harvard's Jeffrey Sachs flew over to Russia — handing them economic schemes that let billionaire oligarchs steal most of the country's wealth.

Military contractors poured money into lobbying efforts by old pals of the Bush family to extend NATO right up to the borders of Russia itself. George Kennan, the U.S. diplomat who invented the policy of "containment" of Communism, warned at the time that such expansion would be "the most fateful error of American policy in the entire post–Cold War era."

For my own part, as a graduate student at Hawaii Pacific University, working on my master's in military science and operational studies, I wrote in the school newspaper that NATO should be disbanded after the U.S.-led air attacks on civilians in Yugoslavia.

We should have acted as magnanimous partners with the Russian people in a joint victory against Communist dictatorship. That is how the United States treated the people of Germany and Japan, after bitter fighting in World War II. Instead, our elites essentially pounced on Eastern Europe, seeking to make it a part of the EU, NATO, and the American sphere of influence.

We would set the terms going forward and guarantee the outcome. The Clinton administration convinced newly independent Ukraine to give up its nuclear weapons — the one thing that would have forever guaranteed its sovereignty. In return? We promised to police its integrity against Russia.

Are we ready to fight a shooting war right now against Putin's Russia to keep that promise? I hope not. That foolish promise both left Ukraine forever vulnerable and kept our hooks in the country. So did our CIA's involvement in the 2013 coup against the (pro-Russian) winner of Ukraine's elections. There's even audio of the U.S. ambassador mulling over whom we should pick as Ukraine's president.

Would we, the United States, tolerate Vladimir Putin meddling this way in Mexico or Canada? How long would we leave such a regime in place?

What worries me more than the current Ukraine War is our future conflict with China. We insist that we do not object to China as a nation, race, or culture. We only object to the Chinese Communist Party (CCP), with a long history of mass murder, that currently keeps Uyghur Muslims in concentration camps.

Should the Chinese people believe us, though? Our track record with how we treated post-Communist Russia suggests that they shouldn't. When the CCP tells its people that our concerns over Taiwan, Hong Kong, or the Uyghurs aren't sincere — that they're "imperialist" evidence of "anti-China" sentiment, the Chinese sadly have good reasons to believe it.

Yes, it was enormously tempting to take ruthless advantage of the Soviet Union's collapse for short-term American interests. But part of American exceptionalism is that we should resist such selfish, Machiavellian behavior. If we want people to see America as a model and an ally in fighting for freedom, we can't give in to such passions.

Russians didn't collude with Donald Trump for him to win the 2016 election. But they did find him refreshing. He stopped peddling all the high-minded, idealistic rhetoric that had masked American power-mongering from 1991 onward. He spoke of America's national interests and real security needs. The Russians were relieved at the end of hypocritical happy talk. They refrained from aggressive actions and responded to Trump's firm policies.

And we see how Russia has responded to the chaos and weakness prevailing under The Secret Committee Formerly Known as Joe Biden. It has pounced, and there's little we can do short of risking destruction.

How will China exploit the power vacuum in the White House? Let's pray for the people of Taiwan.

Poison Gaslighting Ukraine, Biden Seeks a Bloody Quagmire

April 14, 2022

I haven't written here in a while. I spent the past few weeks traveling and visited our medical team on the Ukraine border with Poland. I oversaw delivery of aid we raised for Ukrainians through the Vulnerable People Project. The victims of Vladimir Putin's war are no abstraction to me. I've met hundreds of them and helped some get to safety in Poland, even using networks of previous Afghan refugees we resettled after America's crass surrender there. I ask that you pray in particular for young women fleeing the conflict. They are the prime targets of human trafficking rings, which are using the chaos to capture and exploit fresh new victims.

I know that there are real atrocities taking place, some of them at the hands of Chechen mercenaries, whom the Russians unleashed on Ukraine. That's a bitter irony, since twenty years ago Chechnya itself was devastated at Putin's orders. I've seen firsthand the courage of frontline Ukrainian soldiers. They don't want their country conquered.

But I worry more and more about how elites in the West are exploiting this conflict. The United States and NATO are rightly unwilling to risk a nuclear conflict by fighting Russia directly. So they're pouring arms into Ukraine and, apparently, urging Ukraine's leadership not to negotiate for peace. Instead, as John Zmirak has warned here, Joe Biden and others in the globalist/neoconservative elites seem to favor crippling Russia for the next ten or twenty years. They want to bog Russia down in a bloody "quagmire," which would leave Ukraine a blasted, uninhabitable hellhole. They'd destroy the country to "save" it.

And sadly, America's leadership class is very skilled at doing exactly that: applying sufficient force to wreck a place but not to redeem it. Ask the people of South Vietnam, Cambodia, Laos, Iraq, and Afghanistan how much they benefited from trillions in U.S. aid and thousands of U.S. deaths.

It's one thing to scoff at negotiating when you're facing Nazi Germany and have a realistic plan for bringing that regime to its knees. It's a rare case when we can afford the moral luxury of demanding unconditional surrender — or "regime change." Apart from such righteous crusades against almost pure evil, some 99 percent of wars throughout human history have ended via a negotiated peace. Ideally, such a peace will resolve some of the grievances on both sides that provoked the conflict. Otherwise, you're simply planting the seeds of a new war twenty or thirty short years later.

The Russian government broke international law and outraged the global conscience by resorting to military force. But it didn't start this invasion in a vacuum. There are some real concerns that Russia had, which the West ignored and encouraged Ukraine to scoff at. For example, hinting that Ukraine might join a military alliance like NATO aimed at Russia — an empty tease since it's obvious that NATO can't muster the unanimous vote needed.

The Russian government won't end its attack on Ukraine without resolving some of its concerns — not unless it is comprehensively defeated on the battlefield. Ukraine cannot do that, and NATO won't. Any U.S. effort to do so would mean dancing on the knife edge of a potential nuclear war, the more so since Vladimir Putin would rightly fear losing his job or his life for surrendering.

It's all well and good for a bumbling front man like Joe Biden to mutter some phrases his speechwriters cribbed from Churchill, then blame domestic chaos, energy shortages, and exploding inflation on Putin. Americans are suffering, and this is one way to distract them, through sleight of hand.

But the people I met in Ukraine don't deserve to have their country used as a punching bag for the benefit of Western politicians. Nor is it wise for Ukraine's leaders to put too much faith in American promises and rhetoric. Not when our top generals are openly admitting that they hope to turn Ukraine into a killing field for Russians, with no off-ramp in sight. For every Russian conscript killed, how many Ukrainian civilians will have to die? How many cities must be devastated to help the Democrats in the upcoming midterm elections?

Make no mistake. That's a main concern of the Biden administration. Expect it to serve as an obstacle to peace efforts at least until those elections are over. Tragically, it serves their cynical interests to keep American voters' eyes on foreign atrocities, instead of the local gas pumps or school board meetings. And Ukrainians will die as a side effect of Biden's poison gaslighting.

The same administration that favors legal infanticide and jail time for pro-life whistleblowers is willing to pile up bodies in Kyiv and Odesa. Ukrainians need to know that their fair-weather friends are using them as human shields for their failed and failing policies. And they need to get busy with real peace efforts quickly. Or else they'll end up in the same place as previous U.S. allies in Saigon, Baghdad, and Kabul.

Remembering Allies Who Saved Our Soldiers' Lives

May 30, 2022

What you leave behind is not what is engraved on stone monuments, but what is woven into the lives of others.

— Pericles

If we want Memorial Day to be more than a day for appliance sales, we need to remember its meaning — not merely in our hearts or with our words, but with our deeds. Memorial Day is the occasion when we honor fallen service members across the American military. This year, we have sadly had to add those thirteen warriors who died at Abbey Gate during Joe Biden's botched withdrawal from Afghanistan. We remember them this Memorial Day when our media elites and politicians have already forgotten them.

We must act to honor the sacrifice of our courageous service members. That means guaranteeing them the benefits and services they earned, of course. But it also means helping to finish the mission for which they suffered and died — even in places where our civilian leadership coldly decided to cut and run.

America isn't used to waging long wars and losing them. We still think of ourselves in terms of V-E Day and V-J Day — of grateful civilians waving American flags at our forces, calling them "liberators."

But in recent decades, our leaders have grown more careless about when and where they send our brave servicepeople. So we have found ourselves in conflicts we could not contain — and with leaders who couldn't or wouldn't manage responsible outcomes. First Vietnam, and then Iraq, and then Afghanistan loom in our memories.

In each case, the courage, competence, and self-sacrifice of American fighters were not matched by civilian leadership. In each country, those who'd aided the U.S. forces and shared our dream of freedom paid a bitter price. Our failure to protect them doubtless made the next assignment for U.S. forces more difficult and dangerous: People wondered whether it was safe to help the Americans. Thousands of U.S. lives will ride on that question the next time our leaders see fit to intervene somewhere.

If you move in veterans' circles, you already know this: Servicemen and women who came back from Afghanistan are devastated and ashamed by Joe Biden's surrender of that country. The price of Biden's eagerness to flee haunts these brave men and women. It ought to haunt us all.

The United States under President Trump had stabilized the military situation in Afghanistan and reduced American casualties to almost nothing. The United States possessed vastly expensive, strategically important military bases in a geopolitically crucial country. A small American garrison stood as the lynchpin holding together a pro-American government. The Biden administration didn't continue to negotiate from Trump's position of strength. Instead, it seemed to panic and left behind for a terrorist regime allied to China a vast arsenal of American weapons and equipment. And our own people and our allies paid a bitter price, which is still rising.

Biden abandoned a country clearly ill-prepared for our exit to chaotic rule by fanatics. He stranded U.S. citizens, pulling out our troops before even reclaiming our civilians. Even worse, this sudden and unprovided U.S. surrender doomed to persecution some one hundred thousand Afghans who'd served shoulder to shoulder with American men and women in uniform. The State Department admits that a majority of Afghans who earned Special Immigrant Visas during the war got left behind. The Taliban is hunting them while you read these words.

When I traveled with the Peshmerga near the front lines in their war against ISIS, I heard a powerful proverb. A former high-ranking Iraqi military leader said, "There are two ways to be an Iraqi. Either our sand is in your blood, or your blood is in our sand."

Likewise, there are different ways to become an American. Surely one of them is fighting alongside Americans against vicious extremists in the shared cause of human decency. That's why the U.S. Congress agreed to grant special visas to Afghans who'd really earned them. The Biden administration, where veterans are scant, has not honored America's word.

This Memorial Day, the best way we can honor those servicemen and women who made the ultimate sacrifice, especially the 2,448 warriors who died in

Afghanistan, is to work to bring home to the United States the Afghans who saved countless American lives, who bled alongside our soldiers.

The U.S. Army Rangers have a creed. It includes this phrase: "I will never leave a fallen comrade to fall into the hands of the enemy, and under no circumstances will I ever embarrass my country." The Biden administration clearly never felt such a sentiment. We'll have to teach it to them.

Ukraine, Don't Surrender to Putin or to the LGBTQMYNAMEISLEGION Machine

June 16, 2023

On June 9, 2023, in Kyiv, Ukraine, I delivered a message to pro-patriotic, pro-family Ukrainians attending the "Life, Dignity, Victory" summit there. Here is the text:

It is a privilege to be a participant at this historic "Life, Dignity, Victory" summit, sponsored by the Chalice of Mercy foundation. I founded the Vulnerable People Project over twenty years ago to stand with communities facing ethnic cleansing, genocide, and total war. The fundamental truth I have learned in two decades of standing with the vulnerable is this:

> *Vulnerable communities are made up of strong people placed in seemingly impossible situations.*

But when thoughtful people are inspired to stand with them, the impossible becomes possible, and the vulnerable can triumph over their aggressors.

As a husband, as a father of seven, and as a grandfather, I see my work through the lens of fatherhood. The thought of the children of Ukraine experiencing terror, suffering, and loss has inspired me to leave my own family, on the other side of the world, and be here with you today — to stand with the husbands, fathers, and grandfathers of Ukraine as they fight to honor the sacrifices of their forefathers, the security of their families, and the destiny of their yet unborn descendants.

The people of Ukraine are engaged as a nation in a solemn struggle for something sacred. Right now, you fight for your national independence and historical borders.

Ukraine's culture, faith, language, and boundaries were gifted to you by your ancestors. They're the fruit of uncountable sacrifices by millions of your forefathers: farmers and tradesmen, herders and craftsmen, mothers and nuns, priests and apostles and soldiers. Their names are lost to history but remembered by God in Heaven. Most of our names here today will likewise go unremembered — it's the fate of ordinary people, those of us who don't carve our fame in the history books by acts either famous or infamous.

But each of us leaves a legacy in the work we did, the children we raised, the souls we touched, and our simple acts of love. And in the fabric and texture and historical reality that is Ukraine, you see the accumulated legacy of a people — your people, your ancestors who sweated and bled to leave a world behind for you. And for your children. And for the Faith that sustained them through persecution and poverty, conquest and occupation.

It couldn't be clearer. Your legacy is being threatened. To shrug and allow foreign invaders to erase your culture and rob you of your posterity is the gravest kind of impiety. But that is not what Ukrainians have chosen, as the world now sees each day on the news from the battlefronts.

Borders are important. When colonizers and occupiers impose their will on helpless countries, they draw arbitrary lines that efface history, erase cultures, divide communities, and provoke future wars. Organic borders that reflect a nation's history and respect its integrity are critically important, as Ukrainians all know.

We see that people need more than borders. They need self-determination, genuine freedom, the liberty that comes only with the gospel of Jesus Christ, and the noble view of humanity that follows close behind it. When the people of Ukraine prevail and preserve its boundaries, when Ukraine regains every square inch of its sovereign territory, I pray it happens soon with minimal loss of lives.

What then? Will that come with renewed sovereignty and a real independence? Will it be the free Ukraine your ancestors dreamt of and fought for? Will the nation carry on its culture, faith, traditions, and all those sacred values that solid borders exist to protect?

While physical borders are important, cultural and spiritual borders are even more important. We protect our borders to preserve life, culture, and dignity. Your cultural and spiritual borders must be defended with the same daring and fortitude with which you are fighting to defend Ukraine from Russia's war of aggression.

Will Ukraine trade Russian colonizers and occupiers for post-Christian, post-Western ones? Will it turn over its children to the counselors and therapists who now in America quietly recruit kids for sex-change procedures, puberty blockers, hormone therapy, and surgical castration of boys — often without the consent or even the knowledge of their parents? Will Ukraine let Planned Parenthood — which designed the murderous One Child Policy on behalf of the Red Chinese government — open clinics in Kyiv that would rob you of a generation of children, a new Holodomor in service of a new godless ideology of evil, to finish the job that Joseph Stalin started?

In a Ukraine colonized by destructive ideologies, the ordinary citizens will not rule themselves any more than they did behind the Iron Curtain.

I think everyone here will stand with me and say, "Absolutely not!" You will say, "We are not fighting to trade one set of foreign masters for another, to swap out openly brutal and thuggish colonial masters who rule with the iron fist, for smoother, slicker, manipulative masters who rule by the velvet glove."

I believe, and I pray, that you will not let foreign special interests and media masters throw away the fruits of your suffering, squandering not only the blood spilt in this war, but the blood, sweat, and tears of a thousand years of ancestors.

I'd like to close with the final words of a book I published nine years ago, warning the world against repeating the horrors that tormented the twentieth century. I hope we can issue a Ukrainian edition, because it's something I think you might find helpful. The title is *The Race to Save Our Century.* Here's how it ends:

> We can treat people as if they were robots, ghosts, or beasts. We can starve, enslave, imprison them, or kill them. But that doesn't change the reality. If we look up, and also within, we will find the mysterious image and likeness of God. We will discover the truth that we and our neighbors have an incomparable beauty and worth. A dignity that no one can take away.
>
> Our thousand-year reichs, our workers' paradises, our brave new worlds, are ghastly fantasies that human beings create, and that history duly comes along and exposes. And what is left behind, bruised and battered but still unbowed, is the face of Man — as noble and as beautiful as Adam reaching out his hand to the God who made him.
>
> We will remember that, and we will do what is needed. We will feel from the depths of our hearts to the highest flights of our imagination a love of the good, a hatred of cruelty and smallness of soul, and a loyalty to each and

every member of our family, the human family. We will fight to enshrine the basic principles of decency in our political, economic, and personal lives. We will have courage. We will prevail.

Slava Ukraini, Heroyam Slava! (Glory to Ukraine, glory to the heroes!)

RFK Jr. Is Right: We Need to Disband NATO, Which Has Morphed into a Suicide Pact

June 24, 2024

Thanks to the recklessness of the Biden regime and its overseas cat's-paws, we are closer to nuclear war than we've been since the Cuban Missile Crisis.

Are you willing to die, along with your entire family and everyone you've ever known, to restore the 1961 borders of Ukraine instead of reaching a compromise and a ceasefire in its war with Russia? How about to ensure that LGBT ideology advances in Catholic Poland? Do you support the German establishment's efforts to outlaw its most popular, patriotic political party? Or the EU's blackmail of Hungary, fining it millions of dollars a day as long as it refuses to cede control of its immigration policy to Brussels?

Because those are the de facto missions of NATO, and the European Union, which it protects with billions of borrowed U.S. dollars. Rather than having those nations spend money on their own defense, they can spend ours to censor their media, persecute biblical preachers who object to trans ideology, prosecute homeschoolers, and seize land from farmers in the name of preventing "climate change."

The European Union was pioneered by faithful Catholic defenders of Western civilization who wished to escape the fratricidal slaughters driven by violent nationalism. But secularized elites inexorably took control of it and now use its institutional power to persecute Christians and patriots. NATO is now the military arm of those elites both in Europe and America.

The anti-Christian oligarchs who rule Western Europe, increasingly *despite* the will of those countries' peoples, rely on the NATO alliance to secure their independence with the threat that the United States will launch a suicidal nuclear war in defense of (you name the place: Turkey, Latvia, Finland, etc.). In theory, if Turkey went to war with Greece (not an absurd scenario at this point), we'd be committed to fight for each side against the other.

How did we get here? How did a treaty organization created to stop Stalinist Communism from conquering postwar Western Europe morph into an ideological evil empire all its own, decades after the real threat vanished and the Soviet empire collapsed into a shrinking, impoverished Russia that's essentially an oil and gas patch with an oversized, outdated army?

Robert F. Kennedy Jr., who's willing to ask tough questions about Big Pharma's dictatorial power grab during the COVID panic, is raising similarly brave questions about the role of NATO. As the *New York Post* reported, RFK recently said, "It is insane to even keep NATO going. Russia lost the cold war."

If you listen to intelligence expert Mike Benz, it wasn't the West that won that war so much as the intelligence agencies in the United States and Europe, who'd pioneered the Internet (funded by the U.S. Department of Defense's DARPA). They'd developed elaborate tools for influencing, even controlling, public opinion online to undermine the Soviets.

After 1991, they didn't pack up that tool kit; instead, they started employing it against conservatives, nationalists, and Christians who bucked the agenda of secular globalists. Remember how YouTube promised to censor anyone who disagreed with the WHO during the COVID panic? How Facebook agreed when the CIA told it to silence talk about Hunter Biden's laptop until after the 2020 election? Those weren't outliers. They were the Matrix working as intended.

Robert F. Kennedy is courageous, but he's a little late to the party. The great Christian conservative and Cold Warrior Patrick Buchanan called for NATO's disbanding in several of his prophetic books during the 1990s, especially *A Republic, Not an Empire.* In 2000, I was proud to help Buchanan as a delegate in the Reform Party during his quixotic attempt to sideline globalist George W. Bush.

I have my own track record on this issue. I was so appalled by the way the Clinton administration abused NATO to bomb Yugoslav civilians in 1999 that as a humble graduate student in military science at Hawaii Pacific University, I published my own piece in the student paper echoing Buchanan's call to end NATO (see page 49). The response? Some administrators tried to get me kicked out of the program. (When you start taking flak, you know you are over the target.)

World War III Already Happened — Just Not in the West

July 5, 2024

Recently, my colleague John Zmirak warned of the Biden regime's approving reckless actions that risk an open war with Russia — and likely her allies, which now include China and Iran. And he's right about the present danger of our proxy war with Russia in Ukraine escalating quickly, from at least half a million Ukrainian and Russian dead to unimaginable millions of Germans, Poles, Frenchmen, Britons, and Americans. U.S.-made and -piloted drones attacking Russian civilians in Crimea: How is that not a provocation verging on madness?

It doesn't help that our president, who holds the nuclear codes, is a shambling husk of a man who clearly isn't making the key decisions for our country. Who is? We don't even know. It's a secret. Did I somehow miss the relevant clause in our Constitution that provides for anonymous handlers to lead us? At least with King George III, we knew who was really in charge.

But I want to step back from the brink for a moment and try to understand how we got here. Not just to the very edge of an apocalyptic conflict but to the state of roiling chaos that prevails all across the West and pervades the Muslim world; to the gathering repression in Europe, Canada, and even the D.C. gulag of out-of-touch elites wielding all their power to gaslight, silence, and reeducate their citizens.

We all know the official story, the "Warren Commission" version of the conflict across the globe: It's between the noble, progressive forces of individual freedom represented by Western elites ... and everything else in the world, which is dark, irrational, and evil. That includes all world religions, except for the sanitized versions that airbrush out traditional morality and replace concern for the afterlife with some "social gospel" or another.

The West is ruled for the moment by enlightened advocates of sexual liberation, revolutionary technologies such as AI, and bioengineering that some hope will drag human life out for centuries. Self-assured experts and billionaire activists offer to take over the world's food supply, seize control of energy supplies, buy up all the farmland, and inject the children of the world with bold new vaccines for the diseases they're secretly producing in government labs. They promise us clean energy, forty-five new genders, diversity, equity, and inclusion.

But standing in the way of the brave new world on offer are the murky forces of darkness, repression, misinformation, and "hate." The enemy comes in many shapes and sizes, of course — since most of the human race does not subscribe to the Davos vision of a Great Reset ruled from the top down by a tiny cabal of veal-white Ivy League graduates. Maybe it's American Deplorable voters who object to lawless open borders and plummeting wages; or patriotic Frenchmen who wonder why a historic church burns down at least once a month; Dutch farmers who want to keep working their ancestors' land; Hungarians who think they should be able to choose their own national leaders.

These are the targets today of our bloodless, power-hungry elites, and they're the readers for whom I wrote *The Great Campaign Against the Great Reset.* But what if I told you that this is just the second wave of repression, subversion, and violence launched by our self-appointed leaders? What if much of the chaos afflicting the West today was, in fact, the result of the past thirty years of delusional social engineering and reckless wars?

What if World War III already happened, in fact — if a tsunami of violence and disruption struck large parts of the world, and we in the West are now just experiencing the aftershock?

My Vulnerable People Project seeks to aid the most afflicted, marginalized human beings around the world — the victims who pay the price for the reckless decisions of our leaders, whose countries have been shattered and families devastated, whom most of us usually forget about after the last American soldiers are pulled out of the region and our diplomats have scuttled onto the last helicopter out of town. We provide coal for Afghans suffering in the wake of America's failed intervention there; we sought safe refuges for Yazidis and Iraqi Christians after America shattered that state too.

In my travels, I see things most Americans never dream of. For instance, I pass through medieval villages in Spain and see them full of desperate Syrian refugees begging for handouts. And I ask myself: *Do these people want to be here? Why were millions of Muslims driven to leave their ancestral villages and their countries to live as strangers in an alien culture, whose own Christian heritage (from Lisbon to Warsaw) is being liquidated by elites in favor of pansexual globalism?*

And the answer, sadly, is clear. Our shallow, badly educated, intellectually incurious but massively self-confident leaders have been playing a game of Risk for decades, except with human pieces on the global board. The mainstream "Right" and "Left," from George W. Bush to Hillary Clinton and Barack Obama, didn't really disagree on all that much in the end. We saw how cozy they all were at John McCain's funeral, a massive bipartisan lovefest of our rulers. Remember Bush virtually smooching with Michelle Obama? Bush let us know what he thought of American Deplorables (most of his party's voters) when he lumped in the January 6 election protestors as "children of the same foul spirit" as the 9/11 hijackers.

Our elites all agreed that the United States needed to secure its oil supplies — that we needed to keep any Muslim power from becoming all that strong, lest it threaten those supplies or pose a threat to Israel. The best way for us to do that? To set the various countries in the region at each other's throats, keep them fighting among themselves. Remember how the United States encouraged Iraq to invade Iran and provided Saddam Hussein with chemical weapons? That idea killed between one and two million people and yielded nothing for either country. But it kept each one of them weak.

Then came the first Gulf War, when the United States "accidentally" failed to make clear to Iraq that we wouldn't tolerate an invasion of Kuwait. And our Congress was flooded with lobbyists, including lying witnesses who claimed that Iraqis threw Kuwaiti babies out of incubators. That war killed some two hundred thousand people, mostly Iraqi civilians. Our soldiers were ordered to bulldoze and bury alive thousands of Iraqi soldiers on the infamous "highway of death." One American traumatized by taking part in that massacre was ... Timothy McVeigh. Be careful creating monsters. Sometimes they come back home to roost.

We cynically urged the Kurds to rise up against Hussein and then watched as he slaughtered them. We "contained" Iraq with crippling, savage sanctions that caused the deaths of 1.5 million Iraqis, mostly children, according to UNICEF. I'll never forget then–Secretary of State Madeleine Albright saying, "The price, we think, the price is worth it."

Then came 9/11, provoked by U.S. troops patrolling Saudi Arabia in the wake of the first Gulf War, which was made possible by the slack, apathetic leadership of

George W. Bush. That attack was seized on as a pretext for "remaking" the whole Muslim world, as American neoconservatives called for the United States to invade and occupy more than a dozen countries. In the end, we invaded only two but ruined both of them.

In Afghanistan, we insisted we would impose Western liberalism and democracy in a region profoundly inhospitable to either concept. In Iraq, we smashed the government and ruling party and created a hellhole of chaos that led to the genocide of seven hundred thousand Christians and other minorities. At least we imposed gun control in Iraq, disarming the very groups that were targeted by terrorists (who strangely failed to turn in their guns; go figure!).

When Barack Obama came to power, in part on the promise of pulling out of Iraq, his administration switched from military occupation to massive, savage drone strikes, killing thousands of Muslim civilians around the world, sowing hatred for Westerners and Christians instead of the oligarchs responsible for the policy.

In the "Arab Spring," we wielded Western "soft power" among the populations of fragile Arab countries to encourage "democracy." We used the Internet (developed first as a weapon by the Defense Department's DARPA and carefully managed by the CIA, as we learned during the Hunter Biden laptop scandal) to sow discontent, to encourage dissidents, and to overthrow long-existing regimes. We used NATO to bomb Libya into anarchy, creating a civil war and reigniting the trade in black slaves.

Now, with the war between Israel and Gaza, we're seeing an entire region rendered uninhabitable, with civilians paying the price for their extremist leaders. But why were the people of Gaza driven to embrace groups such as Hamas? A few decades back, most Arabs supported secular socialist parties that centered on nationalism and didn't persecute Christians. Was it climate change that goaded religious extremism all through the Muslim world? Just bad luck? Some law of nature?

Or were the people of a huge swath of the world, from North Africa through central Asia, the victims of an arrogant, high-handed, and selfish civilizational war, waged by secularists in power against Muslims around the world and Christians here at home?

Those are questions worth pondering, aren't they?

What We Wish Donald Trump Would Say to Prime Minister Netanyahu

July 26, 2024

The following is a transcript of what former and future President Donald Trump ought to have said to Israeli Prime Minister Benjamin Netanyahu at Mar-a-Lago.

It's a real pleasure to meet you again, Bibi. The last time we worked together, it was a much different world, a much safer world for ordinary, peaceful people, from Tel Aviv to Kyiv to Kabul, and for Americans too.

Leadership matters, and when the leader of the possibly most powerful force for good on earth is either weak or delusional, the bad guys out there get emboldened. I don't think for one minute that the United States under my leadership would have seen a Russia that dared to invade Ukraine. Nor do I think that Hamas would have attempted the massacres of October 7 aimed at your people. Certainly, the Taliban allied to China would not be sitting on $90 billion of U.S. military hardware.

You know I believe in nations, in borders, and in being tough. I certainly understand and support Israel's effort to crush Hamas's forces. As someone with a Jewish child and grandchildren, I find it sickening, just sickening, to see the open Jew-hatred exploding around the world, including at schools I attended long ago, in much happier times.

I think you know that under a second Trump administration, the United States would have Israel's back in a much more productive and thoughtful way than at any point in U.S. history. We have the same enemies. We share the same core values. We can talk to each other honestly.

But you know I'm also a realist. I believe that making deals is an art — I wrote a little book about that; I'll make sure you get a copy before you leave. I don't want to make the perfect the enemy of the pretty good. That's why I've had to make compromises, give ground, even piss off some of the core people in my own political base who want to go too far, too fast, and end up shooting themselves in the foot.

This means I need to tell you some things that you might not enjoy hearing. But I'm saying them for your good and for the good of the beautiful people you represent and serve in that amazing country they created. I am a Zionist. By that, I mean that I want there to be an Israel, as I want there to be a Finland, an Armenia, and an Albania. Israel exists and has every right to protect itself. It deserves the support of the world.

But it won't be able to defend itself forever if it loses all that support. I'm shocked at how quickly and powerfully that support has drained away in many Western countries. Radical parties aligned with the crazy Left have come to power in France and Britain. And the Left here in America is getting wilder and more reckless every day. As you saw on your visit, mobs in our nation's capital attacked the American flags outside Union Station and replaced them with Palestinian flags. The likely Democratic nominee, Kamala Harris, refused to do her job as vice president by presiding over your speech to Congress. None of these signs are good. If I were an Israeli, they'd make me very nervous.

America benefits greatly from having a democratic ally in the Middle East. Compared with any other country in the world, our history demonstrates our friendliness toward the Jewish people. That's why so many Jews came here, and they have enriched us in so many ways. But even more, I must say, Israel needs America. It's not going to find in Russia or China trustworthy friends. It doesn't want to face Iran and ISIS and Hamas out on an ice floe by itself. God forbid.

For the best interests of both our countries and the peace of your region, I need your help in keeping American support for Israel solid and strong. I'm not going to pander, not one little bit, to the anti-Western hatred and radicalism we're seeing at our colleges. But you could make life easier for me, and for religious Christians in my party who want to support Israel for biblical reasons. You could make life a lot easier, Bibi.

I keep seeing reports, including from supporters of mine who are 100 percent in favor of a secure and peaceful Israel, of truly bad behavior by rogue elements of your military — behavior that targets, of all people, the most helpless and harmless people in the region: Christians in Gaza. These people's families and churches have been there for two thousand years. They're mostly of Jewish origin originally, descended from the disciples who walked with Jesus. And some of the IDF's raw recruits are treating them terribly.

First, in the northern part of Gaza where they live, the army has cut off all food. There's one Christian aid group, the Vulnerable People Project, which provides armed guards for synagogues in Nigeria. It tried to bring food to one of those ancient churches and got approval from your government. But by the time its trucks drew near, soldiers had bombed the place to rubble. I saw a video testimony of a Christian girl whose church had been bombed and her home destroyed, family members killed and wounded, by soldiers who then paraded in her underwear and wrote obscenities on her walls.

I actually have a list here of civilian Christian sites, not Hamas hiding holes, that have been destroyed since Israel began its response to the October 7 massacre. Sorry, but I have to take this opportunity to let you know these things, which I'm sure nobody else brings to your attention. Let me just read you this:

- On October 17, the Anglican Al-Ahli Hospital was blown apart by Israeli missile fire, killing hundreds of civilians.
- Two days later, an Israeli airstrike hit St. Porphyrius Church, killing eighteen Christians and wounding dozens more.
- On December 16, Israeli forces targeted the compound of Holy Family Parish; a sniper killed two women after they walked outside and then wounded several men who tried to help them. That same day, Mother Teresa's order, the Missionaries of Charity, saw its convent struck three times by Israeli artillery shells, leaving it uninhabitable.
- Ten days later, Gaza's only Baptist church was destroyed by Israeli tank shells.
- A Byzantine church in Jabalia (northern Gaza) was destroyed by the IDF.
- The Green Shrine in Deir al-Balah, the first Christian monastery built in Palestine during the Byzantine era, was partially damaged.
- Rev. Mitri Raheb, who founded Dar al-Kalima University in Bethlehem, says that all Christian institutions in Gaza have been severely damaged or destroyed.

I know your government doesn't have a policy of doing such harm, any more than ours did when undisciplined soldiers attacked civilians in Vietnam or in Iraq. But we paid a big, bad price for those mistakes, and Israel will pay a price, too, if American Christians — your biggest supporters, bar none! — start hearing from unfriendly media all about these unfortunate incidents.

The horrors of October 7 are being forgotten given all the civilian destruction that has subsequently taken place. Israel can't afford for that to happen. At this point, we need a ceasefire. Once I'm back in office, I'll help you make a beautiful deal, as we did with the Gulf States. We'll put a stop to this madness and give your citizens some peace.

In the meantime, can we work together on fixing these issues, removing the land mines left behind by history and planting instead olive trees that will offer peace and shelter for our children and grandchildren?

Help! I Am an Anti-Palestinian Bigot

August 6, 2024

My organization, the Vulnerable People Project, is advocating for the victims of the war in Gaza. Recently, while shooting interviews for a documentary about Palestinian Christians, I discovered something shameful about myself: I am an anti-Palestinian bigot.

In interview after interview, I caught myself having these surprised thoughts: *Wow, she has a Ph.D.?* As if Palestinians are incapable of intellectual pursuits. *Wow, he's such a nuanced conversationalist.* As if Palestinians are genetically bound to be inarticulate simpletons. *She's so beautiful!* As if Palestinians are ugly as a rule. *He is so thoughtful and empathetic.* As if Palestinians are all childlike narcissists.

When you hear your inner voice talking about Palestinians the way Joe Biden talked about Barack Obama (in 2008, Biden said that the black senator was so "clean" and "articulate"), you know you've got a deeply ingrained prejudice.

America is extremely racially mixed, and most ordinary Americans have no temptation at all toward anti-Semitism. We see Jews in America primarily as fellow Americans, and even Israeli Jews are easily recognizable as belonging to the same broad, free, glorious Western civilization.

But after my unpleasant self-realization during the interviews, I went back through my memories and realized just how deep-seated my anti-Palestinian sentiment is.

When I was in my teens and my friends and I heard about an acquaintance having a run-in with a group of Palestinian boys who were new to the community, our attitude was unmistakable. We were rough kids, and scattered acts of violence and vengeance were normal in our neighborhood. But this was different: The foreigners had attacked one of us. That day, I remember, a big group of us piled into the back of my friend's car armed with baseball bats.

I've been weathering attacks on my reputation and losing donors because of my decision to speak up about the civilian casualties in Gaza. Fifteen thousand dead children. Twenty thousand missing children. And I will not stop speaking up.

But in the face of each Israeli or fellow American who's questioned my advocacy for Palestinians, I've seen my own. I look at these critics as if I'm looking in a mirror. And there, to my own embarrassment, I see bigotry.

The Palestinians I interviewed for my documentary were magnanimous, principled, and compassionate.

Take one woman who fled for her life and lost family members in Gaza. Her church was bombed. Israeli soldiers deliberately humiliated her, rifling through her private things and filming themselves playing with her underwear.

"I don't blame the Israeli soldiers at all," she told me. Many of them are very young, she explained, and they had been civilians just months earlier. "They're barely trained, and they're angry over October 7."

She blamed the politicians of Israel — fallible and, in some cases, cynical actors whom the Israeli public itself distrusts.

My friend Khalil is from Gaza, but he now lives in the West. During our interviews, I have to admit, I was testing him. I was and remain truly worried about the rise of Jew-hatred in the West. When you tell people what the Israeli government is doing in Gaza, as Khalil does, there is a risk of fomenting more of that hatred.

So I pressed Khalil for hours about how to stop American Jew-hatred. Mind you, Khalil is a young, red-blooded man whose father died during the war — and whose eighteen-year-old sister was killed just a few months ago by the Israel Defense Force in Gaza.

Despite those traumas — any one of which could serve as justification for rage — Khalil passed my "test" with flying colors. Not once did he so much as downplay Jew-hatred, and he sincerely advocated for his own people without any hint of animosity toward the Israeli people.

Could our feelings about Palestinians pass the same test?

This year, I've seen mainstream American commentators publicly call for genocide in Gaza. That's not an exaggeration. Israeli officials have said even worse, calling for ethnic cleansing, deliberate mass starvation, Dresden-style firebombings, and more.

And on October 7, my own thoughts weren't any nobler. "Flatten Gaza," I said under my breath as I watched the horrific footage of violence against innocent Israelis.

Benjamin Netanyahu, of course, is taking full advantage of that kind of thinking. He is an ideologue swept away by history, and he seems bent on undermining Israel's true interests the way George W. Bush undermined America's when he invaded Iraq — a tragic decision that led to genocides, the displacement of millions from their homelands throughout the Middle East, and the rise of ISIS.

I don't look down on my Israeli friends for their rhetoric. I'm also not shocked by the rhetoric of some Palestinians now boiling over with vengefulness toward Israel.

But what we need is a harnessing of these sentiments, and a salvaging of the deepest and most legitimate sentiment of all: a healthy pride in one's own people and an eagerness to defend it against injustice.

And for that urgent need, I am looking to former President Donald Trump — a man who, for whatever his faults might be — has a natural revulsion for war.

In order to extricate the world from the brink of catastrophe, we need a Trump administration willing to channel toughness into thoughtfulness and grace and dignity — an administration that recognizes that other peoples and states have their own interests and that, most of the time, we have shared interests.

America has a longstanding alliance with Israel and shares its interests. But Palestinians and Israelis have more obviously shared interests than any other two people groups in the world. And Israel — surrounded by a tinderbox Arab world filled with competing vendettas and historical grievances — cannot afford to be as stupid as the United States has been.

Under the leadership of a strong but sensible, humane but tough United States, the international community still stands a chance of guiding Israel away from the path toward disaster. It's a delicate operation that will require a change of direction that doesn't compromise the rights of the Israeli people when it comes to a sense of pride and dignity.

But if anyone can pull Netanyahu and other Israeli leaders back from allowing the pain of history to drive them to recklessness, it's Trump, who deftly dismantled the reckless foreign-policy approach of Bushism while leaving America still standing tall.

The "Most Moral" Military on Earth?

August 27, 2024

There are two honest, consistent responses to Israel's draconian war in Gaza. One is to be appalled at the large number of civilian casualties, the singling out of Christians (whom Israeli hard-liners despise because they simply will not leave), and the resulting damage to international goodwill for Israel and Jews. One can watch these events and decide that Israel's government is sabotaging that country's future.

Another response is to coldly decide it's worth it — that Israel must give up the pretense of being a compassionate nation and instead play by the cold-blooded, ruthless rules of its region: a Middle East where American-backed dictators routinely gas civilians, cleanse minorities, and exploit ethno-nationalism and religious fanaticism. One might conclude that the Muslims of that region are always either at your throat or at your feet, and you prefer the latter, thank you very much.

I have friends who take each of those positions.

What you can't do honestly and rationally is pretend that what Israel is doing in Gaza is essentially a humanitarian rescue operation, conducted with exquisite care for civilians by soldiers who are essentially blue helmets — except when the utter fanaticism of their primitive enemies forces those peacekeepers to target facilities containing "human shields." Nor can one pretend that, even then, the IDF acts with the maximum concern for civilian lives consistent with success — evincing a higher moral code than any nation on earth, and the U.S. military in particular.

That's just a lie. And as a U.S. infantry veteran with many friends still in the service and a son who served in Iraq, I resent it. Who's telling this lie? A certain kind of neoconservative or liberal internationalist who practices double standards. In the United States and Europe, such people favor high immigration, political secularism, multiculturalism, and Wilsonian rhetoric. But when it comes to Israel, they suddenly turn into practitioners of Realpolitik of a kind that would make Otto von Bismarck blush.

Here are some instances of the "Israel's hands are cleaner than America's" line that's being repeated:

- Col. Richard Kemp's remarks: "Israel: The World's Most Moral Army."
- John Kirby's claim: "We have seen them [the IDF] take actions, sometimes actions that even I'm not sure our own military would take, in terms of informing civilian populations ahead of operations where to go, where not to go."
- Rep. Brad Sherman: "War is chaotic, and urban warfare more so. I believe that Israel is doing as good a job as can be done and is working hard to avoid civilian casualties. Analysts indicate that Israeli efforts in this area are favorable [compared] to U.S. military actions in Fallujah and Mosul. And of course, ISIS forces in Fallujah and Mosul were not firing rockets at the American homeland."
- *The Telegraph* columnist Charles Lipson: "The IDF is still the most moral army on earth."
- And let's take it straight from the source, Benjamin Netanyahu himself: "The [Israeli] army is the most moral army in the world" that "does everything to avoid harming those not involved."

If only this rhetoric were true. My organization, the Vulnerable People Project, spends millions each year protecting the most forgotten victims of genocide and persecution — such as Iraqi Christians, Yazidi, Uyghurs in China, and Jews in Nigeria, whose synagogue we defend with armed security. Our current most urgent project is aid for the besieged, non-violent Christian population of northern Gaza. They have no connection to any form of violence, yet as Palestinian Christians they faced the same brutal fate their Muslim compatriots have endured at the hands of Israel's army.

These Christians have deep attachments to their ancient churches and cemeteries, and the land on which their families have lived since the first century — when their ancestors were among Jesus' first disciples. And the IDF seems determined to drive them out. Unlike their Muslim neighbors, these Christians have nowhere else to go.

Their churches and hospitals get bombed, their homes invaded, their civilians abused by rogue, undisciplined conscripts who seem to blame them for historical anti-Semitism in Europe — as Sunni extremists blamed Iraqi Christians for George W. Bush's invasion. With the Israeli government's approval, the Vulnerable People Project filled a truck with supplies for these helpless civilians. Before it could arrive, the church at which it was destined to arrive had been targeted and destroyed.

Having heard about these incidents firsthand from survivors, I'm inclined not to dismiss as jihadi agitprop reports of other outrages against Christian facilities:

- On October 17, 2023, the Anglican Al-Ahli Hospital was blown apart by Israeli missile fire, killing hundreds of civilians.
- On December 16, 2023, Israeli forces targeted the compound of Holy Family Parish; a sniper killed two women after they walked outside and wounded several men who tried helping them.
- On December 16, 2023, Mother Teresa's order, the Missionaries of Charity, saw its convent struck three times by Israeli artillery shells, leaving it uninhabitable.
- Ten days, later, Gaza's only Baptist church was destroyed by Israeli tank shells.
- On July 7, 2024, Holy Family Catholic School was bombed, and four civilians killed.
- The same day, a Byzantine church in Jabalia (northern Gaza) was destroyed by the IDF.
- Also that day, the Green Shrine in Deir al-Balah, the first Christian monastery built in Palestine during the Byzantine era, was partially damaged.

The BBC has made a comprehensive list of religious sites damaged or destroyed during the IDF's campaign so far.

Now, maybe we should limit the credence we give to reports from international organizations, especially those with documented anti-Zionist bias. But given the quantity of smoke that I've sniffed, it is not unreasonable to think there might be fire here. Therefore, I won't dismiss out of hand the claims of the Institute for Palestine Studies, which include this alarming report:

> The group's [Euro-Med Monitor's] report cited the cutting off all food supplies to Northern Gaza, along with the deliberate targeting of bakeries and water stores throughout the Strip. Israeli attacks also targeted flour shops, bakeries, agricultural zones, fishing boats, and storage centers belonging to relief organizations. As of Nov. 5, 11 bakeries in Gaza had been targeted and destroyed. The distribution of food to displaced families also

> became severely limited due to Israel's ground invasion, further increasing the threat of widespread starvation and famine. It is painfully evident that Israel is deliberately targeting food supplies to Gazan citizens to further their genocidal objectives.

That tracks with the eyewitness accounts I've heard myself. Again, I don't necessarily trust the source — which now shills for the abortion industry — but Amnesty International has marshaled a long list of outrages such as this one:

> The WHO reported that 600 patients and medical personnel were killed in attacks on medical facilities, including 76 ambulances. In the north of Gaza, al-Ahli and al-Shifa hospitals were operating at 5% of capacity while being overwhelmed with wounded and sick people. Hospital bed occupancy was at 310%, according to the Palestinian Red Crescent Society. Its al-Amal hospital in Khan Yunis was targeted with a drone on 24 December, killing a 13-year-old boy.

All of this is to say, it's a bit rich for Israel's most zealous defenders to claim that Gaza is getting kid-glove treatment. For them to slander America's military by claiming that the IDF is morally superior is actually a disgrace — especially as we mark the grim anniversary of Joe Biden's catastrophic surrender in Afghanistan, which saw many U.S. servicemen and women die needlessly.

America also saw heroic efforts by demoralized, departing service personnel to protect Afghan civilians. The Vulnerable People Project has worked with hundreds of serving personnel and veterans to help thousands of Afghan interpreters, longtime partners who saved countless American lives over two decades — whom the Biden administration left stranded and at the mercy of the Taliban (despite previous U.S. promises of providing visas).

Read about the Digital Dunkirk that helped those interpreters escape to safety in neighboring countries, and Dynamo Two, which airlifted many out. The Pineapple Express created an underground railroad for these brave American allies, while military contractors worked for free to save their erstwhile partners. The Vulnerable People Project joined those efforts, along with our own, building a women's hospital, digging wells, securing schools, and delivering "coal for Christmas" to thousands who were freezing.

Americans aren't, for the most part, morally cynical. And our military doesn't customarily play by the grim, amoral rules that prevail in the Middle East — which the IDF seems to be acclimatizing to, "going native," if you will. When we do screw up, such as was documented at Abu Ghraib, we agonize about it and punish those responsible. Indeed, we're still debating the morality of our civilian bombing campaigns in World War II, especially targets such as Dresden, Tokyo, Hiroshima, and Nagasaki.

Personally, I'd find it tragic if Israel, a creation of Western European nations, which claim Christianity as their founding moral principle, is tolerating the destruction of Christianity in its birthplace and, with it, the Palestinian descendants of the original Christians.

Israel should not let its enemies reshape its moral compass in their own image. It's not right; nor is it especially smart.

A Fellow Dad's Letter to President Trump: A Real America-First Agenda

October 16, 2024

Dear Mr. Trump,

First of all, let me say how grateful I am to God that you have dodged all the bullets. For most public figures, I would mean that as a metaphor. And indeed, our profoundly mediocre elites, corrupt to the marrow of their bones, have tried every "soft" means to destroy you via vilification as "Hitler," a four-year Deep State coup, and never-ending lawfare with Soviet prosecutors, Mafia-quality judges, and tame O. J. juries.

Of course, in your case, our rulers know that they belong not in power but hiding in exile, rotting in prison, or in black sites under questioning, so they're willing to go further. They literally want you dead, but you shouldn't take it personally. It's really your voters they hate — the ones they want to break, destroy, and replace.

Maybe it's hard not to take bullets personally. But I want to take a somewhat personal angle here. I write to you as a father, as someone who, like you, has tried to instill in the people I'm raising an ethic of hard work, honesty, and responsibility, not just for themselves but for the most vulnerable among us. You should be very proud of your family, of children whose circumstances could have led them to be decadent, hedonistic wastrels. But they're not. They're fine young people who love you — no doubt because you insisted on molding their characters firmly and fairly.

There's a story from American political history that I love. One summer in the early 1920s, two young men were sweating in the sun doing brutal manual labor. The first lad started talking about his father. Eventually the second guy admitted the identity of his own: then-President Calvin Coolidge. The first said, "If my father were the president, I wouldn't be doing a job like this." The young Coolidge answered, "You would if your father were *my* father."

I think that the America First policy you've boldly reintroduced to our political discourse works the same way. The United States is so disproportionately powerful compared with all its allies that it really does stand in relation to them as a father to teenage sons — which is ironic, considering how old most of those countries are compared with us. But facts are facts: We have, by far, the largest economy, the most powerful military, and the most international influence. We're their leader, and they depend on us.

But in the years since 1991, when the Cold War finally ended, how well has America performed in that role, led as we were by meddlesome, lazy, unprincipled advocates of the New World Order? You could sum up our foreign and immigration policies in a single slogan: Invade the World, Invite the World. Maybe add to that "Enable the World." Our presidents since Ronald Reagan left office have acted like rich, irresponsible dilettantes indulging spoiled, reckless children. In fact, our leaders encouraged some of the worst instincts in our allies, like a playboy dad who let his kids share his stash of drugs and porn.

We kept NATO in place long after it ceased to serve any legitimate purpose. In fact, we broke our agreement by which Mikhail Gorbachev agreed to dissolve the Warsaw Pact, expanding NATO right up to a nervous Russia's borders. Meanwhile, we let those same allies welch on their defense-spending commitments. As if that weren't bad enough, we used our Deep State to teach those countries' intelligence agencies how to smother public opinion — keeping patriotic parties out of power, rigging the outcomes so that, despite the voters' wishes, the countries kept on importing millions of non-Western immigrants to serve as tame new subjects of their liberal elites. Now, with Britain imprisoning citizens for questioning immigration policy and Germany close to outlawing its equivalent of the MAGA movement, we see how well our dependents learned from us. And, of course, there's a useless, grinding war in Ukraine, where our diplomats intervened to avoid a peaceful settlement.

An America First policy toward Europe wouldn't mean narrow national selfishness but, rather, treating our allies as what they are: fully sovereign nations responsible for themselves and answerable to their voters — rather than as provinces in an empire, ruled by jaded satraps who take their cues from Langley, Virginia. Let those countries pull their weight, defend and control their borders, and honor their national heritages rather than compete to remake a continent in the image of the Beltway. Nor should we goad and stoke an outdated, destructive rivalry with a much-reduced Russia.

Looking to Asia, an America First policy would mean expecting countries such as Japan, South Korea, and India to do their part in deterring Chinese expansion — without our making reckless guarantees to start World War III against a shockingly high-tech, enormous military power. We should also make some demands that honor our values. For instance, we could insist that an aggressively nationalist, increasingly intolerant India stop mass persecution of local, indigenous Christians. And, of course, we must bring back to U.S. shores the industries for producing our own medicine, computer chips, and other necessities of life. For too long we've let "economic efficiency" and the stock portfolios of high-dollar political donors trump national security.

In the Middle East, we'd continue to support Israel's security and safety, and broker deals between that state and the saner players in the Muslim world — as you did in the Abraham Accords. We wouldn't encourage disruption, turmoil, and massive human suffering through the region — as your predecessors did via the Iraq War, the Arab Spring, and our outrageous deal to help the regime in Iran hold on to power in return for vague promises about its dangerous nuclear program.

If we are going to invest tens of billions in aid to such countries — which you might well decide to stop — then we need to demand something in return from them. We should at least require of them, as the price of our friendship and aid, a basic level of respect for our values. That would entail several things. First of all, a respect for religious minorities and their rights — from the hunted Yazidis to the Christians of Gaza, whom Israel is currently besieging, bombing, and starving for the sins of their Hamas neighbors. We must recognize that the angry Muslim suburbs of London, Paris, and Berlin are full of the children of refugees our own policies helped to create.

It's not good for Israel or for us when its military engages in actions that feed anti-Semitism globally and offer propaganda that campus anti-Semites can use to terrorize Jewish students. We need to treat Israelis, Europeans, Asians, and everyone like adults — and that means making adult demands of them in return for benefits.

I know that as a wise and loving father, you've made good choices. I saw you make such choices while you were in office, which was a rare window of peace for the peoples of many regions. I pray that when you return to the Oval Office, you can indeed make America great again. It's the only way to make the rest of the world a little closer to good.

Ceasefire Now:
Trump and the Gaza Generation

November 4, 2024

There's no overstating it: President Donald Trump and his voters are about to decide world history. Just ahead of Election Day, I believe it's more than worth it to regroup and call to mind just how historic the Trump movement is in the grand scheme of global events.

It's not often that a brief chapter of history is so momentous that it shapes an entire generation of American voters. The terrorist attacks on 9/11/2001 and the Bush administration's response were one such inflection point. Nothing after that has come close — until Hamas's attack on Israel on October 7 of last year and the relentless bloodshed that has been taking place in Gaza since.

And here's where the historic importance of Trumpism comes in.

It's largely thanks to Trump's influence that politicians today can't so much as present themselves as Republican candidates for office without first denouncing the political establishment's disastrous actions in response to 9/11. The months following the attack were marked by confusion, rashness, and deception. The opportunism, corruption, and political blunders of 2001 and 2002 led to a monster surveillance state, unmanned U.S. drones gunning down civilians in places like Yemen, numerous wars, genocides, and the rise of ISIS.

After Trump's entry into the national political scene, that whole tragic series of events is now almost universally seen as unconscionable — and that new humane view, with its preference for peace and distrust of political elites, is the Trump effect.

Of course, to the political establishment that profits by what Trump calls the "forever wars," the violent deaths of tens of thousands of Palestinian children just in the last year mean nothing. But the suffering of Gaza — the bombings of churches, the women and girls killed by Israel Defense Forces' snipers, the Israeli government's obstruction of aid trucks to tend to the wounded and the starving — means everything to the good-hearted people of America, especially to our young and minority voters.

In fact, what is rising up now among American voters is what might be called the Gaza Generation. And just as distancing ourselves from the post-9/11 actions of the military-industrial complex has become a litmus test for office in the Republican Party today, denouncing Israel's violence against Palestinians will soon become a litmus test too. And, again, thanks to Trumpism, I believe the Gaza Generation will hold *every* major figure in public life to that litmus test, including candidates of both major parties.

Trump was one of the first and remained one of the only consistent voices for peace immediately following 9/11. While others bickered over the Middle East as if it were profitable material to be divided like spoils, invested in or sold out, used or discarded, Trump always seemed to see the human costs in the midst of Western elites' frivolous games of war and plunder.

And he clearly feels the same way about the current situation in Gaza. At a campaign stop just days ago, a young man shouted, "Trump, what do you have to say about Gaza?" Without hesitation, Trump responded: "It's gotta stop.... What we want is peace."

For Trump, the world isn't a war of all against all, where America competes thoughtlessly against adversaries over resources. He has no interest in a chaotic, unpredictable, multipolar world of tense competitions and skirmishes between greedy nations and their proxies throughout the Middle East. His program is to "Make America Great Again," on a unipolar, stable world stage where vulnerable people — and their governments — have reason to trust our leadership and look to it as an upholder of shared interests.

Even in his comments on the conflicts between Middle Eastern nations, Trump doesn't see the interests of the region's peoples as mutually exclusive. He denounces Iranian leaders as leading exporters of terrorism and warns them against reckless aggression in one breath and speaks with compassion and admiration of the Iranian people in the next.

Similarly, not even in the heat of the current conflict between Israel and Hamas does Trump fail to speak with genuine humanity to both Israelis and the people of Palestine.

This election isn't over till it's over, and the last thing we need in the uncertainty of these last few days and hours is complacency. But despite what many Washington,

D.C., advisers would have him think, President Donald Trump could stand to lose more by selling himself short than by overconfidence.

To secure the edge in the final stretch, and to inject our political movement with the crucial last boost of adrenal energy it needs to get over the finish line, President Trump is now in a position to make one last move that would drive home just how historic this political moment — and his movement — really is: Trump can call for a ceasefire in Gaza.

I'm sure there are plenty of weak-kneed political strategists telling Trump it would be a terrible risk. First of all, that's not even true: The polling is clear that, if anything, he'd gain more votes than he could possibly lose by taking this stand for peace. But more importantly, they fail to see the other, much graver risk. I mean the risk of forgetting — or allowing the public to forget — that the whole character and credibility of Trump's prophetic role in global events has always hinged on his courageous opposition to senseless violence and war.

And besides, by calling for a ceasefire, Trump will forever secure his place as the first political figure to understand and lead the Gaza Generation. In the coming one or two election cycles, many politicians will struggle to catch up. No doubt many will fail the test and disappear into history.

But if Trump calls for this ceasefire now, he won't just win the day in American politics for the next four years. He will shape the fate of the world for at least the next four decades.

Trump's Landslide Was a Mandate for Peace, and His Is Now the Peace Party

November 7, 2024

In the last stretch of the 2024 presidential election season, Donald Trump made it clearer than ever that he was pitting the fate of his entire movement against the military-industrial complex and the violence of war.

There has rightly been plenty of talk about the political "realignments" Trumpism has brought about. These historic shifts have resulted in a new populist Right that champions the worker, the migrant, and the poor, on the one hand, and an authoritarian political Left that threatens censorship, fines, and imprisonment on behalf of a decadent elite, on the other.

But the most significant realignment has been a realignment toward peace — a shift that invites the participation of all, from the great innovator and tech mogul Elon Musk and his peers in Silicon Valley to the most recent Muslim migrant worker plying a humble trade in the American Midwest.

The Democratic ticket, meanwhile, championed the establishment that authored the wars and genocides of the past two decades — all while fresh off a catastrophic abandonment of Afghanistan that left thousands of friends and allies at the mercy of the Taliban.

That's the realignment that not only motivated American Christians, military families, and business owners but also drove historic numbers of Latino, Arab, and Somali voters to Trump.

Trump made many significant gestures of solidarity in the last months leading up to his stunning victory on November 5. And they were more than just gestures; they were principled and noble vows that meant all the more because he staked his chances at the ballot box on them.

He offered his friendship — and the friendship of the U.S. government under his now-incoming administration — to the suffering Palestinians of Gaza. He offered the same friendship to the people of Israel, even as the state's unpopular current officials such as Prime Minister Benjamin Netanyahu engage in actions against Gaza's women and children that Trump vowed to confront and put a stop to.

Trump offered friendship to the peoples of Iran and Lebanon — while also calling out the escalatory rhetoric of Iranian and Lebanese leaders who seem as eager for global conflict as Netanyahu in Israel and Washington elites in the United States.

Meanwhile, at home, Trump also built a coalition of lifelong Democrats such as Robert F. Kennedy Jr. and the heroic military veteran Tulsi Gabbard, as well as all-American entertainers and sportsmen such as Dr. Phil, Joe Rogan, Brett Favre, and Harrison Butker. Trump also drew in the support of committed pro-lifers such as Lila Rose and the team at CatholicVote — moral voices who had proved willing to speak out against missteps.

In the end, by the time of his election victory this week, Trump had built up a global mandate centered on the dignity and worth of every human person — especially when he or she is most urgently under threat.

And never are human beings more under threat than when they live in a time ripe for global thermonuclear war.

That possibility is real — a prospect that could at any moment make every person, to quote Winston Churchill, "equal in misery" — from the bombed-out shelter in Gaza to the post-nuclear suburban home in Virginia.

The arrival of a second Trump administration on the global scene could not come at a more opportune time to quell the devastation just waiting to be unleashed by the recklessness of world leaders over the past four years.

Because America has not just elected Trump. Thanks to his outspokenness on behalf of the would-be victims of war, Trump's supporters have just delivered a global peace mandate.

The Israel-Hamas Ceasefire, Semitic Peoples, and the Mystery of Collective Blame

January 18, 2025

During the violence in Gaza that began in 2023, it's been easy to spot serious-minded observers like Gad Saad. He brings real thought to whatever he considers, "wrestles" earnestly with things, and consistently denounces what he calls "tribalism." So it was all the more intriguing when he posted a message to "all Jews around the world" on social media shortly after Israel began its campaign in Gaza: "Consider learning Cantonese or Mandarin and keep your fingers crossed that China allows you in," he wrote in the unique voice of muted hyperbole he uses to communicate sincere alarm. China "might become the only safe place for Jews in 20+ years," he added. "Tragic but true."

After this week's joyous news of the ceasefire deal brokered by the Trump team between Israel and Hamas, it's worth looking back and — unfortunately — also forward to consider this: Why is it that even a classically liberal atheist intellectual like Saad seems to take it as a given that Jews would be forced into tribal defensiveness — held universally to blame for the shocking actions of Israel's corrupt and unpopular Prime Minister Benjamin Netanyahu in Gaza?

Though an atheist, Saad at least holds an honest and therefore pessimistic view of fallen human nature. He is not one to be easily taken in by false ideological enthusiasms, based, as they usually are, on an implicit belief in what the Catholic conservative thinker Russell Kirk called the (erroneous) notion of "the perfectibility of man."

"Before being Jewish, I'm a man of reason, logic, freedom, liberty, science, and common sense," Saad recently wrote. "I wish to have our children live in a world that is free of grotesque and dark theocracies.... If an ideology is inconsistent with universal enlightened Western values then it should be scrutinized and rejected."

Saad has not, in my opinion, himself fallen into an illiberal tribalism that refuses to find fault with the state of Israel because of its status as "the Jewish State." Insofar as he perhaps was tempted to defend Israel's attempted genocide in Gaza based on a belief that the Palestinian people and their cultural heritage are incompatible with "enlightened Western values," I, as a Christian, could never follow him toward that inhumane conclusion.

But I don't think that is where Saad's impressively consistent thinking honestly leads. Rather, I think he's onto something more than is dreamt of in his philosophy: the mystery of collective blame among Semitic peoples.

I have deep personal motives to avoid this mystery rather than write about it.

First of all, as the great Jewish philosopher Hannah Arendt already recognized by the end of the 1950s, denouncing Jew-hatred has become a cheap, easy, and self-serving ritual especially favored by those who are both powerful and eager to remain irresponsible. Comfortable Westerners have made it a pastime to defend Jews so frequently and so officiously that the practice does as much to single out, corral, and "other" Jewry than Jew-hatred itself does. I want no part of that.

Secondly, I and my organization, the Vulnerable People Project, have actively worked to defend and advocate for the innocent Palestinians who suffered through Israel's campaign of ethnic cleansing up until this week. I frankly don't want to give the Palestinians we have served the impression that we've been defending them only as a strategy to fend off an anti-Jewish backlash that their deaths might cause.

In other words, as Christians, we ought to understand that neither Palestinians nor Jews are means to an end. Each Palestinian and each Jew — like each of the rest of us — is made in the image and likeness of the Creator, with an inviolable dignity and worth that transcends political strategies.

But Saad's "wrestling" with Israel's actions in Gaza was what first focused my mind on both Jews and Palestinians simultaneously in the midst of that horrible bloodshed. And what Saad revealed to me — albeit through my own Christian lens — was that these two Semitic peoples share one and the same mystery of collective blame.

Given Saad's grasp of human nature and its inherent faults, I'm sure he knows as well as I do that people are prone to bouts of violent scapegoating against any group of people.

I owe my own last name (Jones) to the fact that my great-grandfather felt the need to change it from Johannes during a brief but truly dangerous rash of anti-German sentiment that overtook the United States during the First World War.

But there's a difference between passing, ordinary human angers like that one and the mystery of collective blame that sticks to Palestinians like Velcro — not for a few years but for a century and more. And there is a difference between the sentiments that rise and fall with wars and the mystery that never fades — the mystery Saad was onto when he warned that the West is capable of wholly driving Jewry into China.

It's a difference somehow both everywhere known and nowhere articulated — hence my naming it a mystery.

"Please remember," Saad recently wrote: "I'm apparently personally responsible for anything that transpired in Gaza because I'm Jewish BUT no Noble Person is responsible for the 44,000+ terror attacks in nearly 70 countries since 9/11 alone."

I can corroborate half of his point from experience: During the time I've spent in the region, I've certainly encountered Middle Easterners who cast collective blame on Jews. But I have never encountered locals who cast the same kind of blame on the United States and other Western nations. Even after all the great damage Western superpowers have inflicted on them, these anti-Israel locals — many of them of Semitic peoples — are likely to blame the West not as much for hurting them as for "helping the Jews."

But I say I can corroborate only half of Saad's point. The other half is the blind spot — the mysterious thing that evades the understanding not only of Saad but of the whole world, if it were possible.

Because when Saad spoke sarcastically of the "Noble Person" who is never held blameworthy, he was, in fact, joining much of the world in casting blame on that person.

And Saad's blame was not directed at the power brokers of the West who leveled the Middle East, meddled in its customs, drew artificial barriers, and fomented radicalism and genocidal hatreds.

No. Rather, like the descendants of his Semitic ancestors in the Middle East whom I have met with, and like an ever-present, bloodthirsty element in the churning world of Western opinion, Saad chose a Semite to blame.

And yes, it is not a stretch to say he blamed, at least indirectly and by association, the Palestinian himself.

My American Apology to the Ukrainian People

March 3, 2025

Dear Men and Women of Ukraine,

This is a short note to express my profound regret, the sorrow and shame I feel as an American when I think about your country, which I hope my countrymen share ... and my promise to do what I can to make things right in the future.

No, this has nothing to do with the clash between our politicians, as seen on TV last week in our country's White House. Nor am I writing because I want U.S. troops in Ukraine or even to see our country continue to prolong your war with Russia by selling weapons to Ukraine. I know from the lips of our own Gen. Mark Milley that America's intent was never to liberate Ukraine but instead to "make Russia bleed." We were willing to fight to the last Ukrainian man, woman, and child, in pursuit of that cynical aim.

Like most Americans, I support President Donald Trump's courageous effort to end the violence now, via compromise and diplomacy, including territorial trade-offs. From the horrors of the Russian Civil War, to the man-made famine Stalin imposed on your people, to the brutal Nazi invasion and cruel Soviet reconquest, your country has suffered more than almost any on earth for the past one hundred years. Enough is enough.

I want to apologize instead for our Deep State, our political class, and our media — our self-selected elites whose real loyalty is to their fellow oligarchs worldwide. They, as much as anyone — even anyone in Russia — are at fault for the death, ruin, and suffering that scar your beautiful country. Our elites pressured Ukraine to give up its nuclear weapons, which could have been a permanent guarantee of your independence — in return for a piece of paper, an unconstitutional non-treaty that our Senate never ratified and that has no force of law. That guarantee from Bill Clinton might as well have been scrawled on a bar napkin.

But the politicians you inherited chose to put faith in it. They saw that America's ruling class was eager to break the promise it had made to Mikhail Gorbachev not to expand NATO eastward — as the price of the Warsaw Pact peacefully dissolving. Our elites, as corrupt as yours, talked friendship and freedom to Russia while helping to loot the country's assets and forging one military alliance after another, right up to Russia's borders. Then they acted surprised when a shell-shocked, bankrupt Russia found itself a brutal strongman — as if they'd never cracked a single history book.

Our military-industrial complex, which dominated both parties, goaded our country into useless wars in the Middle East, cashing $3 trillion in checks along the way. When that grift finally petered out like blood in the sand, they turned their hungry eyes to your country. As sharks who scent blood in the water, they saw the tensions between Ukraine and Russia as a golden opportunity.

As Victoria Nuland, the former U.S. ambassador to NATO, admitted (actually boasted) in 2016, the Obama administration saw Putin's seizure of Crimea as a chance to make Ukraine an offer it couldn't refuse. Our CIA and USAID flooded a frightened Ukraine with cash and spies. They bought the loyalty of Ukrainian public officials, making them beholden not to your voters but to our secret agents. They set up abortion clinics and transgender activist groups and made the price of our "aid" the acceptance of the West's most toxic cultural exports.

When the Ukrainian people overthrew their pro-Russia president in 2013, our Deep State hijacked that revolution. Nuland was caught on the phone in a recording mulling over the names of whom she might appoint to rule your country.

Did our elites really think that a Russia led by a former KGB colonel steeped in chauvinist "Great Russian" nationalism would swallow such behavior? When the Soviets put nuclear missiles in their de facto colony of Cuba, our president planned an invasion, and walked right up to the brink of a full-scale nuclear war. Did the spooks in Washington really think that Putin was more of a peacenik than John F. Kennedy?

Of course they didn't. They didn't expect Donald Trump to run for office, much less defeat Hillary Clinton. They were sure she'd be elected and would thank them for their efforts. She'd carry on their policy, designed to force a conflict with Russia and cut off its cheap energy exports to Europe. Instead, trillions of dollars would go to corrupt energy companies, such as Burisma, in which our elites (such as the Biden family) had heavily invested. The arms companies in which our elites held stock, such as BlackRock, would profit hand over fist selling weapons to "help" Ukraine defend herself.

Our politicians, deprived of Middle Eastern wars, could swagger around talking tough about "standing up to Russia." And if need be, our Deep State could smear its enemies as "Russian colluders." They invented a fake conspiracy theory and tried to run Donald Trump out of office, as you'll recall. Some fifty-one leaders of our intelligence community signed a letter claiming that Hunter Biden's crime-diary laptop was "Russian disinformation" — and then, when people disagreed, our CIA pressured social media to censor the dissenters.

None of this is the fault of the Ukrainian people. It's hardly even the fault of the American people, except insofar as we've let ourselves be governed by such criminals. But you are the ones paying the price in blood and tears. Our politicians boast in unguarded moments that the money we've sent to Ukraine we really paid to ourselves because most of it went to U.S. defense contractors — as Robert F. Kennedy Jr. pointed out during his campaign.

But, of course, when they're making speeches, these powerbrokers speak instead of "defending democracy" and "saving" the people of Ukraine. They're lying. They care even less about your people than they do about our people. We're all just pawns in their astronomically high-stakes chess game, and pawns were made to be sacrificed.

More than a million people have already been killed or wounded in this ghastly, avoidable war. Donald Trump has a passion for peace, and he plans to end the war. I pray he succeeds. And I will go on praying for Ukraine, setting up real aid programs there and living the Faith I share with so many good people in your proud country.

Forget the Gold Card — We Need a "Red Card" for America's Afghan Partners

March 16, 2025

The second term of President Donald Trump is already iconic. A would-be assassin shot him, the government tried to put him in prison, and he still came out on top. Better yet, along the way he never lost touch with his loyal backers, whose affection for him has only grown, and he even picked up some new supporters from every background. Trump has created a new sense of optimism after years of uncertainty and distrust between conservatives and their government.

As he put it during his speech to Congress earlier this month: "America is back" and entering its "Golden Age." Trump promised in the address that the United States would soon begin selling the $5 million "Gold Card," a clever play on the Green Card. The cards will ensure that "the most successful job-creating people from all over the world" will opt to "buy a path to U.S. citizenship," Trump said Tuesday.

"America is back."

"Gold."

Those words are still stuck in my head two weeks later as I continue to work with my team at the Vulnerable People Project to serve our friends in Afghanistan, where the Biden administration bungled the 2021 withdrawal of U.S. forces, sparking chaos and violence and leaving American partners at the mercy of a new Taliban government.

The Gold Card proposal remains stuck in my head too, and it brings to mind another obvious idea, one that I hope Trump will soon adopt as his own: a card for foreign nationals who have already paid an expense worth more than $5 million.

I mean the brave men and women who served alongside our troops in Afghanistan over the twenty years of our occupation, only to be abandoned and to find themselves hunted by a vengeful Taliban that will never forgive them for supporting America's mission.

These Afghan translators, intelligence support staffers, and others didn't just offer money. They gave themselves and their families. They put their very lives and those of their spouses and children in America's hands. The Vulnerable People Project has been serving these forgotten heroes.

As I wrote with my Afghan friend Prince Wafa in May 2022, Biden's surrender

> doomed to persecution some one hundred thousand Afghans who'd served shoulder to shoulder with American men and women in uniform. The State Department admits that a majority of Afghans who earned Special Immigrant Visas during the war got left behind. The Taliban is hunting them while you read these words.

Those words still hold true. So do these:

> The best way we can honor those servicemen and women who made the ultimate sacrifice, especially the 2,448 warriors who died in Afghanistan, is to work to bring home to the United States the Afghans who saved countless American lives, who bled alongside our soldiers.
>
> The U.S. Army Rangers have a creed. It includes this phrase: "I will never leave a fallen comrade to fall into the hands of the enemy, and under no circumstances will I ever embarrass my country." The Biden administration clearly never felt such a sentiment. We'll have to teach it to them.

In the coming weeks, in fact, I will be traveling to visit the safe houses my team and I have created and monitored ever since the fall of Afghanistan — as the Taliban government there continues threats of violence against our friends. But also, and for obvious reasons, Pakistan and Iran have only become more and more inhospitable to our friends. Pakistan oppresses them, and Iran has even been conscripting and forcing them to fight against Ukraine — using the threat of expelling them and their families back to Afghanistan.

As an army vet myself, I will never abandon these comrades. Never.

Trump, who had ordered the withdrawal from Afghanistan, would have done a much better job executing it than Biden, a disastrously incompetent leader. The president now has an opportunity to rectify one of the worst mistakes his successor made. As Trump has said, he won last year's election decisively, though the odds were stacked against him, and now he has a moral mandate to undo Biden policies that the American public found reprehensible.

Trump knows that among the disgraced Biden administration's most universally hated crimes was its dishonorable abandonment of our friends in Afghanistan — a historic wrong that perhaps only the equally historic return of Trump could reverse.

He can do it with a policy just as obvious and easily achievable as selling the Gold Card: by offering our Afghan allies a path to citizenship as a reward for their great sacrifices to American interests.

And since they have proved themselves willing to pay with their blood, call it the Red Card.

My Palestinian Friends Taught Me How to Combat Anti-Semitism

March 31, 2025

I didn't set out to learn about anti-Semitism from Palestinians. But I did.

My organization, the Vulnerable People Project, has worked for years to serve vulnerable communities everywhere, from Afghanistan to Chinese-occupied East Turkistan to Nigeria to Gaza. And if there's one thing I've learned, it's that the first step to defending the vulnerable is to see them clearly.

A characteristic event that makes a group of people vulnerable occurs when the powerful elites of the world turn their backs on them and even make it socially costly to stand with them. It's then that you find you can't defend them at all unless you really love them, because love is the only thing that makes those social costs worth it to you — win or lose.

But if you can't defend someone you don't love, you also can't love what you don't see — or a people you don't know.

Until I listened to the voices of my Palestinian friends, I did not see or know the Semitic people.

I thought I did. I was an American Catholic, steeped in the language of Catholic social teaching and the American founding — the language of human dignity. I knew the slogans. I'd been to Bethlehem, walked the Via Dolorosa, touched the stone where Christ's body was prepared for burial. I imagined myself to be an advocate for peace.

But something ugly lived in my blind spots: a comfortable, unexamined anti-Palestinian bias wrapped in piety and slogans about "standing with Israel." It took a war to reveal it.

Then came the voices of my friends. Rev. Munther Isaac, the courageous Lutheran pastor in Bethlehem, was one of the first to break through to me. He didn't speak in slogans. He spoke with pain, patience, and prophetic clarity. "We are not collateral damage," he said, pleading with Western Christians to remember that Palestinians are not abstractions in someone else's theology.

His latest book, *Christ in the Rubble,* is both a cry of lament and a fierce act of hope. In it, Isaac dares to proclaim the presence of Christ — not in conquest, not in the ideology of an empire, but in the bombed-out ruins of Gaza, in the tears of weeping mothers.

I listened to Khalil Sayegh, a Christian from Gaza who refused to conform to either side's propaganda. A man deeply committed to peace, and no less committed to truth, Khalil told me how the Israeli siege, the bombings, the checkpoints, and the walls had shaped his childhood. And he told me about Hamas — about the fear he and his family endured under their rule. He rejected both the ideology of armed resistance and the ideology of ethnic supremacy. He wanted a future. For his people. For the Jewish people. For all of us.

Khalil's convictions were not born in any abstract study. He lost his sister and his father to the violence of the Israeli military. They were not statistics; their deaths wounded him deeply and shaped his soul. And still, he speaks without hatred. Still, he calls for peace. Still, he refuses to return evil for evil. In that, he taught me more about resisting anti-Semitism than any book I've read or speech I've heard.

Listening to Khalil and Isaac didn't just teach me about Palestinians. It taught me how to see the hatred I had allowed to calcify inside me — hatred I had mistaken for virtue. And it taught me something else: that the struggle against anti-Semitism and the struggle against anti-Palestinianism are not opposites. They are the same fight, as I wrote in a piece at *The American Conservative.* This one battle will be won only by those with enough moral clarity to reject collective blame and ideological hate — wherever it festers.

The face of Christ is disfigured wherever innocent blood is shed, whether in Sderot or in Rafah, whether in a synagogue in Pittsburgh or in a church in Gaza. To love the Jewish people is to defend them from the genocidal hatred that enabled the Holocaust to be perpetrated while the world half-knowingly looked the other way. And to love the Palestinian people is to defend them from the genocidal hatred that has already normalized the slaughter of tens of thousands of their children in our own time.

We are witnessing a global rise in anti-Semitism. It must be condemned with no ambiguity.

But do not fool yourself: If you cannot condemn the mass killing of Palestinian children today, the ethnic cleansing of Gaza, the use of starvation as a weapon of war, the hatred spewed in our churches and on our screens in the name of Christ — then, when the mob turns again on the Jewish people, you will not have the courage to stand with them any more than you had the courage to stand with the Palestinian people.

We train our hearts in justice, or we train them in cowardice. There is no neutral ground.

Anti-Semitism is a demonic hatred, and so is anti-Palestinianism. But here is the difference: One is socially accepted, while the other, in most polite circles, is rightly reviled. I have seen donors pull their money from ministries that defend Palestinians. I have watched good men become silent.

And I'll confess this too: I have been tempted to silence — or at least, I have been tempted to speak more softly.

Speaking out against anti-Semitism is important. Speaking out against anti-Palestinian hate is urgent — and today, it is more difficult.

There is no contradiction here. The true lover of the Jewish people must be a friend to the Palestinians. And the true defender of the Palestinians must oppose Jew-hatred wherever it lurks.

Christians should be the first to speak up. Sadly, we are often the last.

My Palestinian friends have shown me what moral clarity looks like in the darkness. They have taught me to see Christ in the wounded — whether crucified by Hamas or by the Israeli Air Force.

And they have shown me that there is no road to peace, no road to justice, that does not begin with the refusal to hate.

Imagine Treating Ukrainians as Ends in the Themselves

March 31, 2025

It seems that everyone engaged in world politics now, both in the United States and in Europe, has a position on Ukraine — what really happened there, who's at fault, who deserves to win, and what their nation's government ought to be doing about it. From leaders of NATO countries that are outlawing opposition political parties and imprisoning people for Facebook posts — all in defense of democracy — to embittered "red-pilled" Americans who wish we had our own Putin, the stances are all staked out on the ideological battleground.

These people disagree with each other fiercely and call each other names. They want radically opposite outcomes to the Ukraine-Russia war. They accuse their opponents of callously risking either a Russian invasion of Scotland or a nuclear World War III. But after years of careful reading and listening, I have found a common thread uniting all these self-styled Ukraine whisperers. Perhaps it can even serve as a common ground that brings them all together.

What's interesting is that none of them actually care about the people who live in Ukraine. Whether they live or die, prosper or flee, go back to grinding poverty, or abort and trans themselves out of existence, none of the people who talk about Ukraine really care. They treat Ukrainians like counters in a dorm-room game of Risk — in which, as those who've played it will recall, control of Ukraine is key to winning. (Okay, Ukraine and the Middle East, but the Risk players already goad us into wars for that region too.) Or pawns in a chess game, which, of course, can be sacrificed for any strategic advantage.

I take the eccentric position that the most important thing to worry about in the Ukraine War is the Ukrainian people. Since it is their country (not ours), their interests ought to come first, then second, then third. Only after that should we investigate how a given stance on the country benefits our national interests and ideological goals. Indeed, if the well-being of real live Ukrainians requires it, we might even have to take the "L" and sacrifice some worthy project we had in mind, rather than pay for it in the blood and misery of hapless foreign citizens.

To determine what really would benefit Ukrainians, we must sift through the many partisan claims and biased histories surrounding that country — and as best we can, figure out what's really true. As scientists say about data, "Garbage in, garbage out." If our starting point isn't a solid understanding of genuine facts, we're going to push policies that are grounded in wishful thinking. And that's how you get conflicts like the Iraq War, which end up benefiting organizations like ISIS.

Based on very wide reading, talks on the ground in Ukraine with citizens and soldiers, and what I learned from my friends in the U.S. intelligence community, I believe the following facts are solid:

- The West took ruthless advantage of Russian weakness after the Soviet collapse in 1991. After promising not to expand NATO as Mikhail Gorbachev's price for disbanding the Warsaw Pact, we did exactly that — pushing that nuclear alliance right up to Russia's borders instead of inviting Russia in or dissolving NATO as now obsolete. Russia rightly sees NATO membership for Ukraine the way U.S. leaders saw nuclear missiles in Cuba in 1962.
- U.S. President Bill Clinton convinced the impoverished, inexperienced leaders of newly independent Ukraine to surrender their best guarantee of independence — the nuclear arsenal they'd inherited — in return for a nonbinding, unratified non-treaty that might as well have been written on a bar napkin. Our foreign-policy elites insist on treating that document as if it were part of the U.S. Bill of Rights.
- Vladimir Putin took ruthless advantage of NATO expansion to weaponize Russian nationalism and revive old chauvinist notions of Ukraine as "Little Russia," a perpetual province to be ruled from Moscow — as if a common heritage in the tenth century could erase the terror famine Russians imposed on Ukrainians in the 1930s.
- The American Deep State, especially the CIA and its front organization USAID, has opportunistically seized upon the real desire of Ukrainians for genuine independence in order to try reshaping the country as a puppet of Western elites. Ukraine's government and civil society were hijacked and honeycombed by U.S. agents and representatives. They, in turn, treated

> the country as a laboratory for social engineering experiments, from U.S.-funded abortion clinics to trans grooming in schools. Accepting such poisonous policies was the price of getting Western aid to resist the Russians, as one pro-life Ukrainian Christian after another told me in tears.

As I warned in a Kyiv address in 2023:

> Will Ukraine trade Russian colonizers and occupiers for post-Christian, post-Western ones? Will it turn over its children to the counselors and therapists who now in America quietly recruit kids for sex-change procedures, puberty blockers, hormone therapy, and surgical castration of boys — often without the consent or even the knowledge of their parents? Will Ukraine let Planned Parenthood — which designed the murderous One Child Policy on behalf of the Red Chinese government — open clinics in Kyiv that would rob you of a generation of children, a new Holodomor in service of a new godless ideology of evil, to finish the job that Joseph Stalin started?

Russia's government has, in turn, weaponized the perverse social agenda of Western elites to paint itself as the defender of Christian values and legitimate nationalism, even as it waged a vicious war of conquest against a long-suffering nation. Vladimir Putin's invasion is an act of naked aggression driven by a delusional, quasi-spiritual ideology that bears more in common with occult totalitarianism than Christian conservatism. His philosophical muse, Aleksandr Dugin — an admirer of Satanists and cultists — has been called "Putin's brain," and it shows. Russia's war has brought death to civilians, repression to churches, and devastation to a Christian nation already bruised by a century of suffering. No Christian should be seduced by Moscow's propaganda.

With all of these facts read into the record, what should we hope for? What should we do? We should work for a compromise peace as soon as possible rather than stoke an unending conflict to "make Russia bleed" (U.S. Gen. Mark Milley's goal) in the name of making impossible reconquests of unsustainable regions — such as Crimea, which Russia will never surrender.

President Trump's efforts to serve as a good-faith, neutral arbitrator, rather than a distant, callous warmonger, deserve our support and prayers. We ought to seek peace not because we are jaded and don't give a fig about Ukrainians but for the exact opposite reason. We care about those people's lives far more than icy neoconservative geopolitical amateurs with Ukraine flags in their Bluesky profiles and BlackRock stock in their portfolios. That's why we don't want to abort or transition Ukraine's children to another gender, or send its young men to die for pie in the sky.

To me, that's the proper patriotic and Christian stance. But hey, maybe I'm a weirdo.

Follow Pope Leo's Lead: Defend the Christian Presence in the Holy Land

May 15, 2025

In a beautiful address to Eastern Christian pilgrims in Rome, Pope Leo XIV this week showed that the tenets of our Catholic Faith are more than platitudes. In particular, he applied Catholic principles plainly and unflinchingly to the plight of the Christian communities in Bethlehem, located in the West Bank, and in Gaza — defending their right to remain secure where they are. By implication, the pope's address invites us all to stand in solidarity with these churches and against Israeli prime minister Benjamin Netanyahu's campaign of ethnic cleansing in the region.

When we have the courage to articulate it clearly and without compromise, the gospel of Jesus Christ always stands as a sign of contradiction — with real and sometimes costly implications. My fellow members of the pro-life movement know that well. So do Christian defenders of marriage and childhood innocence against the LGBTQ movement.

But Pope Leo now reminds us to stand up for another hard truth: This same gospel tells us that there is such a thing as a Holy Land, a historical place that mankind ought to hold sacred because it is where God worked out His plan of salvation for us.

Quoting his namesake Pope Leo XIII and Pope St. John Paul the Great, our new pope said that "the work of human redemption began in the East," giving the Christian community in the Holy Land "a unique and privileged role as the original setting where the Church was born."

Pope Leo also quoted Pope Francis's frequent references to what he called "martyr Churches," applying that phrase first and foremost to the Church of "the Holy Land," and only after that to the churches in Ukraine, Lebanon, Syria, and elsewhere.

"I thank God for those Christians — Eastern and Latin alike — who, above all in the Middle East, persevere and remain in their homelands, resisting the temptation to abandon them," Pope Leo said. "Christians must be given the opportunity, and not just in words, to remain in their native lands with all the rights needed for a secure existence. Please, let us strive for this!"

Pope Leo's courageous message could not be more timely. As I wrote in January of this year, just after visiting Palestinian communities in the West Bank, my friend Alice Kisiya will tell you how "the Israeli military and Civil Administration have used" their campaign against Gaza since October 7, 2023, "as an 'excuse' to even more aggressively undermine Palestinians' rightful claims to their own homes, businesses, and farmlands" in and around Bethlehem.

But while the lives of Palestinian Christians in Gaza and the West Bank are surrounded by politics, the sacredness of their communities is far greater than any partisan political concern. These Eastern Church communities, in fact, are "the beating heart of the free world," I argued:

> As a Christian, I won't shy away from professing my own understanding of the significance of the ancient Christian community there in the West Bank — the community in which Christ was born.
>
> Families like the ones Alice fights for in the West Bank descend directly from those who were in the upper room when the Holy Spirit first knit the Church together. And it was that Church which, through centuries of courageous and costly preaching about the dignity of every human being as made in the image and likeness of God, gave us the world we have today.
>
> It was this ancient Christian community's world-reforming ethic of radical solidarity between all peoples that would give rise to Christendom, and then to the humanizing political principles by which we would govern ourselves.
>
> The Magna Carta, the Constitution of the United States, the abolition of slavery in Europe and then in the United States, the United Nations Charter of Human Rights — all of these stem from God's presentation of Himself as our fellow man in the arms of His Mother in Bethlehem.

I pray that Christians in America will follow Pope Leo's lead and also come to a deep understanding that when he stands up for Palestinian Christian communities, he is ultimately standing up for us in the West. And I pray that we join him in the fight, knowing that the fight for the East is, in fact, a battle for the heart of the West.

Tens of thousands of Palestinians, including Christians and mostly civilian women and children, have already died. Survivors are now starving behind an Israeli blockade against humanitarian aid. Both Pope Leo and President Donald Trump are pressing for an immediate ceasefire and for the corridors for aid to be opened. And my organization, the Vulnerable People Project, stands ready to send in trucks full of supplies, including diapers for babies born in the midst of unspeakable violence.

One of our trucks will be sent in honor of Pope Francis, who advocated for the Church in Gaza with his last breaths. Another is in honor of Pope Leo XIV, and a third will be sent in honor of Trump for telling Netanyahu to his face that he must relent and allow us to feed these innocents.

"Rising up from this horror," Pope Leo said in his address this week, "from the slaughter of so many young people, which ought to provoke outrage because lives are being sacrificed in the name of military conquest, there resounds an appeal: the appeal not so much of the Pope, but of Christ himself, who repeats: 'Peace be with you!' "

"For my part, I will make every effort so that this peace may prevail," the Holy Father added:

> The Holy See is always ready to help bring enemies together, face to face, to talk to one another, so that peoples everywhere may once more find hope and recover the dignity they deserve, the dignity of peace. The peoples of our world desire peace, and to their leaders I appeal with all my heart: Let us meet, let us talk, let us negotiate! War is never inevitable. Weapons can and must be silenced, for they do not resolve problems but only increase them. Those who make history are the peacemakers, not those who sow seeds of suffering.... The Church will never tire of repeating: let weapons be silenced.

Chapter 3

FREEDOM

Immigration: "Where Tenderness Leads to the Gas Chamber"

August 6, 2014

My title here is a famous quote from Flannery O'Connor. What exactly did she mean by saying, "Tenderness leads to the gas chamber"?

Was she citing the Nazis' kindness to animals (Adolf Hitler was an anti-hunting vegetarian)? Or was she thinking of Planned Parenthood founder Margaret Sanger, whose stories of overburdened poor mothers made the case for sterilizing them?

Just like Sanger, too many Americans in 2014 want to feel like really good, compassionate people — without paying the price. We want cheap grace, easy miracles, and automatic progress.

And that explains why we don't secure our country's borders.

We want people to like us. To think that we're "nice." We want to feel nice, and to experience nice things — like comfort, safety, leisure, and that warm, fuzzy feeling that comes from taking easy moral stances that get us applauded by our peers. We don't want to brush up against real poverty or injustice, even if that is the price of fixing them.

This lust for the nice explains why so many otherwise sensible Christians have gotten drunk with their own sheer goodness and "openness" on the subject of immigration.

Here are the facts: Americans have voted for certain immigration laws, which have been widely disregarded for many years. The Americans who benefited most were employers who use cheap labor, whose workers get hurt building houses and then get dropped off at the public emergency ward.

The citizens who suffered were embattled blue-collar workers, honest business owners who pay fair wages to legal workers, and ordinary law-abiding taxpayers.

The amnesty granted in 1986 to a few million immigrants was supposed to march in lockstep with strict enforcement of workplace verification — but the cheap-labor lobby protested, and President Ronald Reagan backed down. The result was a law that offered amnesty, but did nothing to prevent the ongoing exploitation of workers in the shadow economy or create order on our borders.

What we need today is a rational, statesmanlike compromise that combines a hardcore seriousness about enforcing our laws with some measure of mercy toward millions of people who already live among us. But that compromise has failed.

A year ago, many Americans would have been willing to support a "path to citizenship" — provided it was accompanied by real, honest, comprehensive efforts to make sure that another such amnesty would never be needed again. I angered many of my own conservative friends in 2012 by advocating a "path to citizenship," conditioned on rock-solid enforcement of our labor laws and serious border security.

But liberal Democrats hungry for votes and cynical Republicans in hock to low-paying employers combined to kill such a compromise. Every measure for really guaranteeing our borders was stripped out or watered down, rendering the "path to citizenship" a lure to future migrants in the underground economy, just like the 1986 bill that so flagrantly failed — and attracted eleven million more people to join the ranks of the exploited.

What is worse, far worse, is the ripple effect that talk of "amnesty" without enforcement has had throughout our poorer neighbors. As Fox News reports:

> Tens of thousands of illegal immigrants have flocked to the U.S. in recent months, believing the Dream Act, as well as a 2008 law that grants an asylum hearing to any child not from a border nation, and the White House policy known as "prosecutorial discretion" means once they arrive, they'll never have to go back.

Newspapers, TV shows, and social media throughout Latin America are reporting the very same thing — effectively running ads for the ruthless "coyotes" (human traffickers) who promise to deliver children safely to America. In England, the *Daily Mail* has published appalling pictures of the victims of immigrant smugglers, who are getting rich on the rumor of an impending U.S. amnesty.

Residents of border states will tell you about the "rape trees," full of panties torn from trafficked women who were brutalized and dumped in the desert. Even without the cartel-connected, heavily armed coyotes, travel through the desert can be deadly — as Gilberto Ramos learned.

As *The Washington Post* reports, that fifteen-year-old boy left Guatemala to come to America in search of work that could fund his mother's treatment for epilepsy.

He wore a white plastic rosary she gave him — which Gilberto was still wearing when authorities found his desiccated body.

Gilberto died so that Americans could feel good about themselves.

We want to be seen as the kind of people who selflessly "welcome the stranger." We want to eat quesadillas and wield a few phrases in butchered Spanish, and sneer at the "xenophobes" who tell us about the rape trees. We want to enjoy the low, low prices made possible by cheap, unprotected labor — and we don't want to hear about the price that other people will pay.

True grace, actual empathy, and genuine compassion are not fleeting emotions that flicker through our heads and stir our hearts, like a glimpse of porn. Instead, they are firmly rooted in reality, in the truth. And the truth is that without political order, without the firm enforcement of democratic laws, what reigns instead is chaos. And chaos is the natural habitat for the human traffickers, rapists, drug smugglers and other exploiters of the helpless. Until we as a nation make the hard choices needed to impose a just order on the influx of immigrants, we are all responsible for the suffering that results.

Reclaiming the Safety Net: The Challenge for Social Justice Catholics

November 3, 2014

Where does the idea come from of having a social "safety net" to help the poorest and most vulnerable among us? It seems like an obvious and inevitable fact to most of us today, apart from some radical individualists who believe that the poor should sink or swim. But it hasn't always existed. The ancient pagan world made little provision for the weak or unlucky. In Greece, the desperately poor might sell themselves into slavery; in Rome, the needy became hangers-on and parasitical "clients" of the wealthy and powerful. Even the "bread and circuses" offered to the Roman plebes was not really poor relief but a social lubricant designed to keep the mob politically pliant.

The first record we have in the West of systematic aid for the less fortunate appears in the Hebrew Bible, where the prophets demanded that the better off provide for widows and orphans, and the Law prevented extortionate treatment of the poor — even enjoining the Jubilee, a periodic cancellation of debts and redistribution of income. Inspired by Jesus' almost incessant talk of the importance of caring for the poor, the early Church quickly developed her own system of charity, distributed by deacons to the needy, Christian and pagan alike.

The most famous incident from that period was surely the story of St. Lawrence, arrested by the Romans and ordered to produce the Church's reputed treasures. He called together the widows, orphans, and paupers who were supported by Christian charity and presented them to the Romans, saying, "These are the Church's treasures." On one level, Lawrence was simply, almost sarcastically, showing his persecutors where the Church had spent the money they were looking for. More profoundly, he was demonstrating to pagans a profound Christian principle: To us, the human person is the greatest treasure on earth. We see our eternal salvation as conditional on whether or not we recognize, honor, and act on that truth — whether we rescue that treasure when it is endangered, preserve it from harm, and defend its transcendent dignity. When Julian the Apostate tried to restore paganism across the empire, he found himself frustrated by the massive goodwill won by Christian charity toward the poor, which his pagan allies saw no earthly reason to imitate.

Since then, in one form or another, the Church has always been engaged in doing what we traditionally call the Corporal Works of Mercy. Laymen, clergy, and religious alike saw it as their solemn obligation to feed the hungry, give drink to the thirsty, clothe the naked, harbor the homeless, visit the sick, ransom the captive, and bury the dead. Sometimes the local or royal government would play a part in that effort, but much more often it was seen as the Church's duty, to be provided out of the lands possessed by bishops or monks, or the funds raised by pious laymen and entrusted to their local pastors and abbots for that purpose. One of the worst blows struck against the poor in Western history was the destruction of monasticism in much of Europe. In England especially, Henry VIII's seizure of the monasteries at one stroke deprived the poor of their educators, hospitals, and soup kitchens. It would be centuries before the English state stepped in to fill some of the vacuum it had created. In the interim, the poor were largely left to fend for themselves and were controlled by strict laws against both begging and vagrancy — and savage punishments for theft, including mutilation and death.

Our modern Western vision of social justice for the poor and the vulnerable is unimaginable without its biblical, Christian background. The concept of a social safety net is a profound and fragile artifact of Christian civilization, and I think it is quite unclear how long this idea will survive the collapse of Christian faith. We saw with the rise of totalitarianism in the twentieth century how quickly people cut off from faith can forget the moral values that they'd inherited from their believing ancestors and adhere to brutal and antihuman visions of the Good, which conceive and treat human beings as less than persons. The burden of my recent book, *The Race to Save Our Century*, is the rise of such "Subhumanism" and its roots in the failure of faith.

Dostoevsky warned in *The Devils* that "if God does not exist, all things are permissible." He might have added that many other things seem pointless, wasteful, or futile. Without belief in a God whose image each one of us bears, we do begin to wonder, as the Germans did, whether some lives are "unworthy of life." Today, some 90 percent of preborn babies diagnosed with Down syndrome in America are routinely aborted by their parents. In the Catholic kingdom of Belgium, euthanasia is legal for sick children, with the permission of their parents. In Switzerland, depressed patients are presented with the "treatment option" of assisted suicide. What will be the fate of the elderly all across aging societies such as Europe and Japan, where grandparents will soon appear as luxuries that society cannot afford? Assaults on the sanctity of life will only increase, as our vision of the human person grows dimmer and more degraded.

As the Christian roots of our post-Christian societies fade with each generation, it will take a prophetic witness of believers to keep alive the idea of human dignity. We must see that our work on behalf of the poor contributes to that dignity and reflects its roots in the person of Jesus Christ — or else it will utterly fail, becoming merely a means of quelling social unrest and solving social problems — that is, bread and circuses.

How can we ensure that our work for the poor remains distinctly Christian and that our activities build up their human dignity? How do we keep from breathing in the all-pervasive ideology of our age — the "lowest common denominator" of Utilitarian Hedonism, which asserts that the good of human life is to accumulate happy moments and, at all costs, avoid suffering? Make no mistake, that theory is the unspoken common ground that unites the most powerful liberals and conservatives alike, though they differ on how to achieve it. Of course, as Christians we do not fetishize suffering, and the Church has always worked to alleviate it where possible. But we hold to a higher and much more challenging vision of human dignity, a more human and dignified notion of what real happiness means. We see happiness as coming from a life well lived, one grounded in virtue and aimed at a relationship with a loving, eternal God. When we strive to aid people in danger or in need, we can never use means that degrade their intrinsic dignity, undermine their attempts at building up the virtues, or reduce them to abstract "problems" we need to solve. If we do, we ourselves will fail to build up the virtues and will starve our own relationships with Christ.

For all these reasons, we cannot subcontract our duties toward the "least of Jesus' brothers" to the programs of an impersonal secular state. You and I are called to perform the works of mercy ourselves — not to buy indulgences through our taxes to hire strangers to do them for us. It is all too easy to forget the full humanity of people we never see, to dispose of them and their needs with grandiose programs or blasé slogans. We fall into patronizing pity, or resentful indifference, toward masses of faceless strangers whose personal failures and sufferings are boiled down into pie charts, bar graphs, and "metrics." The well-known socialist statesman Joseph Stalin recognized this when he quipped, "A single death is a tragedy. A million deaths is a statistic."

The challenge for social justice Catholics today is to refuse the thirty pieces of silver offered by statesmen in return for compromise about the killing of the innocent.

How can you and I avoid lapsing into such toxic cynicism? There is only one way, I think, and it's one that Pope Pius XI enshrined at the heart of Catholic social teaching. We must use as a litmus test of all our works and plans the fundamental principle he called Subsidiarity. Put simply, in bumper sticker language, what he meant was, "Think globally, act locally." Whatever we can do as private citizens, families, churches, and members of civil society we *must* do. Only what we find, empirically, that we simply cannot accomplish should be entrusted to local government. The residue of problems that elude local government's reach should be bumped up to state government. It is only those intractable issues that really require national legislation that we should hand over to that most distant and unaccountable actor, the nation-state. The federal government, being the bluntest instrument, should be our absolute last resort. Too often, it seems that those with a heart for the poor have mistaken the Church's preferential option for the poor for a preferential option for the federal government.

We must encounter the poor people who live near us and act toward them as genuine brothers and sisters, finding ways to offer them opportunities and assistance that respect their full humanity, including their potential to become and remain self-sufficient. None of us would want his or her children to be perpetually dependent. Why should we accept that fate for our neighbors?

Because it is easier, cleaner, and cheaper — at least in the short run. So instead of working at soup kitchens or crisis pregnancy centers, visiting prisoners and helping homeless people to find affordable housing, we drop a dollar into second-collection baskets and vote for politicians who promise to take the poor off our consciences. We see panhandlers and think to ourselves, "I gave at the office — the IRS office." Worst of all, some of us are willing to compromise fundamental issues of human dignity for the sake of advancing state-based solutions to poverty.

The poorest, most vulnerable human beings in America today are preborn children, whom dishonest Supreme Court decisions and complacent elite opinion abandon to destruction, for any reason, through all nine months of pregnancy. Anyone who supports such laws does not deserve the name of Christian. Such people should not present themselves for Holy Communion in Catholic churches, and if they do, according to canon law, pastors should refuse to give it to them. No Catholic may endorse or support any candidate who does not favor full legal protection for the preborn — regardless of his or her stance on lesser prudential questions. If we scoff at the least of Jesus' brothers, who today are unborn babies, He warned us what we would hear from Him on Judgment Day: "Depart from me, you cursed, into the eternal fire prepared for the devil and his angels" (Matt. 25:41). That's a phrase that "pro-choice" or otherwise compromised Catholics should meditate on, every day.

The challenge for social justice Catholics today is to refuse the thirty pieces of silver offered by statesmen in return for compromise about the killing of the innocent. To reject the false compassion that accepts the sin and abandons the sinner. To leave the place of comfort, where we can sit alongside philanthropists giving TED talks and NGO leaders who party with Bono, and go out to face rejection, scorn, and spitting. That might mean manning the barricades, praying outside abortion clinics. Or teaching the undiluted Gospel of Life in the teeth of sophisticates' sneers. Or defending the goodness and holiness of marriage against its powerful, wealthy enemies. Or refusing Holy Communion to the vice president of the United States and then facing the consequences.

We are each called to different works, but our call is the same: to the foot of the Cross. If we find ourselves far from it, we know we have gone astray.

Editor's Note: Jason Jones delivered this address at the Notre Dame Center for Ethics and Culture's Poverty Conference on October 31.

Gun Rights: Human Rights Guaranteed by Natural Law

April 1, 2016

In arguing for the wisest public-policy proposals to bind our fellow citizens, we must look to the broad vision of human flourishing and the common good that we draw from our Christian heritage.

Doing so prevents us from lapsing into the most common deadly errors that pervade a culture enfeebled by a cheap utilitarianism, which sees the goal of government as maximizing the number of happy moments for the greatest number of voters. We must look to natural law, the law of human flourishing that God wrote on our hearts, which is equally available to pagans and to Christians

Citing Church documents — none of them with infallible authority, by the way — is a feeble means to persuade our fellow citizens and is unnecessary anyway. We have all the tools we need in our God-given reason and the wholesome civic traditions we inherited from British Common Law, whose medieval origins ensured that it served the dignity of the human person, a dignity reinforced by Christ's Incarnation.

On the issue of gun rights and gun control, we are speaking of perhaps the most basic human right imaginable: the right to defend yourself and your family against an immediate threat of violence — either against your person or your hard-earned property. The primary function of the state is more effectively to guard our lives, liberties, and property from aggression, coercion, and theft.

But the state cannot be everywhere, nor would we want it to be. Given that, there will always be situations in which citizens must defend themselves and their families against immediate threats from criminals. That is their inalienable right, and for the state to deprive them of that right would be intrinsically evil. No situation justifies doing what is intrinsically evil. Therefore, no argument of public policy, no appeal to some "seamless garment" or sentimentalized version of Christian nonviolence, could ever justify preventing citizens from protecting themselves from violence.

In seeking the common good, of course, we see that rights hang in tension. We must preserve public order and make sure that one person's attempt to exercise his rights and protect his human dignity does not infringe on someone else's rights and dignity. Someone who wishes to protect his property from trespassing children, for instance, may surround it with a fence, but not a lethal electric fence. Our efforts to defend our rights must be proportional to the threat and must not directly or through negligence harm the innocent.

Therefore, the state has good reason to regulate the level of lethal force available to private citizens, to make sure that it is proportional to the threats they may face. This means that there is no one-size-fits-all firearms regulation appropriate to all people everywhere. Christians living in the lawless parts of Syria, for instance, may well have to own and operate military-grade weapons to protect their families from the depredations of ISIS. For U.S. citizens, such weapons would be totally disproportionate.

In many American cities, violent crime is a constant threat to citizens' well-being — not only to their safety and that of their children but to the fruits of their hard work. The home, the car, the possessions that a member of the working poor has managed to accumulate might have taken him many years to acquire and could prove impossible to replace. But short of full-on surveillance, there is no way for the state to provide such citizens adequate protection. So these citizens must be allowed to arm themselves in a proportionate manner.

The laws governing self-defense should rightly center first and foremost on the absolute right of each human being, the image of God, to protect himself and his family — not on the calculations of distant bureaucrats or the wistful imaginings of high-minded idealists.

On top of our right to defend ourselves against the daily threat of lawless people, we also have a right to resist the lawless actions of government. In virtually every case, this will take the form of going to court or voting in elections. However, we have seen that governments are just as tainted by Original Sin as any human institution. They can turn to evil with devastating force. According to scholar R. J. Rummel, *governments in the twentieth century killed some 262 million people* — not including casualties of war. In most cases, those civilians were totally unarmed and hence unable to defend their most basic rights.

We know well that totalitarian governments such as the Bolsheviks and the Nazis made it among their first priorities to confiscate all private weapons from their citizens — where previous, well-meaning progressive governments had not already done so. The resistance movements that pushed back against the government brutalities relied on private weapons that still survived among the populace.

This grim history tells us that the American Founders were wise indeed to put a constitutional protection on the right to private firearms in our country's central document. They did so out of respect for natural law and our human dignity as images of God.

Dear Catholics of Mexico and America: Let's Talk Border Control

October 11, 2017

Since the election of President Donald Trump, American and Mexican bishops have issued statement after statement about border enforcement and migration. Unfortunately, each of their pronouncements is more heated and unhelpful than the last.

When the Archdiocese of Mexico accused Mexican businessmen of "treason" for supporting Donald Trump's border wall, I wrote an open letter to the Mexican bishops. By publicly shaming their flock at the outset, these bishops were squandering an opportunity for leadership. I begged them to reconsider.

Similarly, when my friend Steve Bannon expressed his opinion about DACA, several Church leaders attacked him publicly. When they did so, they showed their failure to grasp a point Bannon made in the first place: when it comes to policy issues like these, we're all equals who deserve a hearing, and a bishop is just "another guy with an opinion" — not a moral authority who must be obeyed on pain of sin.

Bannon's argument was straight out of the *Catechism*. It's the distinction between:

1. *The absolute and binding moral principles of our Faith.* Bishops are meant to lead laymen like you, me, and Steve Bannon by painting the bright-red lines of faith and morals that we are bound to follow. Laymen can't dissent from these principles and still consider themselves Catholics in any meaningful sense.
2. *Prudential questions as to how to enact those principles in the world.* Laymen have a duty to take the lead in Christianizing the world around us in everything we do, working always toward a humane culture that is hospitable to our fellow men. Taking our cues from the timeless teachings of the Church, we should robustly debate how best to apply them in business, politics, art, and activism.

When bishops throw the full weight of their moral authority around, recklessly applying it to prudential policy questions, they discourage us from fulfilling our duty as laypeople to engage in the kind of reasoned, respectful debate that is so needed today.

I don't even agree with Bannon's position on DACA. But it's acceptable for him to express it. What is absolutely unacceptable is that Catholic laymen can't seem to have a respectful conversation on prudential questions of policy without their own shepherds attempting to shut down the debate with moral condemnations.

Imagine if bishops were to do the same on absolute moral issues such as abortion and natural sexuality — as they should! When was the last time we heard a bishop aggressively intervene in the midst of a discussion on LGBT identity politics to slam a layman on the liberal side of the debate?

Here's my brief, good-faith effort to set aside all the heated rhetoric and restart the border conversation in a more humane, respectful, and truly Catholic way.

First, I am thankful that President Trump has made it a priority to secure the border between the United States and Mexico and to implement mandatory verifications of worker eligibility in the United States.

Just like Americans, I believe Mexicans have good reason to see the wisdom of these policies.

For too long, the border has been controlled not by elected governments, but by violent gangs and by people smugglers, who abuse vulnerable people on both sides. Thousands of Mexicans have died in the chaos. Americans have suffered too.

The people of both our nations have also struggled economically. When Mexicans enter the United States illegally to find work, they can't appeal to our labor and safety laws. Instead, they find themselves trapped in an underground economy that takes advantage of migrants and undercuts American workers' wages.

The economic reality of foreign workers in the United States has existed for so long that it raises another policy question: the status of Dreamers and the continuation of DACA.

Dreamers were raised here, they were educated here, they married here, and they work here. Their culture, their friends, and their coworkers are American. In many cases, even their spouses are American, and not even of Mexican descent.

I have Mexican friends, and I have American Dreamer friends whose parents migrated from Mexico some twenty years ago. I can tell you, these Dreamers are not Mexicans. They are Americans.

I was glad to see President Trump make a similar observation when he recently tweeted, "Does anybody really want to throw out good, educated and accomplished young people who have jobs, some serving in the military?"

Since Dreamers are Americans in fact, it is only right that they should be Americans by law.

As an American and a Catholic layman, I feel it's my duty to begin this dialogue. I hope my Catholic brothers and sisters both in Mexico and America will join me. We shouldn't be aiming for each other's throats. We should aim for the common good and a win-win solution that benefits both the people of Mexico and the people of the United States.

Each of our great nations has the right to control its border. And when we do, we defend the rights of our people. A secure border and a mandatory employee verification system for workers in the United States will move both our nations toward a much more humane future.

"Why I Got Arrested Protesting the Lockdown": An Interview with John Zmirak

May 4, 2020

JOHN ZMIRAK (JZ). I saw that sweet pic of you getting arrested. What happened?

JASON JONES (JJ). I'm in trouble with the lawless governor of Hawaii and the mayor of Honolulu. Or more accurately, I'm in trouble with distant, un-American, unelected bureaucrats. They're working their will through Governor Ige and Mayor Caldwell. I was arrested on Friday for participating in the #ReOpen Hawaii event.

JZ. What did you observe about law enforcement at the reopen Hawaii protest? How were they acting? What were their orders, as far as you could tell?

JJ. Initially, I was relieved. It looked like we would have a short rally, express our grievances with the mayor and governor, and then head home for a barbecue with the family. About thirty minutes in, I noticed three separate groups of police officers. They began to move in from all three available directions in a standard cordon operation. This made my blood boil. I couldn't believe our mayor would order police to use military tactics against the families of Hawaii.

JZ. What do you object to about the lockdown orders in Hawaii? Are they unconstitutional, needless, or irrational?

JJ. Simply put: Because they amount to an illegal prior restraint on our right to free speech and our right to freedom of assembly, the order was unconstitutional, and it should not have been enforced.

JZ. What groups were involved in the protest? What about the efforts of Michigan's Gretchen Whitmer to label such protests as "white supremacist"?

JJ. This is Hawaii; it's hard to make that claim. A man arrested with me is a Samoan chief. I was there with my Chinese wife and *hapa* (Hawaiian for "mixed") children. The event looked like Hawaii: Hawaiian, Samoan, Filipino, Chinese, Japanese. It was a good mix of our state — a lot of small business owners. I also saw a prominent pastor from Calvary Chapel Honolulu.

JZ. Do you see the actions of so many blue-state governors as ominous? Part of a real threat to liberty? Or just the fruit of panic and incompetence?

JJ. Regardless of motive or intention, the response by our governors is an ominous threat to liberty. Our state and local officials are behaving as thoughtless sock puppets. Distant, unelected bureaucrats are working their will through our governors and mayors. They give no thought to the local realities and needs of the communities impacted by Orwellian government overreach. It is vital in the preservation of liberty that we revitalize those institutions that shelter us from distant ideologues.

JZ. Do you see Americans as giving in to panic, and surrendering fundamental liberties based on weak or speculative evidence? Is this a trial run by enemies of liberty to see how "Reichstag fire" panic can be weaponized to steal our rights?

JJ. We have surrendered our inherited freedoms without a fight. We will see if we will have to fight to regain them. Or if, by the grace of God, men like de Blasio and Cuomo surrender their totalitarian powers peacefully.

JZ. Are nursing-home patients being kept safe in Hawaii? Or is your state forcing nursing homes to take in COVID patients, endangering the vulnerable, like New York, New Jersey, and California?

JJ. Hawaii has a long, rich history of caring for the elderly. I have not heard news reports either way. It is unimaginable that the crimes against the elderly in New York and in Canada could happen in Hawaii. In fact, our commitment to the elderly and vulnerable leaves us open to easier manipulation by the dishonest media and victimist politicians

JZ. How are the homeless, who live on remote beaches in Hawaii, being treated by the authorities?

JJ. The homeless problem in Hawaii is complex and unique. They could have left our homeless community unmolested. Instead, the city and county of Honolulu have relocated thousands of them amid the crisis, several times. The relocation has made it more challenging for private nonprofits and church groups that serve them and meet their needs.

JZ. What's your message to Americans in states with overreaching lockdown orders?

JJ. We must pressure our states to open up. The lockdown has catastrophic unintended consequences. The depressed are committing suicide. People are not getting necessary medical tests and treatment. There's a real threat of hunger and famine in Africa, Asia, the Middle East, and South America.

JZ. What are the next steps that you're taking?

JJ. My next legal step is filing a complaint, a motion for a restraining order, and hopefully, a trial. I am filing against the governor, the mayor, and the chief of police.

How Many African and Asian Kids Will Leftists Starve Just to Beat Donald Trump?

May 14, 2020

How many African and Asian kids will Leftists starve just to beat Donald Trump? That's an honest question. It's one you should pose to Leftists who favor extending America's lockdown indefinitely — who may have even convinced themselves that they care about the vulnerable.

First, we had to flatten our way of life "long enough to flatten the curve." We crushed the curve. Even in New York City, the hospital system was never overwhelmed. Now there are thousands of empty hospital beds, even there. Healthcare providers are going broke, since "inessential" procedures stay banned. You know, trivial medical interventions like cancer screenings, root canals, and knee replacements — Botox-level frivolities like that. We can worry much later about the casualties these bans cause. Or we don't have to, since they won't get tallied or reported. And certainly not blamed on the lockdown hawks.

The next goalpost was "till we have enough masks and ventilators." That one whizzed past so quickly we barely noticed it. Mention it now, and you just seem stupid. "That's so ... mid-April 2020," the smart set will scoff. "Why don't you listen to ... Science? Believe facts over truth! Trust Dr. Fauci, omigod you religious fanatics!" That may or may not be a direct quote by Joseph Biden. We couldn't quite make out his words.

How about the goalpost "till we have secured nursing homes and protected the most vulnerable, who account for almost half the deaths in many states"? Just kidding. The Left never cared about that. Just ask Joe Biden's virus expert Ezekiel Emanuel, who invokes the "duty to die" at age seventy-five, after which he would deny old folks life-saving medicine. Or the governors of massive blue states California, New Jersey, Pennsylvania, and New York, who, for many deadly weeks — sit down for this one, because it sounds like something made up by guys in tinfoil hats — dumped virus patients at nursing homes. A growing backlash, which started largely at *The Stream*, soon spread to Fox News. Now some of these governors are finally backing down, reluctantly. So there are still old folks left alive in those states, despite their governors.

What are the goalposts now? Do they stand at "till we have a reliable vaccine and have forced everyone in America to take it"? That's a safe one, since five years will likely pass, with no guarantees on that score.

We think we know the real goalposts: Till the limping, battered economy drives enough blue-collar workers to deaths of despair, closes enough small businesses, and makes sufficient Americans 100 percent dependent on government money to induce a national Stockholm syndrome. Then, like a traumatized, battered Patty Hearst, Americans will numbly reach out and vote for their captors, the Democrats. The very next day, the media sirens will sound the "All Clear!"

Perhaps we're being unfair. Maybe the people who cheered the destruction of Gen. Mike Flynn, of Brett Kavanaugh and Mark Judge, of Nick Sandmann, Carter Page, and George Papadopoulos aren't as ruthlessly addicted to power as we suspect.

There's one way to find out. Ask them how many African kids they're willing to starve to beat Donald Trump and retake the U.S. Senate. No, really, we'd like the number. Is it one million, five, or ten? How many fragile countries devoid of white, Christian males are they willing to plunge into civil war? We already know that there's no limit to the pain the Left will inflict on America's working class. But to be fair, lots of them are white, and many voted for Donald Trump. They might do so again. So they kind of... deserve it. ("Bad voter, bad! No job for you! Get back in your crate.")

But what did the children of Sudan, Syria, and Pakistan ever do to our elites in Park Slope and Georgetown? Why should they suffer?

And suffer they will. We warned people back on April 13 at *The Stream*. At the time, the only people warning about the threat of global hunger and instability were a few heroes inside the Trump administration. Of course, the media laughed them off. If you're a person single-mindedly focused on grabbing power at any cost, you tend to project your priorities onto others. So, few repeated their warnings.

But these genuine humanitarians whom President Trump tasked with preventing a global food catastrophe kept on working. They somewhat flattened the hunger curve, but it's still liable to crush millions.

Especially inspiring is the work of Ambassador Kip Tom. A family farmer, he serves as America's ambassador to the United Nations Agencies for Food and Agriculture in Rome. He's traveling the globe on creepy, empty airplanes trying to keep intact the fragile chain connecting food producers here in America with hungry nations sliding helplessly toward the brink of catastrophe. Meanwhile, record swarms of locusts ravage African nations, destroying their food stocks. Ambassador Tom warned the world:

> When people can't feed themselves, they lose hope, and when they lose hope, they migrate. When they migrate, we know they become one of the 20 million victims who get involved in human trafficking, or they get involved in arms movement, or in a worst-case scenario, they get involved in extremism.

That's happening in Africa and the Middle East right now. How long before it spreads to Latin America too?

David Beasley, executive director of the United Nations World Food Programme (WFP) is another hero in this battle. He's globe-trotting trying to stave off a man-made human catastrophe. On May 8, Beasley issued a grim prediction. As the Atlantic Council reports:

> Up to 300,000 people could starve to death every day if the COVID-19 pandemic ruptures global food supply chains — even more than the roughly 275,000 people who have died of the disease worldwide so far. . . .
>
> He [Beasley] added: "If farmers can't get food to the marketplace, it impacts the rest of the population. And if farmers aren't out there planting, then next fall when it's harvest time, there'll be serious food shortages. In Sudan, for example, there's flooding. And desert locusts are consuming a million acres of just-planted crops. You've got a perfect storm of extraordinary proportions coming together right now."
>
> According to Beasley, 821 million people go to bed at night chronically hungry; another 135 million are acutely food-insecure. But as COVID-19 wrecks the global food supply chain, that number could more than double to 265 million — roughly the population of Indonesia.
>
> "Acute means you're on the brink of starvation," he said. "On any given day, we feed about 100 million people, of which 30 million get their only food from us. You can go a few weeks exposed to a disease, but you can't go two weeks without food."
>
> If economic deterioration continues and supply chains break down, he said, "you could have 150,000 to 300,000 people die of starvation every day for several months — at a minimum."

Maybe you don't believe Ambassador Tom. Or Mr. Beasley. Or us. You think we're being callous, partisan MAGA zealots who don't "believe science"? Fine. Don't listen to us.

How about *The New Yorker*? Maybe we can agree it's not a GOP mouthpiece controlled by the Christian Right or the Koch brothers. Here's the latest headline from *The New Yorker:* "COVID-19 Will Lead to 'Catastrophic' Hunger." In it, we hear from Arif Husain. He's the chief economist and director of research, assessment, and monitoring at the WFP. Husain notes the sudden spike in the millions of people suffering from "chronic hunger." That means that

> regardless of people's circumstances, they go to bed hungry; it's just normal for them. And that number, four years ago, in 2016, was seven hundred and ninety-six million. At the end of 2019, that number was eight hundred and twenty-one million.

Husain then points to a second number, the total of those suffering "acute hunger." That means people who normally are as well nourished as we are. But their situation is fragile, and emergencies deprive them of food. That total has shot up as well, even before the virus: "That number, in 2016, was eighty million. At the end of 2019, that number was a hundred and thirty-five million. That's almost a seventy per cent increase."

All of that's just background. With the massive disruptions of the food chain supply, and economic damage thanks to our indiscriminate lockdown? Husain predicts our policies will make

> an already really bad situation catastrophically bad. And what we are projecting, as we speak, is that there will be an additional hundred and thirty million people who will become acutely hungry in 2020.

Or listen to *The Nation,* the furthest-left mainstream magazine in America. It reported on May 4:

> Even as people around the world grapple with the medical and economic consequences of the Covid-19 pandemic, many are also facing yet another great calamity: food scarcity. Either for lack of funds or lack of supply (or both), poor and newly jobless families are finding it increasingly difficult to

> obtain the food they need. With both economic contraction and joblessness expected to accelerate in the coming months, the number of families facing food insecurity and starvation is bound to soar....
>
> The curbs on international trade and travel imposed by governments around the world in response to the pandemic have also played havoc with global supply lines. Many ships and planes remain idle because of such restrictions (or because key employees are sick or afraid to show up for work), slowing the delivery of vital supplies and adding to a surge in food prices. In East Africa, international efforts to combat a historic plague of crop-devouring locusts are being hampered by a slowdown in the delivery of pesticides.

The United States is the world's breadbasket. Our highly efficient, safe, clean food exports are one of the last lifelines of hundreds of millions of the poorest people on earth. And our politicians are wantonly sabotaging that life-saving mechanism, allegedly to protect us from a disease we're all going to be exposed to, sooner or later.

How do these people sleep at night?

Conserving Liberalism: A Manifesto for the Class of 2020

May 31, 2020

Dear Class of 2020,

You probably feel it in your bones. This year ought to be the beginning of your great adventure. Adults should be encouraging you to set out into the world and change it for the better.

Instead, what you're hearing from school announcements, corporate commercials, and government press conferences is "#StayHome."

But wait, it gets creepier.

Suddenly you're also supposed to treat hugs, high fives, and handshakes like attacks instead of signs of affection and to parrot weird, unnatural phrases like "contact tracing," "together apart," and "social distancing."

And you're seeing the effects everywhere. Cops show up and ticket kids for skateboarding in the open air at the park. Lovers glance nervously around before they kiss in public. Some of them get so tired of the "social distancing" surveillance state that they despair and just break up.

And it's not just Big Brother.

"Karen" from across the street might call the police if you forget to wear a mask next time you take the trash out. That one girl a year ahead of you who's home from UC Berkeley? She downloaded a government contact-tracing app and put you on a list. Maybe even your favorite teacher. He used to encourage you to pursue your dream of becoming a deep-sea diver, a filmmaker, or a civil rights lawyer. But now he tells you to forget it and just get used to the "new normal."

What you're witnessing is a battle between real, freedom-loving classical liberalism and illiberalism.

The old liberalism is the overarching philosophy that makes a country free, prosperous, healthy, and secure. It's the reason parents in America tell their kids they can be anything they want when they grow up. Because, up until now, they could.

While I was growing up in a free (liberal) America, no disaster could hold me back. Kids like me had the freedom to take traumatic events as inciting incidents and calls to adventure, not paralyzing "new normals" that would hang over us for the rest of our lives.

Like you, I, too, didn't get to walk for my high school graduation. I dropped out of high school shortly after my seventeenth birthday and joined the army.

And you know what? Since then, I've gotten two degrees, served on two presidential campaigns, and produced several award-winning films. Nobody I met along the way cared that I was a high school dropout, and it never held me back.

Illiberalism can take any number of forms because illiberal people will use any event as an excuse to paralyze the world (for instance, a tragic, criminal, police abuse of force). They're doing it now, using a flu pandemic to suppress our nation's freedom, control its wealth, threaten our health, and rob us of the security of a stable world not in the control of the unpredictable whims of petty tyrants.

Now they're telling you there's no guarantee you'll have the freedom to pursue your dreams in a career you're passionate about. They're shooing you away from mentally and spiritually healthy activities, like time spent with friends playing Frisbee in the park. They're even denying you the right to a private life, secure from the scrutiny of a new surveillance-obsessed regime that hems you in for your own good.

For them, the "new normal" means it would be abnormal for you to question why the world is closing in around you. It means that whatever teachers, health officials, and bureaucrats in distant capital buildings decide to do with you is just how it has to be. It means you have no role to play in shaping the future.

In other words, the normal they're trying to foist on you is illiberalism.

So, for you, the question isn't hypothetical: Will you accept the illiberal future they're bringing about, or will you fight for liberalism?

To help you decide, let's take a look at representatives of each option.

Bill Gates was once a free spirit, just as we all should be when we first set out into the world. He dropped out of Harvard to pursue a career in computer technology. He cofounded the tech giant Microsoft and went on to become one of the wealthiest, most powerful men in the world.

And with all that wealth and power, how did he react to the crisis we're all living through today? He contacted the highest levels of world governments, arranged interviews with media megacorporations, and spread an urgent, fearful message: Stay inside.

In fact, Gates has gone so far as to say we should never feel secure again. Freedom, prosperity, health, and security: All of those things have to wait. Governments must develop a vaccine, and everyone must be vaccinated. Until then, life must come to a halt. Do nothing until someone in authority tells you to.

Elon Musk was a dropout too. He dropped out of a Stanford University Ph.D. program to pursue a tech career. He's now one of the most successful people in the world. On top of that, he's made it his goal to get the first human beings to Mars, almost one hundred million miles away.

When government officials locked everything down (including Musk's factory in Alameda County, California), he didn't just shrug and accept it. His employees were hurting and wanted to get back to work. His own instincts told him his mission was more important to the world than the petty tyrants of Alameda County. But most importantly, he looked to the future and the role he feels called to play in it.

He looked to Mars.

After a few months of waiting, watching, and careful research, he made a decision. He opened his factory, attended the opening himself, and publicly called on local officials to arrest him (but not his workers) if they had a problem with it.

Alameda County backed down.

Bill Gates started out as a bright young kid with a vision. Today, with his faded pink cardigan and thick glasses, his wearied hunch and his nervous laugh, he's become the personification of the illiberal new normal.

You can find illiberals like Gates on both sides of the political aisle. They're fearful, repressive, and controlling. Their first instinct in a crisis is always to call down the wrath of higher authorities to punish and control their neighbors — whether that means calling the cops, drumming up a Twitter mob, or imposing a new lockdown order.

But when Musk got famous for the big role he was playing in human history, people noticed another thing about him.

He's kind of weird.

More importantly, he didn't stop being weird when he got famous. He still tells interviewers his bizarre theories about AI. He still laughs at inappropriate memes. He fell in love with a strange musician who goes by the single name "Grimes." They had a baby and named him "X Æ A-12."

Musk represents another possible new normal. It's the new normal of liberalism.

And liberals, thank God, can also be found on both sides of American politics. On the Left, you have people like Elon Musk, Joe Rogan, and Dave Rubin; on the Right, people like Tucker Carlson, Peter Thiel, and Ron Paul.

I'm proud to have these people alongside me as I fight for a truly liberal future. And I promise I'll fight hard for you, to make sure you can live in freedom, prosperity, health, and security after your graduation.

But finally, Class of 2020, you have to ask yourself if you'll fight too.

And you'll be off to a good start already if you just consider the stakes: Will your future be huddling indoors waiting for orders? Or will it be on a rocket headed to Mars?

Don't Give Joe Biden the Best Years of Your Life

July 15, 2021

It's one of my most deeply held convictions, and I believe it's also a universal one. We all know it instinctively: *We ought to leave the world a better place than we found it.*

At the very least, we should leave our children and grandchildren with the same good experiences and opportunities we had.

That's the thought that came to mind when I saw a recent statement from Joe Biden. "Twelve years [of education] is no longer enough today to compete in the 21st Century," he said. "That's why the American Families Plan guarantees four additional years of public education for every person in America — two years of universal, high-quality pre-school and two years of free community college."

When you and I spend our energies building up a heritage for our children, it's a beautiful thing. But when the head of the government's executive branch says he has an "agenda" that will "guarantee" two years of preschool and two years of "free" community college, it's another thing entirely.

In fact, let's just say it straight: It means agents of the state are coming to take over. In particular, they're coming to take over two things: Americans' earliest childhood years and the most formative years of their young adulthood.

Speaking for myself, those were four of the best years of my life. And I won't keep quiet while government bureaucrats plot to rob our posterity of those wonderful years.

By the grace of God, I didn't spend my preschool years in a preschool.

My father left for the army when I was three years old. While my teen mom worked as a waitress, I was left to my own devices along with my little brother. All I remember about my life from three to five is a world of boundless horizons and endless adventure.

I got a lot out of those years of stalking Nazi forces with "rifles" pulled from fallen tree branches, outwitting neighborhood spies, and sailing on an ocean of pavement while my brother and I took turns walking the plank.

But then came my K–12 education. It was miserable.

By third grade, I was already ditching classes regularly to revisit the world I'd grown to love before entering the system. I'd wander around in the prairie behind my house and let my imagination run wild. It was worth the punishments I got at school. To a kid like me, school was already a kind of punishment itself.

Toward the end of middle school I cut out even more often. But by then, I was starting to trade in rocks and sticks for books and artwork. I loitered in bookstores and museums. By high school, I attended classes less than half the time, and I dropped out at the age of seventeen to join the army.

A few years later, after I served, I found my first good experience in formal American education. I signed up for classes at Leeward Community College on the west side of Oahu, Hawaii.

There, I finally excelled.

It was easy to stay inspired and diligent at Leeward. I was surrounded by such unique, energetic, and creative people.

My classmates included wise older men leaving behind decades of labor on now-defunct plantations to study for a new line of work — ambitious new migrants, excited and determined to make their way in America. Veterans, heroes, single moms, and escapees from authoritarian regimes. Some went on to become brilliant media figures and thoughtful, dedicated elected officials.

The school's culinary program made the best breakfast I ever had. I miss those mornings of "Loco moco" and passion-orange-guava juice.

I can honestly say that my community college education made everything I've accomplished possible. The books I've written, the movies I've produced, my apostolate: none of that would have happened without it.

I later came to understand what made the magic of Leeward Community College possible in the first place: skin in the game. That's right, it cost us something to attend. Not much (I paid off my community college debt in two years!), but enough to represent a real and personal commitment.

And that little barrier to entry proved to be a path to freedom. After all, it meant that everyone at Leeward was there because he really wanted to be there. How different from my public high school, where so many were in class only because they were compelled to be. More importantly, our skin in the college game meant that we related to one another differently: as mutual caretakers of a shared world. A world in which we were each buying a real share.

That was a magic you can't manufacture or plan from the outside. By definition, it was a magic that happens in the absence of the sort of enforced provision that Biden has in mind. A magic that came from us, the students investing our talents and time.

Throughout my life ever since, I've learned to look for and find that magic in many other wonderful communities throughout the world. It always comes from real people making real gambles with their lives.

And as a husband and father, I also learned that nowhere is this magic more present than in the family. And I've made sure my children got a good start playing with sticks and enjoying their own years of endless adventure.

It's thanks to the four most beautiful and formative years of my life that I can see the danger in the Biden administration's plans.

Preparing the way for our descendants isn't some static, abstract objective that bureaucrats can blueprint, graph, and "guarantee" through the machinery of a state.

No, the task of bettering our world belongs to us. To ordinary individuals and families who know firsthand our own dreams and desires, and those of our children.

History has shown that authorities and systems of government are no match for the natural genius of free individuals, families, and communities. In fact, one of the most brilliant things about America's founding was our constitutional principle of providing the framework and stability of the rule of law, while leaving most of society's flourishing in the hands of the people.

Now, in a time of tumult and rapid change, we can't afford to forget what America's political order has given to us as a heritage — nor how well it's worked for us, and how poorly things will go for future Americans if we allow it to be snuffed out.

Banality, Evil, and Romney

March 16, 2022

A few days ago, my friend John Zmirak begged Americans to remember the blowhards, fools, and amateur Machiavellians who steered Europe into suicide: the twenty million dead and unspeakable destruction of World War I, which made the world safe for Communism and the Holocaust. He had to beg because it's difficult.

Dear reader, can you name a single one of the diplomats, prime ministers, or other civilian leaders whose incompetence led to that war? You can't. They are forgotten. Because they were forgettable. Not one of them had the vision to see the ruination that lay just beyond the brink. They weren't even vividly evil, but merely contemptible.

The greatest crimes in history aren't all conceived by visionary madmen. Some such crimes instead simply accumulate, as the waste products of thousands of wicked decisions made for venal or cowardly reasons by little, forgettable men. Like rat droppings on a battlefield.

For instance, the decision to import African slaves into the Americas. That started with a few greedy conquistadors and grasping Arab traders. It led to a vast system of cruelty, the American Civil War, Jim Crow, race riots, and (in our day) Critical Race Theory. Can you name a single slave trader?

But sometimes Providence operates to reveal the mechanism of mass-production injustice, by casting a cold, clear light on one of the cogs that turns its wheels. By studying how such functionaries end up enabling tremendous evil, we can learn how to reject such temptations in our own lives. We can instead shoulder the cross and obey the dictates of our conscience. We can train ourselves to swim upstream against a powerful current of groupthink that threatens the powerless and the forgotten.

Using her own classical worldview, philosopher Hannah Arendt observed the case of Adolf Eichmann during his trial in Jerusalem for his key role in planning the Holocaust. He hadn't written the anti-Semitic pamphlets that laid the groundwork for genocide. He didn't join bloodied ex-veterans in gunning down political enemies in the streets of German cities. Eichmann wasn't a demonic orator like Hitler or a master manipulator like Joseph Goebbels.

Eichmann was a functionary, a doggedly thorough bureaucrat. When higher-ups set him a task, he turned the whole of his narrow, stunted self to carrying it out — obsessively, like a machine without an "off" switch. Early on, he was given the task of getting Jews out of Europe, to Palestine. So he worked at that fanatically. When Nazi leaders decided instead to exterminate Jews like insects, Eichmann bloodlessly shifted to that task. He made the trains run on time, not reflecting on whether they were full of coal or women and children. He obeyed his marching orders, even if they told him to march millions straight into the incinerators.

As Arendt wrote of this toxic little man:

> Eichmann was not Iago and not Macbeth, and nothing would have been farther from his mind than to determine with Richard III "to prove a villain." Except for an extraordinary diligence in looking out for his personal advancement, he had no motives at all.... He merely, to put the matter colloquially, never realized what he was doing.... It was sheer thoughtlessness — something by no means identical with stupidity — that predisposed him to become one of the greatest criminals of that period. And if this is "banal" and even funny, if with the best will in the world one cannot extract any diabolical or demonic profundity from Eichmann, this is still far from calling it commonplace.... That such remoteness from reality and such thoughtlessness can wreak more havoc than all the evil instincts taken together which, perhaps, are inherent in man — that was, in fact, the lesson one could learn in Jerusalem.

All of which brings me, quite naturally, to Mitt Romney. The United States might very well blunder into a shooting war with Russia. If cities full of civilians get roasted in nuclear fire, Romney is one of the small and thoughtless men who will have caused it. Or we might just lose our constitutional freedom of speech and end up one of those countries (like Russia and Ukraine) where political dissidents end up in prison. If we do, Mitt Romney will have played a larger part than almost anyone. Still, nobody's likely to name one of our gulags after him. Like a food smudge in the history books, he's just too hard to remember.

Mitt Romney has supported every call for aggressive war by the United States since 2001. He backed our disastrous Iraq War and our nation-building fantasy in

Afghanistan. He encouraged our blustering Cold War with a post-Communist Russia, calling it America's "enemy." And now he urges reckless escalation over Ukraine, instead of a negotiated peace, which is on the table.

Even worse, he talks like one of Vladimir Putin's own secret police about his fellow Americans. For differing with him on foreign policy, he accused the great, independent-minded Democrat Tulsi Gabbard of "treason." Think about that. Legally, to commit treason, you must give "aid and comfort" to a country with whom the United States is at war. So, in Romney's mind, we are already at war with a nuclear-armed Russia. In fact, it's the act of a traitor to try to de-escalate the conflict.

That's not how free countries work. It's how petty bureaucrats inside the East German Stasi or Nazi Gestapo falsely labeled dissenters, to justify imprisoning them. Yet we have a prominent U.S. senator, embarrassingly a former Republican nominee for president, spouting such poison.

But I don't believe that Romney is even a convinced militarist, a jacked-up neocon fantasist who dreams of the United States occupying Moscow; because militarism is, in its own sick way, a principle. And Romney has never shown evidence of holding fast to any political or moral principle at any point in his life. He has, at various points, been pro-abortion and pro-life; aggressively pro-LGBT, then tepidly pro-family. He talked up the claims of auto workers when he sought votes in Michigan, then sneered at the working poor when he quipped before a dinner party for millionaires.

Romney seems less like a human being than some lost and frightened cyborg, whose original programming got deleted, so now he seeks a new set of algorithms. Once his calculating faculty concludes that a given set of actions suits his all-consuming ambition, he slides into gear as coolly as lubricated titanium. He sets out to terminate anyone or anything that seems to him an obstacle.

We are a country of free men and women, with the right to speak our minds. If we cannot hear various viewpoints on crucial questions like yes or no on a nuclear war, then what does that even mean? Is this the "freedom" we claim to champion for Ukraine? Mitt Romney has no answer because he can't even understand the question. Those robotic eyes of his look out to us but not at us, as if they were x-raying our bones and scanning our brains.

The only question you'll ever really see in eyes such as those are "What's in it for me?"

Martha's Vineyard: Virtue-Signaling and Victimism

September 17, 2022

This notice on our front door is by way of explaining the sign in our yard. You know, the one that reads:

In This House We Believe

Black Lives Matter

Women's Rights Are Human Rights

No Human Is Illegal

Science Is Real

Love Is Love

Kindness Is Everything

We're concerned that some people may have innocently misinterpreted that sign. The fact that you are standing some seventeen feet on our side of the property line to read this note suggests that you might be one of them. (Our apologies if you're just the Amazon delivery person! Just leave the package on the porch.) Along with most of the other proud residents of Martha's Vineyard, we stand in firm solidarity with the marginalized. In the course of the past few years, an observant person would have seen that very clearly. We have hosted fundraisers, organized online petitions, made generous donations, and spoken out in public on behalf of crucial causes:

- Undocumented migrants in Texas
- Austere Muslim religious scholars in London and Paris
- Transgender athletes seeking inclusion in school and professional sports
- Victims of environmental racism in West Virginia
- Women seeking reproductive rights in Latin America
- Victims of gun violence, including police violence

A decent, educated, responsible fellow citizen would have registered these gestures as what they were meant to be: exquisitely clear signals of the kind of people we are and the virtues we practice here. Even those who, for their own (dark, dogmatic) reasons, disagree with these positions ought to respect them, to see that they are motivated by only the best intentions; that, in fact, they are part of a coherent, long-term worldview that looks beyond today's petty concerns and our own local worries, to plan out a livable future for everyone on our planet for centuries to come — even those too poorly educated or negatively conditioned to realize that it's for their own good.

Some of the people who fail (or refuse) to understand this cold, scientific fact have reacted harshly to us. In fact, if we're being candid, they have behaved atrociously. The illegitimately chosen governors of states full of election deniers that reject women's Choice, Texas and (ahem!) Florida, for instance. They have subjected our community here to an unprecedented siege for several days. In a move that award-winning filmmaker and national treasure Ken Burns aptly compared to the Nazi deportations of Jews, these governors kidnapped some fifty or more (we lost count — it seemed like thousands!) undocumented migrants and forced them on our community.

Border towns in Texas have had time to acclimatize themselves to the free movement of people across the arbitrary line dividing land that America stole from Mexico from territory it didn't. Especially since the legitimate election of President Joe Biden. By stark contrast, Martha's Vineyard has no facilities to receive such migrants. They were just ... dumped here like bags of trash and started wandering around. (Which mixes the metaphor a bit, come to think of it. Sorry! We're overwhelmed here, completely at the end of our last nerves.)

Some of our residents were frightened. Others confused. Some homeowners mistook the victims of the Republican governors for their own nannies and gardeners and tried to address these newcomers in their best Kitchen Spanish. To no avail.

As this threat spread throughout the community, most of us sheltered in place inside our homes and phoned the U.S. senators whom we've most generously supported. It took unconscionable hours before the Massachusetts National Guard could respond to this emergency and safely remove these unfortunate pawns of cynical MAGA power politics to a nearby military base. Life could return to normal, at least on the surface, giving us the chance to begin to process our trauma. Only time will tell how long such healing might take for the first responders.

We have been saddened and somewhat surprised by the lack of national sympathy for our afflicted community. We hadn't realized that even the "red states" contained this many haters. Yes, there, we said it. We have been inundated on social media with vile, unspeakable comments from the worst kind of people, rife with offensive epithets and (of course!) grammatical errors.

More substantively, a few MAGA apologists who seem to have somehow graduated from second- and third-tier colleges have tried to daub out in paragraphs a list of accusations, aimed at all of us. They complain that we do not concern ourselves with what they call the "truly marginalized" of society:

- Uyghur Muslims oppressed by China
- Child workers forced to mine rare-earth elements to make batteries for electric cars
- Persecuted Christians in the Middle East and Africa
- Yazidis hunted in Muslim countries
- Afghans who opposed the Taliban, now pursued by that country's new government
- Women in crisis pregnancies who wish to bear their children
- Americans in poor towns on the border
- Victims of human trafficking groups that control the U.S. border

Such charges betray a profound ignorance of our hearts, our minds, and our very selves. We are fully aware that as citizens, even privileged ones, we cannot address every situation where human beings suffer. We cannot even avoid making hard choices that might (unavoidably, oops!) inflict additional suffering on some people, somewhere, somehow. As progressives, humanists, and futurists, we must make the proper calculations in order to maximize happiness in the biosphere for all its stakeholders, whatever their species.

We know that there is a planetary ecological climate crisis. The Science is settled, just as it was on the proper treatment and prevention of COVID, and the safety and efficacy of vaccines produced by international corporations. If any species, much less our own, is to survive and thrive, we must resolve this crisis, whatever the cost. That means that those of us who understand the crisis and dutifully follow the Science must manage the planet — its politics, economy, communications, and culture. There's no more room for old-fashioned values like "debate" or "popular government." Not when the life of our planet is at stake.

With this in mind, we in communities like Martha's Vineyard must strategically select the issues where we engage our compassion, to dovetail with those where it maximizes our leverage over the global economy and politics. This is rational altruism at its best. We must use — no, better, recycle! — the suffering around us to help us put our loving hands on the levers of power, so we can use them for Good. As John Lennon once, unforgettably, said, "Imagine all the people."

That's what we do here. We imagine people. That's what it means to be a practicing Victimist.

With all of that in mind, please turn right around and march yourself off our property, before our private security people arrive. You have already triggered the infrared sensors, and their Prius vans are on their way.

Remember When the Left Actually Served a Purpose?

February 27, 2023

It might mark me out as a Boomer, but I can actually recall when liberals and progressives served a legitimate function. I know, I know, that "sounds crazy," but hear me out. Go back and watch an old episode of *All in the Family*, for instance. Yes, "Meathead" was fuzzy-headed, Utopian, and frequently self-righteous, and Archie Bunker was right to mock him.

But Meathead was also right about a number of things. For instance, he disapproved of genuine racist statements and thoughtless bigoted attitudes, which Archie used to express. Well, that was useful, wasn't it?

There was a time when those on the left were the main advocates of genuine racial justice, even reconciliation — while William F. Buckley of *National Review* was defending literacy tests that stopped blacks from voting.

Likewise, they supported the legitimate goals first sought by women's "liberation," of equality under law. Of course, progressives didn't know where to stop, and they quickly embraced the escalating, extreme demands of zealots, such as abortion on demand.

The Left forgot that the impulse to defend citizens' dignity and offer them fair treatment arose entirely from the Christian vision of the person — and soon saw churches themselves not as allies but enemies. Now it's up to conservatives, many of them non-white, to revive the civil rights movement's goal of treating people according to the "content of their characters."

The Left once championed an end to censorship and paternalistic government attempts to manipulate public opinion. No more. Now liberals are all-in on letting billion-dollar corporations work with the FBI to censor our medical information and stifle open debate. Left-wingers of principle such as Matt Taibbi and Glenn Greenwald became pariahs for daring to dissent.

The Left once served as a reflexive check on our leaders' impulse to overthrow foreign governments and intervene in foreign wars, often at the behest of big corporations who pulled on senators' purse strings. Can you remember that? We saw a few remnants of the former antiwar Left criticizing Bill Clinton's attack on Yugoslavia and George W. Bush's pointless attack on Iraq. But their heart was hardly in it by that point.

The big money had poured into the Left from crafty defense contractors, who assured them that Left-wing presidents, too, could wield their bombs and bullets ... to promote progressive goals. And pretty quickly the antiwar movement dried up and blew away. Now you can hardly find a Democrat willing to criticize nuclear brinkmanship over Ukraine. It's up to libertarians and America First realists to try to apply some brakes before the next August 1914.

Now, with the horrific ecological disaster in East Palestine, Ohio, we see that the Left has abandoned the environment too. I'm old enough to remember when Lefties would be outraged at mushroom clouds of toxic gas spreading over U.S. cities, poisoning water supplies, farms, and citizens too poor to get out of town.

So where is the outrage now? Where are the protest marches, the congressional hearings grilling the secretary of transportation over a catastrophe on his watch on his railways? Where are the grassroots groups who used to lobby intensely for breathable air, drinkable water, and uncontaminated soil?

They have all been bought and paid for. They bought the well-funded line that "climate change" is the universal issue, trumping everything else and rendering all other questions moot. Conveniently, there are huge corporations ready and willing to get rich offering electric cars, wind farms, and solar panels. The World Economic Forum is a club of billionaires who offer to take over control of the wealth of the planet in order to "build it back better" via a "Great Reset."

When Lynyrd Skynyrd was touring and the Rolling Stones still could dance, progressives would have been screaming their lungs out over such an oligarchical conspiracy. But in our time? You can hear the crickets. Or maybe that's the sound of thirty pieces of silver getting slipped into millions of pockets. From a movement that sought to preserve a livable earth for our posterity, the environmentalist cause now warns people not to have any children at all. Which leaves them exactly what stake in the future of the planet?

So once again, we're going to need the political Right to pick up a legitimate cause that the Left abandoned out of a paucity of principle. We need to remember that Republican Theodore Roosevelt steamrollered big business and established our system of national parks. He drew on religious and patriotic sentiment to champion preserving our country's God-given beauty and the wonders of nature. (This at a time when social Darwinism was driving progressives like Margaret Sanger to forcibly sterilize immigrants who flunked culturally biased IQ tests.)

You can't build a society on blinkered self-interest, an obsession with the present over the future, and sneering contempt for the past. But all these impulses have taken over the movements on the Left, which now chase cheap, easy victories instead of moral, long-term goals. It's left to the churches, the farmers, the patriotic small-towners, and the cussed independent thinkers to rebuild a conservation movement that actually cares about the country and its citizens.

Letting the World's Poorest Freeze in the Dark

December 11, 2023

In the Western world, we eagerly anticipate the arrival of Christmas Day and the winter break, a season filled with joy. However, for millions of our fellow earth dwellers, it will be a season of darkness and cold. Throughout my journey, I have encountered thousands of families who lack the necessities of life that we often take for granted.

In our world's impoverished and conflict-ridden areas, the lack of food, clean water, and rudimentary shelter continues to pose a significant challenge. Access to energy becomes particularly crucial during winter, as many of these communities find themselves vulnerable.

Astonishingly, there seems to be a striking neglect in addressing the urgent energy needs of the most vulnerable at the ongoing United Nations Climate Change Conference — the twenty-eighth chapter of the Conference of the Parties (COP28) — as attention is fruitlessly absorbed by futuristic climate forecasts and policies that hold little relevance to the socioeconomic well-being of people.

Dubai is currently playing host to the COP28 climate meet, attracting a swarm of private jets and an assembly of politicians, along with approximately sixty-five thousand other participants. This gathering marks the most emission-intensive climate conference of the calendar year.

It's quite ironic that these individuals, who frequently travel on private jets and commercial airlines across the globe, are advocating for some of the world's most impoverished people to relinquish their basic right to access energy for survival.

The call for ending fossil fuel use has been around for a while, and there are finally some people who have voiced their strong displeasure toward policies that are disastrous to the energy security of the world.

One of them is Sultan Al Jaber, the host of this year's UN COP28 event. In an event at the conference, the sultan said, "There is no science out there, or no scenario out there, that says that the phase-out of fossil fuel is what's going to achieve 1.5C [referring to the temperature warming mark that policymakers want to achieve]."

He further questioned the apparent lack of solutions to meet the energy needs that are currently being met by fossil fuels. "Please help me, show me the roadmap for a phase-out of fossil fuel that will allow for sustainable socioeconomic development, unless you want to take the world back into caves," asked the sultan.

The comments made by the president of COP28 are indeed accurate. Take, for example, the plight of the impoverished residents in the conflict-affected regions of Gaza, Ukraine, and Afghanistan. They endure highly unstable economic conditions and lack access to essential resources for survival. As winter sets in, they are left to fend for themselves in the bitter cold.

According to the International Energy Agency (IEA), approximately 2.6 billion people in the world still lack access to clean cooking facilities, and 1.4 billion people lack access to electricity. Most of these individuals reside in sub-Saharan Africa and Asia, where energy poverty is a pressing issue, and they rely on traditional biomass fuels, such as wood, charcoal, and animal waste, for cooking and heating.

Winters can be extremely harsh, with temperatures plummeting well below freezing. For those living in poorly insulated homes, particularly in mountainous regions or high-altitude plateaus, coal-fired stoves provide a crucial source of warmth, preventing hypothermia, respiratory illnesses, and even death. For instance, in Mongolia, where temperatures can drop to as low as -40°C (-40°F), coal is the primary source of heating for nearly 90 percent of the population.

For these communities, coal remains a lifeline, providing an affordable and accessible source of energy for heating during harsh winters. Coal is relatively affordable and readily available, making it an essential lifeline for millions of families struggling to meet their basic heating and cooking needs.

Ignoring the significance of coal in these regions not only risks exacerbating energy poverty but also endangers the lives of millions who are defenseless against the harsh realities of cold weather.

This is why the Vulnerable People Project is launching its third annual Coal for Christmas campaign. This year, they will supply more than twenty million hours of heat and more than two million meals for poor and forgotten communities in Afghanistan, Nigeria, Malawi, Mongolia, Pakistan, Gaza, and other places.

The campaign launched on the feast of St. Nicholas, Wednesday December 6, and will run through Christmas and into the New Year. More information on it can be found at Coalforchristmas.org, vulnerablepeopleproject.com.

Champion the poorest. Speak up for the vulnerable. Support the underprivileged. The well-being of the weak must come before empty gestures of environmental virtue in our world.

The WHO Lied. Thousands Died. And Millions Got Locked Down, Dumbed Down, or Injured by the Vax

May 16, 2024

In a classic work by J. R. R. Tolkien — a learned skeptic of power-grabbing elites and self-credentialed experts — Samwise Gamgee talks to his old friend Frodo about the perilous path they are treading toward Mordor: "We shouldn't be here at all, if we'd known more about it before we started. But I suppose it's often that way." In the broken, post-tyranny world refashioned by the COVID panic, we know how such hunted hobbits feel. We wonder if the Shire can ever be the same again.

The COVID virus, fashioned in secret as a weapon, was wielded like Sauron's One Ring, a totem with which to terrorize and brainwash billions, always in service of just one simple outcome: control. Dominion by the few over the many, wealth massively transferred from small businesses to trillion-dollar conglomerates, sacred rights such as freedom to worship, to speak, and to gather stripped away like wool from sheep.

Like the black-robed, flying Ringwraiths, political leaders and media moguls devotedly served their globalist masters. They issued their diktats, and we were expected to crouch in our homes and obey. We couldn't shop or go to work or to church, and we were expected to vote by mail — though Sauron's minions could riot unimpeded in the streets. If we tried to dissent, we were censored. Even experts in their fields found themselves silenced and professionally persecuted.

As I wrote over at Substack:

> Social media giants such as YouTube shut down the accounts of famous epidemiologists and vaccine researchers such as Dr. Robert Malone, silencing free debate about the best responses to COVID, with the explanation that it was simply following the WHO's guidance? But most of us just took that in stride: Oh, our free speech just got stripped away by billion-dollar corporations working with unelected foreign bureaucrats, allegedly to "save lives." What else is new?

> The COVID panic was a test-run for full-on totalitarian thought control, justified by a "crisis." That experiment succeeded beyond its authors' wildest dreams.

Now the same World Health Organization that led the cover-up of the real origins of COVID (a U.S.-funded Chinese bioweapons lab), championed murderous lockdowns, and forced an untested vaccine into our bodies is reaching out again to grasp the One Ring of power.

The WHO is meeting later this month to sign a treaty that would override the constitutions of every country that agrees to it. Twenty-two out of fifty U.S. attorneys general just signed a chilling letter warning Americans what's at stake:

> As the chief legal officers of our States, we oppose two instruments under negotiation that could give the World Health Organization (WHO) unprecedented and unconstitutional powers over the United States and her people....
>
> To varying degrees, these measures would threaten national sovereignty, undermine states' authority, and imperil constitutionally guaranteed freedoms. Ultimately, the goal of these instruments isn't to protect public health. It's to cede authority to the WHO — specifically its Director-General — to restrict our citizens' rights to freedom of speech, privacy, movement (especially travel across borders) and informed consent.

Let's remember what happened just four years ago, when the WHO flexed its muscles. Allegedly to "stop the spread" of an already uncontrollable virus, the organization declared a global health emergency, imploring all countries to impose COVID lockdowns. The warden imprisoning us in the United States was Dr. Anthony Fauci, who'd helped fund the research that initially created COVID. Fauci used his bully pulpit to mislead elected officials with false information on COVID's origins and how it spreads; to demand that everyone wear useless containment measures like masks; to exaggerate the disease's virulence and morbidity. And most dangerous of all: He helped impose on us potentially deadly vaccines disguised as lifesaving devices.

With a global propaganda campaign of shaming and fear, the WHO managed to shut down the economic activity of the entire world. The useless, fascist lockdowns crashed thousands of businesses, caused mass unemployment, and incinerated hundreds of billions of dollars in wealth in a vast bonfire, which hurt the world's poorest disproportionately — depriving millions in Africa of medicine, food, and fuel. The COVID panic caused the highest economic uncertainty in decades, surpassing the impact of 9/11 and even the 2008 economic crisis.

Marko Kolanovic, a strategist at JP Morgan, argues that governments were "spooked" into imposing lockdowns: "Unlike rigorous testing of new drugs, lockdowns were administered with little consideration that they might not only cause economic devastation but potentially more deaths than COVID-19 itself."

In 2021, states with the strictest lockdowns, such as Hawaii, California, Massachusetts, New Jersey, and New York, exhibited some of the highest unemployment rates in the country. The exploding joblessness helped bid wages down for those who could even find work. Middle- and lower-income families in the United States bore the brunt, with "nearly one-in-five middle-income families . . . receiving unemployment benefits in 2020." One in three adults in lower-income households reported unemployment for at least part of 2020.

School closures robbed children of more than a year of school and harmed their mental health in incalculable ways — to protect them from COVID, which posed little real health risk to most. Studies in the United States showed that "the loss of connectedness in one's social network was heavily associated with poorer psychological distress and mental health during the early months of the 2020 pandemic."

In richer nations, blue- and pink-collar workers in sectors such as tourism, hospitality, and retail were laid off in droves, reduced to dependence on government checks. Not everyone can work via Zoom — a fact that proved impossible to convey to editors and journalists.

The impact on food security was particularly severe in low-income countries. Millions who already lived hand-to-mouth struggled to afford necessities, pushing them deeper into hunger and malnutrition. A study in Bangladesh showed that the "COVID-19 lockdown had a significant impact on household food insecurity, dietary diversity as well as acute malnutrition in children." Even in wealthy Britain, one in four adults became at risk of hunger and potential malnutrition.

Multiple poor countries witnessed widespread internal displacements where millions of migrant workers living in the big cities returned to their villages, since they no longer had work or housing. But with buses and trains canceled, many walked barefoot for hundreds of miles to reach their villages. Casualties were inevitable.

Sadly, many of them would not get their jobs back when things returned to normalcy, worsening the plight of their entire extended families. In India alone, around 230 million people were pushed into poverty.

No one needed to go through this man-made nightmare. It was all a fake, a fraud, an exercise in social engineering, as part of a grasp at power — a power more absolute than any totalitarian dictator or system has ever come close to achieving. And all of it was sold to us based on a lie: that COVID was uniquely dangerous. You would think, if that were true, that governors in blue states would have kept COVID patients far away from the most vulnerable, the elderly. Instead, those public officials dumped COVID patients by the thousands in nursing homes. That duly spiked the death stats, justifying the ongoing lockdown, plus ensuring that we would have insecure mail-in balloting just in time for the 2020 election. (But that was surely just some weird coincidence.)

We know from the data in Africa that COVID was not radically more dangerous than other well-known diseases. Toby Green, writing for RUSI, notes:

> The African continent has registered fewer than 260,000 Covid deaths in three-and-a-half years, and over 100,000 have been in South Africa alone. On a continent where around 12 million people die every year, this is a 0.75% increase over 3 years; removing South Africa from the equation, this becomes a 0.25% increase. Even accounting for missed diagnoses, mortality impacts have been very low.

Green writes that "in addition to the inflationary pressures, other factors such as access to electricity, school closures (and loss of associated nutrition), premature marriage for adolescent girls, and restrictions on the informal market on which 85% of African workers depend all had major impacts on the lived experience of poverty" due to lockdowns.

A 2022 Afrobarometer public policy report concluded that "government orders closing borders, restricting domestic travel, closing businesses . . . are likely to have had much more far-reaching effects on trade, sales, employment, and personal income."

Further, by shoving experimental vaccines into their bodies, the WHO–Big Pharma nexus has violated the dignity of billions and impacted their health forever. Billions now live with the scars not of the virus but of the vaccines themselves — which may well be fueling an epidemic of heart problems and exotic cancers.

What can men do in the face of such reckless evil? Sam Gamgee observed to Frodo that heroes in the old stories, the best stories, "had lots of chances, like us, of turning back, only they didn't. And if they had, we shouldn't know, because they'd have been forgotten."

We must not flinch from the fight. As Tolkien's whole magnificent tale managed to prove, "Even the smallest person can change the course of the future."

Tech Brahmins Should Look at Indian Dysfunction First

January 3, 2025

We get it. You tech bros are trying to help us. You see America languishing compared with its global competitors. That's why some of you pitched in at some point to help defeat Kamala Harris and her coalition of grabbers and smashers. A few of you even openly endorsed Donald Trump, as Elon Musk and Vivek Ramaswamy did, to their credit. Many more of you are now stepping up to offer your services and your advice, as the transition continues.

But some of that advice is frankly misplaced and aimed in the wrong direction. Some of it has offended core Trump supporters, especially the populists and activists who fought against savage lawfare, served time on trumped-up January 6–related charges, battled election fraud, and protested the COVID panic lockdowns (for which I got arrested), and otherwise paid a real, tangible price for supporting a MAGA movement that Joe Biden labeled "semi-fascism" in a nationally televised speech.

People like us were particularly put off by Ramaswamy's tin-eared comments concerning H-1B visas and the cultural deficits that allegedly make American workers less competitive. He wrote on X:

> Our American culture has venerated mediocrity over excellence for way too long (at least since the 90s and likely longer). That doesn't start in college, it starts YOUNG.
>
> A culture that celebrates the prom queen over the math olympiad champ, or the jock over the valedictorian, will not produce the best engineers.
>
> A culture that venerates Cory from "Boy Meets World," or Zach & Slater over Screech in "Saved by the Bell," or "Stefan" over Steve Urkel in "Family Matters," will not produce the best engineers.

He praised hard-driving immigrant parents by comparison and called for

> more movies like Whiplash, fewer reruns of "Friends." More math tutoring, fewer sleepovers. More weekend science competitions, fewer Saturday

morning cartoons. More books, less TV. More creating, less "chillin." More extracurriculars, less "hanging out at the mall."

Now, some conservatives interpreted these comments as tough love, a call for Americans to return to old-fashioned virtues and the Protestant work ethic, or something. Many others were deeply offended and said so. They were duly labeled "racist," "woke Right," or worse.

Ramaswamy didn't make clear how letting corporations import indentured workers from the third world, who can't quit working for the company that got them into the country without getting deported, would help solve any of the cultural problems he diagnosed among Americans. Maybe via brutal, Darwinian competition? Or perhaps he meant to say that Americans had no business restricting the import of driven, hungry migrants until we cleaned up our act and parented like tiger moms.

Whatever he meant, on behalf of my fellow Americans, I'd like to call on him and his allies — including Elon Musk and Peter Thiel — to turn their attention to a nation that needs their help more urgently than we do. A place where cultural problems waste human potential on a much vaster scale and cause enormous, needless suffering and division. I'm speaking of India.

Through my nonprofit, the Vulnerable People Project, I try to help those around the world who belong to groups that are targeted for oppression or singled out for neglect. We advocate for Afghans who allied with the United States and now face persecution; for civilians in Gaza caught up in Israel's war of retribution; for Nigerian Christians and Jews who suffer for their faith. And along with all of those, we work on behalf of Indians abused by their extremist, ethno-nationalist government because they are either Christians or Dalits ("Untouchables").

India's three hundred million Dalits continue to face widespread discrimination, violence, and oppression. According to the United Nations, almost a third of the Dalit community, or some one hundred million people, still live in poverty.

Dalits continue to be assigned to the most undesirable tasks, such as manual scavenging — cleaning excreta from toilets by hand, skinning animals, and disposing of dead bodies. In 2023, at least 90 sanitary workers in India died on the job. From 2017 to 2022, 373 people are reported to have died cleaning hazardous sewers and septic tanks.

Every year, thousands of Dalits, especially women, are subjected to rape, torture, acid attacks, and murder. The stories are so common, and the practice is so endemic, that news media don't bother to report most of these atrocities because they are not considered to be news.

As I wrote at *The Stream*, India's Christians (whose communities date back to the first century AD) are equally oppressed for different reasons.

> Open Doors categorizes the persecution of Christians alongside "Iran, Pakistan, Afghanistan — and worse than Saudi Arabia or China."
>
> The signatories highlight the anti-Christian violence in the state of Manipur, which has displaced more than 65,000 believers and seen more than 400 churches bulldozed or burned down "with the sanction of the Indian state."
>
> Moreover, more than 2,500 Christians were forcibly displaced as Hindu mobs attacked, looted, and destroyed homes between December 2022 and February 2023 because residents refused to convert to Hinduism.

Beyond the Christians and Dalits, India is home to some two hundred million Muslims, one of the world's largest Muslim populations, but since Prime Minister Narendra Modi's reelection in 2019, the government has pushed controversial policies that trample Muslims' rights, restrict religious freedoms, and are intended to disenfranchise millions of Muslims.

A 2019 report by the India-based nongovernmental organization Common Cause found that half of police surveyed showed anti-Muslim bias, making them less likely to intervene to stop crimes against Muslims.

In recent years, state and national courts and government bodies have sometimes overturned convictions or withdrawn cases that accused Hindus of involvement in violence against Muslims.

In addition, authorities have turned to extrajudicial means to punish Muslims, through a practice critics call "bulldozer justice." In 2022, authorities in several states destroyed people's homes, alleging that the demolished buildings lacked proper permits.

What drives a putatively democratic, multireligious society such as India to tolerate such horrors? A religiously based racism more appalling than anything we ever experienced in America.

> So far as the Hindus are concerned, all power has remained for many centuries in the hands of a small group of hereditary exploiters whose life and interests even today are antagonistic to the welfare of the masses in India.

So wrote Swami Dharma Theertha, a high-caste Hindu who rebelled against the caste system. In his *History of Hindu Imperialism*, a landmark text of resistance, Theertha explains:

> Brahmanism is the name used by historians to denote the exploiters and their civilization. It may be defined as a system of socio-religious domination and exploitation ... based on caste, priestcraft, and false philosophy.

The racial slur *Untermensch* ("subhuman"), borrowed by the Nazis from the eugenicist Lothrop Stoddard in their campaign to dehumanize Jews and other non-Aryans, would be an appropriate category to understand how the Untouchable (Dalit) is regarded in the Hindu caste hierarchy.

A flurry of academic studies in peer-reviewed journals and books by university publishers have demonstrated the infiltration and dominance of caste hierarchy, hegemony, and discrimination by Indian Hindu high-caste individuals in American companies, especially in the IT sector. Are those the kinds of companies we want to see expanding in America?

Which nation needs a thorough cultural conversion, to stop wasting the talents of countless people — America, with its phone-preoccupied Zoomers, or India, with its hundreds of millions of people oppressed for their religion or the imaginary taint they inherited by getting born in the lowest caste?

So the Vulnerable People Project is calling on Ramaswamy, Musk, Thiel, and every tech entrepreneur concerned about maximizing innovation and enhancing human potential, to pressure the Indian government on this long list of abuses. Furthermore, we call on the U.S. government to accept migrants from India only from groups currently being oppressed by its bigoted government — not from the Brahmin elites who crack the whip and sometimes have the gall to accuse blue-collar Americans of "racism."

The hypocrisy is not lost on us.

Elon Musk Loves to Solve Other People's Problems . . . Not His Own

January 8, 2025

Imagine a devoted Christian wife and mother who was so preoccupied with distant philanthropic projects that she did nothing for the poor who were her neighbors and, in fact, neglected her own family — driving her husband and children into misery and despair. Actually, you don't have to imagine such a character, since Charles Dickens did that for us in the form of Mrs. Jellyby in *Bleak House*. As Jim Forest wrote at *Touchstone*:

> [Mrs. Jellyby] resolutely devotes every waking hour to the "Borrioboola-Gha venture." The reader never discovers the details of the endeavor except that it involves the settlement of impoverished Britons among African natives with the goal of supporting themselves through coffee growing.
>
> Mrs. Jellyby is convinced that no other undertaking in life is so worthwhile, or would solve so many problems at a stroke. . . . [She] is so wedded to her work that she has no time for her several children, with the exception of Caddy, a daughter she has conscripted as her secretary. Ink-spattered Caddy puts in nearly as many hours as her mother in the daily task of answering letters and sending out literature about Borrioboola-Gha.
>
> Caddy, however, has come to hate the very word "Africa" or any word that has the remotest suggestion of causes. For her, causes simply mean the ruin of family life. Mrs. Jellyby's husband eventually becomes suicidal and, though surviving despair, is last seen in the book with his head resting despondently on a wall.
>
> In the book's postscript, we discover that the Borrioboola-Gha project failed after the local king sold the project's volunteers into slavery in order to buy rum.

Or you could just follow the public life of Elon Musk. On several important issues, Musk has become a folk hero to conservatives — just not on any issues where he'd have to make any sacrifices or inconvenience himself. Instead, Musk weighs in on subjects distant from his interests, where the price of improving things will be paid by somebody else. And he's often right.

Musk was right to support Donald Trump over the babbling nonentity Kamala Harris — or whoever was actually going to run the country had she won the election. (Probably the same Obama-appointed Deep State hacks who have been running it the past four years in the name of Joe Biden.) And he's right that our government is massively wasteful, definitely in need of a penny-pinching overhaul by the Department of Government Efficiency (DOGE), which Musk has offered to help run.

But advising Trump to cut funding to government programs won't cost Musk anything — and, in fact, would grant him almost unprecedented power as a private citizen who didn't face confirmation by the Senate. Government contractors right now have every reason to try to get on Elon Musk's good side.

Musk was right that Twitter (now X) had become a tightly censored, politically suffocating echo chamber, thanks to the mass-banning of conservatives and Christians. His purchase of Twitter was risky, or seemed so at the time. People claimed that he was crazy. But, in fact, buying Twitter has given Musk astonishing global influence — and will amply repay his purchase price with all the data he scrapes from it to fuel his own AI enterprise, Grok. So, not really a sacrifice on his part.

Furthermore, it's not at all clear that Musk really believes in free speech after all. Conservative Treehouse has an article revealing the political bias that Musk and his engineers are building into X and Grok. It isn't pretty; in fact, it sounds a lot like the "social credit" scoring system used by the Chinese Communist Party — a longtime Musk business partner:

> Elon Musk and his Twitter (X platform) engineers have an Artificial Intelligence (AI) user engagement and information system known as Grok. Essentially, you can ask AI Grok questions, and it provides responses based on the coded values of the engineers who built it.

Some users asked Grok to evaluate their X posts and got answers such as this:

> These posts might be subject to reduced reach because they could be perceived as promoting skepticism, conspiracy, or negativity towards individuals, institutions, or the media.

When a user asked how to avoid being censored, Grok gave this response:

> Don't criticize your government, don't criticize foreign governments, don't talk about conspiracy theories ... and don't accuse government officials or members of the media of malfeasance or dishonesty.

The Conservative Treehouse continues:

> These are the parameters built by Elon Musk and his Twitter engineers....
>
> These same coded values are being created by the same tech engineers who are currently building out the surveillance state technological interface with [the] government. This same perspective, what Palantir CEO Alex Karp described as "coded values," is being written into the code within Palantir facial recognition and targeting software. The U.S. Government has already signed billions in contracts with Palantir (Peter Thiel) for these AI products.

So maybe Musk isn't exactly a free-speech hero — just someone who aspires to take Big Brother's place.

Musk is fighting hard against the authoritarian Leftist government in Britain over the epidemic of rapes committed by Pakistani men against young British women. He's exposing a decades-old cover-up by police and the British government, who refused to protect these young women or prosecute their assailants for fear of stoking "racism." Bravo, so far. Again, on this issue that poses no risk to Musk's personal interests or businesses, he's taking a worthy stand.

But when it comes to the impact of immigration on society, Musk isn't always consistent. He threatened to "go to war" over the issue of expanding H-1B visas that tech companies use to extract cheap labor from indentured foreign workers. And here Musk profits directly. According to *The National Memo* and *Electrek* magazine:

> "Over the last few days, several current and former Tesla workers reached out to *Electrek* to reveal that Tesla ramped up its use of H-1B visas to replace US workers it let go during a wave of layoffs earlier this year," according to a story by its editor-in-chief, Fred Lambert, that led the website on December 30.
>
> Last April, *Electrek* reported that Tesla dismissed about 15,000 US employees, mostly in Texas and California — but then the company moved to fill those same jobs with imported labor at lower cost.

Now it makes more sense why Musk might want to focus discussions of immigration on faraway horrors in working-class British neighborhoods instead of laid-off Americans at his factory in Texas.

It's admirable that Musk wants to protect young British women by writing Tweets that cost him nothing. But if he's so concerned about young people, you might expect him to care about the child laborers in Africa who get sick and die from mining the cobalt required for electric car batteries. As I've said here before:

> The rare earth minerals (such as cobalt) used for the manufacture of EV batteries are excavated and processed in a pollution-intensive way, poisoning the environment surrounding those plants and impacting hundreds of communities.
>
> Tesla purchases raw materials from the natural resources-mining giants, despite those companies' documented human rights abuses in desperately poor countries such as the Democratic Republic of Congo (DRC). Kamoto Copper Co. is Tesla's primary supplier of cobalt, and while it runs a large mechanized mine, it also buys additional cobalt from area "artisanal" mines, which almost certainly employ child labor, and in some cases forced labor. . . . Critics charge that more than 40,000 child slaves in DRC are forced to work in cobalt mines so that companies like Tesla can produce their electric cars.

So which is it, Elon? Do you want to protect helpless children from exploitation or not? Maybe not when it might cost you tens of millions of dollars to purchase ethically sourced raw materials.

Musk really needs to decide whether he wants to be a freedom fighter or a censor, an immigration reformer or a sweatshop owner, a protector of children or a child-labor tycoon. Let's pray he chooses well.

Chapter 4

FAITH

Mosul's Last Mass

July 1, 2014

"For the first time in 1,600 years there was no Mass in Mosul last Sunday," reports Chaldean archbishop Bashar Warda. An Iraqi city that once was a major center of Christian life is now almost devoid of the sacraments, and its thousands of resident Christians are fleeing Sunni radicals' reign of religious terror.

If the occupation continues, at some point the last church will close, and the last consecrated Host will be consumed — at which point the city will be in one sense devoid of Christ. Think about that for a moment.

Imagine your own city or town, and visualize what it would mean for every church and chapel to close, and the bishop to put the last ciborium in the trunk of his car and drive away. Would the city feel any different to you? Would its shambling life recall a zombie, a body without a soul?

Now think of the cities of Germany after *Kristallnacht*, where not a single synagogue could be seen whose windows had not been smashed, which had not been gutted by the burning of sacred books. Think of those cities in Poland, in Russia, in Greece, where Jews had lived for hundreds or thousands of years — where empty temples and abandoned graveyards now are the only traces left of those cousins of Christ. Walker Percy wrote in *The Thanatos Syndrome* that the fathomless, seemingly senseless hatred of Nazis for Jews had a real and comprehensible motive: the desire to make mankind a god and the need to erase every concrete sign of the real God and of His people.

Ours has been a bleak and bloody century, and if we do not learn its lessons, we will reenact all its crimes.

But the hundred years since 1914 have not been uniquely evil. If we look back at the massacres of previous centuries, we might begin to see the explosion of racist violence in the twentieth century less as a hideous innovation than as the resurgence of a profoundly human temptation. Our dark impulse to exclude and victimize the "other" can be kept at bay only by our consciously cultivating a sense of our common humanity.

It may be that what is unusual is not tribalism but its opposite: universalism, the acceptance of a human dignity uniting the whole human family. The effort of empathy is a costly one, and the task of reviving and reasserting the universal rights of man is one that falls to each generation in turn. It is made no easier when the leading sectors of society in the most powerful nations on earth are morally crippled by a subhumanist view of man, which undermines any argument for self-sacrifice and dissolves transcendent moral norms in the acid of relativism.

It may be true that white Westerners feel too guilty or socially constrained to express racial animus; but as Western societies become ever more diverse, that taboo is eroding. Xenophobic parties are growing in strength across Europe, in response to the reckless embrace by European elites of forced multiculturalism and unchecked mass immigration.

Furthermore, the new groups migrating to Western lands are entirely free of white guilt, and they bring their own bigotries with them. In the absence of a vital moral discourse that reinforces common humanity and human rights, there is no reason to expect these new residents to be magically immune to the historical human temptation of racial groupthink and violence. The violence that marks racial conflict between native-born African Americans and Mexican immigrants in cities like Los Angeles may offer a window into the broader pan-Western future. What is more, it is clear that the lessons the West learned from the racist excesses of the twentieth century were woefully incomplete, amounting to little more than:

- It is wrong for white people to discriminate against others.
- It is wrong for European nations to conquer and colonize non-European nations.
- Because Hitler used ethnic identity as a pretext for murdering people, Western nations must abandon any ethnic or historical basis for their identities — even nations that were conquered and terrorized by Hitler, such as Poland and Ukraine.
- None of these lessons apply to non-Western nations or nonwhite people living in them.

Generals always blunder by planning for and refighting the last war. In the battle against racism, our culture certainly seems preoccupied with preventing such unlikely occurrences as the rise of National Socialism in Germany, while ignoring or excusing the real and lively threats to human dignity that are arising across the world, even in Europe.

Watchdogs who track anti-Semitism in Europe focus much of their attention on tiny, contemptible fringe groups of nationalistic thugs instead of the groups that actually perpetrate most of the anti-Jewish violence across Europe — radicalized Muslims.

Indeed, if we use a more realistic definition of *nationalism,* we will find that Islamist movements today ought to be included in it. They constitute a grave and growing threat to the safety and liberty of hundreds of millions of people — including both non-Muslims and those Muslims who reject the revival of sharia. Religious and ethnic identities often blend and fuse, particularly in the minds of persecutors. So it makes perfect sense to include the worldwide epidemic of religious persecution, most of it perpetrated by radical Muslims, under the headings of racism and nationalism. For these Muslims, there is only one nation: the House of Islam. Everything outside it is the House of War, which they are called to convert or to conquer and control. Non-Muslims in such societies must either convert or accept a kind of Jim Crow status as inferior, humbled, third-class citizens (*dhimmis*) who are forbidden to take part in politics and expected to give way to Muslims in every sphere of life.

This is the goal pursued by Islamists who target Christians in a long list of countries from Nigeria and Sudan to Pakistan and treasured by radical Muslims who dream of breeding and bombing their way to power in England and France. Ancient Christian communities have already been ethnically cleansed from Iraq in the wake of the U.S. invasion, and Christians (among other religious minorities) fear that a similar fate faces them in Syria, should the Al Qaeda–linked rebels in that country overcome its brutal, but religiously neutral, Ba'athist regime. Christians in Egypt face mounting violence as they are made the scapegoats of Islamist frustration in the wake of the military's crackdown on the Muslim Brotherhood.

We must admit to ourselves the ugly fact that Islamism is an ideology and that its hoped-for Caliphate is a virtual nation (like the Greater Germany Hitler dreamed of). Radical, nationalistic, anti-Semitic, and anti-Christian radicals number in the millions and seek to control whole countries through groups like the Muslim Brotherhood, which was only dislodged from Egypt in 2013 through a brutal military coup. Such groups' explicit agendas are both expansionist and totalitarian — openly calling for conquest and for the domination of every sphere of life by their rigid ideology. Such groups are leading what journalist John Allen has called *The Global War on Christians,* although Hindus, Jews, Alawites, secular Muslims, and others also number on their list. In certain ways and for certain groups, it really is 1933 all over again.

Give Us Barabbas!

May 4, 2015

At age seventeen, I lost my unborn daughter to a coerced abortion, and that experience enflamed in me a passion as deep as a fire in a coal mine: to defend the human person from acts of violence. So l launched into pro-life activism, walking door-to-door lobbying strangers, then joining more organized groups, right up to and including presidential candidacies.

Over the course of years, the logic of my beliefs stretched my concern to other threatened people. I have marched, or written, or lobbied, or worked on films in defense of Serbian civilians, Iranian women, Nuba tribesmen, South Sudanese animists, and Assyrian Christians. My work in cities brought me face-to-face with homeless Americans, some of them veterans like me. So I started a series of missions intended to highlight their human dignity. I have helped raise millions of dollars for women in crisis. I have published a book on the roots of twentieth-century genocide.

Studying that subject, and learning that, in the past one hundred years, the modern state murdered some 170 million civilians — not including casualties of war — I realized that the kind of governments ruling nowadays have no business dealing out death. So I came to embrace the idea of a moratorium on the death penalty. Until and unless we see a worldwide resurgence of respect for innocent life, I think that we should pressure our governments to stop executing even the guilty.

But right now I would like to indict a significant swath of those who agree with me on that issue. There's a certain type of person who grabs onto the issue like a fashion accessory. You know the type I'm talking about: the fashionable urban liberal for whom the death penalty is not a profound moral question, deeply connected to the modern contempt for life. No, it's one of those tacky, "red state," redneck things like gun rights, pickup trucks, country music, and going to church. That is, it is something you ritually reject in order to mark off your status as a progressive sophisticate. Like GMOs or NASCAR or homophobia.

These lifestyle anti-deathers never follow the issue closely. You won't find them visiting prisoners on death row or even writing them letters. They aren't involved in crusades like the Innocence Project or in efforts at stomping out the national epidemic of prison rape. They don't help groups like Prison Fellowship, which try to bring hope and healing to convicted criminals. No, the men and women on death row in America are merely abstractions to them, little plastic pawns they move around on the chessboard of their minds — as wispy and insignificant as nameless unborn children. Oh, I had to mention them, because the people I have in mind, who wax passionate over mimosas about the evil of capital punishment are always, to a person, pro-choice when it comes to abortion.

For the longest time, I couldn't wrap my head around that position. I can get how someone who views all life as cheap could favor both abortions and executions — and euthanasia, and cloning, and even the use of nuclear weapons, when it's the utilitarian thing to do.

I can see how sincere pro-lifers make room for capital punishment, since killing the innocent is clearly different from killing the guilty.

What I couldn't for decades understand is how someone can get outraged about the execution of the Boston Marathon bomber — but shrug at the deaths of a million innocent unborn Americans every year. Does the human brain even work that way?

But now I understand. It came to me not long after going to Mass on Palm Sunday. Instead of the Gospel reading that day, what we do is a Passion play. The priest speaks the parts of Jesus, the lector reads the narration, and we in the congregation get to play the Jerusalem mob. That is not as much fun as it sounds, since among our lines is "Crucify him!" and, more importantly, "Give us Barabbas!"

Having to speak those words, to put myself in the sandals of the people who had welcomed Jesus with palm fronds and hosannas and then, days later, demanded that Pilate put him to death, well, it got me thinking. It wasn't as if Barabbas were some beloved resistance leader, as Hollywood movies would have it. No, he was simply a robber and a killer. Five minutes before Pilate offered them the choice between him and Jesus, those people had never heard his name. They knew as little about him as the lifestyle liberal knows about the killers on death row. They knew only one thing: he was guilty, while Jesus was innocent. And that is why they preferred him. And on some level, all of us do.

Because we aren't innocent. We all have things on our conscience. We have all made grave mistakes, even if most of them don't merit hanging. We can empathize with the guilty; can put ourselves in their place. What we cannot apprehend, because we cannot stand it, is the suffering of the innocent. It is simply too appalling. It overwhelms us and crushes us. It demands that we take action. If it really were true that a million innocent people were murdered each year in our country, we'd have to feel very differently about the place and its system of government. We would have to get angry, and underneath that, we would feel profoundly tainted. We'd feel helpless, outraged, and sad.

And who really wants to feel that way? Not the lifestyle liberal, who tells himself he's a humanist in the great Renaissance tradition. He sends checks to animal rescue shelters and buys produce from local farmers. He hopes for peaceful coexistence among the nations and despises all forms of prejudice. But underneath it all, he secretly thinks that man is no more than a brainy ape, and life is a meaningless snuff farce in which the cast members die at the end. Since life is short and futile, he wants his to be cheerful. And the truly innocent, the vulnerable, are a pig's ear found in the punchbowl. He doesn't want to look at them. Instead, he'll drink his chai latte as he tweets: #GiveUsBarabbas.

Our Lady of Guadalupe: A Light for Human Dignity in the Face of a Culture of Death

December 11, 2015

One of the greatest Christian communicators in American history was Archbishop Fulton J. Sheen. Trained in top-level theology, he chose to use his talents to convey the complex truths and deep human insights of Catholic thought to a wide American public. In the 1950s, his prime-time religious TV show (imagine that!), *Life Is Worth Living,* had higher ratings than its rival, *The Milton Berle Show,* a fact which Sheen attributed to his fine top-notch Jewish writers: Matthew, Mark, Luke, and John.

One of the most profound reflections Sheen ever offered was about the tragic gulf that exists between the person each of us should be and the person we really are. As he wrote in *The World's First Love*: "God, too, has within Himself blueprints of everything in the universe. As the architect has in his mind a plan of the house before the house is built, so God has in His Mind an archetypal idea of every flower, bird, tree, springtime, and melody."

But it is not so with man. God has to have two pictures of us: One is what we are, and the other is what we ought to be. He has the model, and He has the reality — the blueprint and the edifice, the score of the music and the way we play it. God has to have these two pictures because in each and every one of us there is some disproportion and want of conformity between the original plan and the way we have worked it out. The image is blurred; the print is faded. For one thing, our personality is not complete in time; we need a renewed body. Then, too, our sins diminish our personality; our evil acts daub the canvas the Master Hand designed. Like unhatched eggs, some of us refuse to be warmed by the Divine Love, which is so necessary for incubation to a higher level. We are in constant need of repairs; our free acts do not coincide with the law of our being; we fall short of all God wants us to be. St. Paul tells us that we were predestined, before the foundations of the world were laid, to become the sons of God. But some of us will not fulfill that hope.

There is, actually, only one person in all humanity of whom God has one picture and in whom there is a perfect conformity between what He wanted her to be and what she is, and that is His own Mother. Most of us are a minus sign, in the sense that we do not fulfill the high hopes the Heavenly Father has for us. But Mary is the equal sign. In the flesh, Mary was already the ideal God intended for her. The model and the copy are perfect; she is all that was foreseen, planned, and dreamed.

Sheen speaks of Mary as she is seen in the Catholic and Orthodox traditions, free of any personal sin, perfectly pleasing to God in all the decisions she has made, through the saving grace of Christ. Hence, Mary is simply the perfect Christian, the one merely human being whose earthly image is exactly what God had in mind for her. She is, in that sense, a window into the very mind of God.

And that window pours light out for the rest of us, stumbling in our uncertainties and sins. Over the centuries, Catholics have believed that Jesus sent — and continues to send — His mother from time to time to appear to certain people, to offer encouragement, or a warning, or to call us to more fervent prayer. Typically, these "apparitions" have been to the poor, the weak, the forgotten in society, but the words of the Mother of God have sometimes changed the fate of nations. That is what happened in Mexico, in early December 1531, when an Indian peasant named Juan Diego, one of the few who had followed the Spanish missionaries who had accompanied the conquistadors into that country, was climbing the hill of Tepeyac. At the top,

> he saw a brilliant light on the summit and heard the strains of celestial music. Filled with wonder, he stopped. Then he heard a feminine voice asking him to ascend. When he reached the top he saw the Blessed Virgin Mary standing in the midst of a glorious light, in heavenly splendor. The beauty of her youthful countenance and her look of loving kindness filled Juan Diego with unspeakable happiness as he listened to the words which she spoke to him in his native language. She told him she was the perfect and eternal Virgin Mary, Mother of the true God, and made known to him her desire that a shrine be built there where she could demonstrate her love, her compassion and her protection. "For I am your merciful Mother," she said, "to you and to all mankind who love me and trust in me and invoke my help. Therefore,

go to the dwelling of the Bishop in Mexico City and say that the Virgin Mary sent you to make known to him her great desire."

Mary did not speak Spanish or wear the courtly clothes of the conquerors. Instead, she appeared as a woman whom Juan Diego might have seen in any village. But she spoke of the love of God for the Mexican people, in a way that no foreign friar could hope to do. So Juan Diego dutifully marched off to the bishop, Fray Juan de Zumarraga, who heard Juan Diego's case but did not believe him. Juan Diego returned to Tepeyac Hill to pray, and Mary sent him back to bother the bishop. At the second meeting, the bishop suggested that Juan Diego ask for some sign of proof. A few days later, the Virgin appeared to Juan Diego and told him to gather roses and bring them to the bishop. Juan Diego was astonished to see, in the midst of winter, an explosion of unfamiliar flowers all around him. He gathered them in his humble tunic (called a "tilma") and carried them to the bishop's palace.

Bishop Zumarraga was stunned by the flowers, of a breed that grew only in his native region of Spain. He was even more taken aback by what had happened to Juan Diego's tilma: It bore a magnificent, mysterious image of the Virgin Mary, pregnant with Jesus. The bishop was convinced. So were the native people of Mexico, who hearkened to the story and flocked to the shrine that Bishop Zumarraga built in Guadalupe, which enshrined the mysterious tilma — an ordinary garment, made of cheap materials that typically decay in just a few years, that never aged or lost its luster over the next five hundred years.

That's a lovely story. But it is much more than that. The image of Mary and Jesus that appeared on that tilma is, in fact, a kind of book — a theology text that teaches us critical lessons that modern man has forgotten. First of all, the image teaches us about human dignity, and where it comes from. If Mary is a perfect reflection of God's vision of her in His own mind, then in this supernatural portrait we have a picture of how God sees mankind: more important than all of nature, since Mary stands on top of the moon, is backlit by the sun, and is clothed in the stars of Heaven. The human person, which our Culture of Death treats as a means to pleasure and power, is, in fact, much more important than the rest of the created universe.

What gives us such dignity and importance? Only the grace of God. Mary's head is not turned by her glory; it is bowed in prayer. She knows that all her importance derives from her Son, that all her virtues are only the fruit of His grace.

We fully retain our dignity only when we unite our will with God's and obey His plan for us. It is perfect obedience to the promptings of grace, not power, learning, or knowledge, that elevates a person. When we try, like Satan, to rise against God's will, we degrade ourselves — as our culture today has diminished the sanctity of life and the value of self-sacrifice, pretending to elevate man while, in fact, reducing him to the level of just one more primate.

This message might seem abstract or unconvincing to modern people. But remember the original audience to whom the Virgin appeared in Mexico: The Indian people of Mexico had, for centuries, been subject to the brutal regime of the Aztecs, who believed in a cult of dark and desperate gods, which could keep themselves and the universe alive only if they were fed by human sacrifice. When the bold Spanish explorer Cortes landed in Mexico, he found an Aztec nation engaged in its own culture of death. Every month, thousands of people from conquered tribes would be dragged up Mexican temples and have their hearts ripped out of their chests — to "feed" the gods and the Aztec upper class, who had come to rely on the sacrifices as a key source of protein. (We still have some of their ghoulish recipes for cooked human flesh.) With only a few hundred troops of his own, Cortes turned to the tribes that fed the sacrifices, who allied with him to obliterate the Aztec kingdom and close its temples.

This was the pagan despair that lurked in the background when the Virgin appeared in Mexico. Few Indians had dared to accept the new and gentle creed of Christ, a God who accepts no bloody sacrifices but offers Himself for us. It seemed too good to be true. But when they saw clothed in their own garments and speaking their own language a Lady who reflected God's love for them in particular, the Mexican people gained the courage to hope. The faith of the Mexican people in Christ can be traced to the tilma of Juan Diego, and it has never failed despite the fiercest persecutions.

In our own age of pagan despair, we look to icons of courage and grace to remind us that goodness is possible. We read the lives of men like Dietrich Bonhoeffer, of women like Mother Teresa, and we search out the people who today are standing for life in the face of death — especially those in the pro-life movement, who face down the law and the media, the courts and the social elites, to defend the weakest, most vulnerable images of God's most precious creation.

The Politics of the Baby Jesus: A Christmas Essay

December 24, 2015

It's always helpful when theological truths are echoed in events of history and in our daily lives. The man whose birth we celebrate today told us plainly, "The truth will make you free" (John 8:32). Now we know that His primary meaning was spiritual, not political: By learning God's real plan for us, we can set aside false gods and worldly idols and order our lives correctly in accord with His will to save us.

That's the real point of Christmas: The God who made us good, and mourned our Fall, rebuilt a bridge for us, so that we could travel to join Him in eternal happiness. He took on our flesh and then spent His life among us and shared our sufferings. He told us the Truth and embodied it in His life, which He offered in reparation for our sins. Jesus became that bridge, which stretched from one arm of the Cross to the other, connecting earth to Heaven across the abyss of death.

Compared with that, it almost seems banal to bring up the political effects of Christianity. But the Incarnation teaches us that nothing is banal, or ever will be again. Not after this. Christ came into our flesh to sanctify it, to heal and redeem every stick of human furniture, every parking lot and convenience store, every courthouse and legislature. He didn't tell us that earthly life is evil, that our natural drives are hopelessly corrupt, or that we should renounce our inbuilt cravings for love, freedom, peace, order, and progeny — and, instead, go hide in a cave and wait for death. That was the despair spread by the Gnostics, who tried to hijack the Church even in the age of the apostles and have persisted ever since. But it wasn't Jesus' teaching. And it wasn't His example: His very first miracle was catering a wedding.

So it's good, right, and proper to look back to earth and follow all the ripples that shook our little pond when the Son of God came down. We will see in their shapes innumerable mementos of Our Lord — lessons about ourselves and what He wants for us, in this life and in the next. Because, in fact, we are shaping what we'll be in eternity right here, right now, at 2 p.m. in Panera, at 2 a.m. on the Internet, at work and at play, just as at prayer. We begin to build the Kingdom right here, in our families and our republic.

The Incarnation of Christ made possible political and economic freedom. In fact, it made them, for the first time, even desirable. Before the epiphany of the greatness of the human person that came with Jesus Christ, no one even thought to desire these things — not for everyone, not as inborn human rights. Outside the noble but self-segregated world of our Jewish forefathers in faith, we have no pre-Christian record of any notion that each man's life is sacred.

Certainly, various tribes, nations, or political castes held their members' lives as precious and protected them against enemies. Roman senators, Spartan citizens, and Aztec priests each looked out for their own. And every human mother clutching her newborn child felt that he was supremely precious. But there was nothing to connect those two realities — the fierce self-defense of a group asserting its interests, and the worldwide primal goodness of *human life itself*. Of a random, anonymous baby, like the thousands whom Romans discarded on the walls of their gleaming city, which Jews and, later, Christians would furtively go and rescue. Like the Babe in the manger. His halo, which we see in so many exquisite paintings of the Nativity, would spread across the world, lighting the head of every child born to woman, forever after.

If human life is sacred and may not be stolen without the threat of eternal punishment, then tyrants and slave masters must always walk in fear. A greater, juster Master holds the upper hand, and He will hold them accountable for their cruelties. To that Master, slaves can make their prayers, and it's His standard they wave when demanding liberty. There's a thin, exquisite, unbreakable, golden thread that links the Hebrews fleeing Pharaoh and Southern slaves praying for freedom, Polish workers faced by Communist bayonets and college students shivering on sidewalks while praying outside abortion clinics. That thread runs straight through the straw and the dung of Bethlehem.

When medieval Englishmen saw their lords assert feudal rights against tyrannical kings, they probably weren't conscious of how Christianity goaded their revolt, underscored their particular rights, and extended them implicitly to serfs as well as warriors. But the seed was planted, and the Magna Carta that was written to protect the privileges of barons now defends even hostile Muslim migrants from abuse at the hands of police. When monks scrawled copies of Roman Law in the hope of preserving order in the wrack of a collapsing empire, they might not have fully realized the mischief that Christianity had made with that pagan law: A code that aristocrats had written to strengthen the state was leavened now by the rights of walking images of Christ. It would rise to undreamed of heights: international law and the UN Declaration of Human Rights.

So when you pray before the manger today, don't think of the next election. Think of the fact that we have elections, and constitutions, and an adversarial system of justice that starts by assuming our innocence and tests every criminal case before a jury of our peers. He built that. He planned and planted it by waking in this manger and walking the way to the Cross. Merry Christmas, one and all.

The Politics of Good Friday: We Must Stand with the Innocent When They Suffer

March 25, 2016

One of the twentieth century's greatest thinkers was the French anthropologist René Girard, whose study of myths across many cultures brought him to stark and disturbing conclusions. Reading the stories of peoples from every corner of the earth, along with the West's, and comparing them with real historical events, taught him one central truth about human society: It is goaded and fragmented by the nature of human desire. We learn what to want by *seeing what other people have*, and that tempts us to try to take it away from them. In Christian terms, this is envy, which Thomas Aquinas considered the worst of the Seven Deadly Sins. Indeed, it was Satan's envy of God that drove him to revolt, and his envy of Adam's happiness that drove him to lure our first parents into sin.

Girard didn't view things in Christian terms, not yet. He was a standard-issue secular French intellectual when he launched his academic career. But studying man's myths and reading his histories, he saw the same pattern repeated over and over again: People imitate each other's desires, and conflict ensues. Not everyone can be top dog, and those who achieve high status are strongly motivated to shove their competitors down. In return, the have-nots are driven to vengefully tear social structures down. With dismal predictability, this conflict turns ugly and bitter and threatens to break society into mutually hostile pieces.

Then some person or group comes up with a solution, an explanation for the chaos and poverty that result when cooperation collapses. No, they don't find the real cause of the problem. That would be too radical. Instead, they locate some person or group on whom they can *pin the blame* for the fighting and mutual hatred. It isn't that our society as a whole has a fundamental problem. No, that's the fault of some evil troublemakers — the Jews, the clergy, the genetically "inferior," or the "fundamentalists" — who are hogging too many resources, or corrupting people's minds, or otherwise throwing sand in society's gears. Destroy them, exile them, imprison them, and all will return to normal.

The tragic thing is that *this mechanism works*. Locate some innocent, harmless person or group, make them a scapegoat for all of society's evils, and, by some bitter magic, society is unified once again — in hatred for the scapegoat and the righteous effort to punish it for its "sins." It won't last forever, of course, and sooner or later, a new scapegoat will need to be found, so the bloody cycle repeats itself over centuries, in every human society. The Nazis, who practiced scapegoating with an almost unmatched intensity, found one victim after another to take the blame for the fact that the real Germany didn't live up to their fantasies: first the Jews, then the handicapped, then the Gypsies, the Slavs ... the list kept on getting longer. As Hannah Arendt noted, by the end of the war, Hitler was planning to sterilize every German afflicted with heart disease or other serious illness.

Seeing this grim phenomenon that crosses human cultures, Girard was tempted to despair. It was only the figure of Jesus that puzzled and fascinated him. Here was a scapegoat, a single man chosen by the angry mob, the secular state, and even the religious authorities, to die as the price of maintaining the fragile peace. But He did not angrily protest his innocence. He forbade his friends to fight on His behalf. From the Cross itself, He offered no rebukes but said instead, "Father, forgive them; for they know not what they do" (Luke 23:34).

And Girard meditated on that. Jesus' story was different from all the others. He had gone to the Cross without protest. In fact, He had even predicted it and had told His apostles that such suffering was critical to His mission. Could the figure of Jesus be exactly what mankind needed, a universal warning against the temptation to follow the crowd in hounding its scapegoats — a reminder, indeed, that each of us will be judged by what we have done for the least among us (see Matt. 25:40), which surely includes the persecuted scapegoat?

From that deep ethical insight, Girard retraced his steps to the Christian faith of his youth, and when he died in 2015, he was perhaps the most famous Catholic intellectual on earth.

In my own way, I found that the painful events of my youth led me to the same truth that René Girard unfolded with scholarly exactitude. I lost my daughter to a forced abortion, and I resolved at age seventeen to spend the rest of my life fighting against such callous cruelty, on behalf of the helpless and marginalized — beginning with the unborn. That led me to other groups who were subject to hate and abuse on the part of the powerful: the Christians of South Sudan, the homeless in U.S. cities, the Christians and Yazidis of ISIS-occupied Syria and Iraq.

I wonder if thinking of Jesus as a scapegoat, and other innocent scapegoats as images of Christ, could serve as the critical backstop against extremism that our politics desperately needs. Whatever you value most — and, as a conservative, I'd have to pick "freedom" — make sure that your pursuit of it doesn't harm the helpless and the vulnerable. Make the effects on the vulnerable the litmus test of your actions and your policies. Do nothing that could turn any innocent person into a scapegoat or deprive him of human dignity. That's a red line you cannot cross.

We need a Good Friday politics. We must internalize the habit of standing with the vulnerable, of defending the unjustly persecuted, as Mary and John stood steadfast with Jesus until He died. We don't want to be with the crowds that chose Barabbas, of course. Nor do we want to be like those apostles who ran away, including Peter.

Instead, we must stand with those who are suffering, even when it seems as if there's no way we can help them except to pray.

Want to Love Your Enemies? Start by Learning to Like People Who Don't Like You

April 16, 2016

Christ tells us to love our enemies. That's hard enough on the face of it, you'd think. But living as privileged Westerners in peace, comfort, and safety makes that commandment even more challenging. Because most of us don't have any enemies. Not really, in the sense that Jesus meant the word. We might have rivals, opponents, ideological foes, alienated ex-friends, and even online stalkers, but few of us have deep, personal enemies — individual people we know by name who have deeply wronged and damaged us, who threaten our lives and our families. Apart from victims of rape, domestic violence, and other crimes, how many of us actually have such enemies?

Things were very different in Darfur, when I visited as part of a mission to dig new wells so the victims of Muslim ethnic cleansing would have access to drinkable water. People I met there would point someone out and say, "That man used to work for a warlord. He and the other soldiers killed my brothers and sisters." Can you imagine living in a dusty village where you'd walk to the marketplace and run into someone like that, several times a month? As the kind of person I am, I fear that I know what I would do: hack off his head on the spot and use it as a soccer ball.

And of course, such acts of vengeance were not unknown. But in societies like Sudan's, where so many crimes piled up in just a few short years, it would have been utterly impossible to reestablish peace without an almost miraculous level of forgiveness. And I saw such miracles happen. I saw people meet and speak with their blood enemies and learn to work together to build a future. So I know that, with God's help, it can happen.

In fact, the example of those forgiving African Christians kind of shames me when I read some stupid or vicious thing that someone has said about me and find myself muttering warrior oaths to "eviscerate" that person. In the absence of genuine enemies, how can we break sinful habits like this?

I think that I've found a way. It entails starting small, using the opportunities that God leaves in my path. So I have resolved to try to like people who don't like me. This is every bit as hard as it sounds at first. When someone rejects my ideas, or mocks one of my projects, or rolls his eyes disdainfully at things that I've said in earnest, it hurts, of course. That's perfectly natural. So I'm schooling myself to silently remember the following questions:

- Was the way that I phrased that needlessly sharp and divisive? Self-aggrandizing and boastful? Perhaps even incoherent?
- Is my "big" personality part of the problem? Is this person a quiet introvert who is tired of high-volume extroverts like me hogging the spotlight?
- Could this person simply be having a terrible day or going through a soul-straining personal or financial trial?
- Might God have sent me this person as an obstacle in order to teach me patience and forgiveness?

I've found that after running through this gauntlet of questions, it's virtually impossible to muster the gumption for hatred or even anger. Instead, I feel a lot lighter, as if I've been freed of a dark and ungainly burden — the "duty" to despise this other person and dismiss everything that he says.

Even better, I then have the privilege to gain from the experience. I can learn from whatever might be (unfortunately) valid in that person's criticism. I can better gauge what I say in the future so that it appeals to a wider range of people. And in cases where I'd previously liked the person because of some admirable quality that he has, I can go right on liking him — even though he doesn't like me!

You might call what I am doing a baby step, and you'd be right. I can't make any promises for what I would do if I were presented with a genuine, Darfur-level enemy. But in an age when social media and political divisions are turning us all into schools of piranhas, I know that my spiritual health demands that I do at least this much, go at least this far today on the long, slow walk of grace. As the AA handbook tells us, "One day at a time."

You Won't Believe What Catholic Social Teaching Really Says

November 20, 2016

You've probably already heard about Culture-of-Death-billionaire-globalist George Soros trying to hijack Pope Francis's 2015 U.S. visit as a campaign tour for Left-wing Democrats. We next learned of pro-abortion "Catholic" front groups that Clinton campaign chair John Podesta hoped to use to overthrow the "middle-ages dictatorship" of the Church.

My own pro-life apostolate was targeted in 2016, when Democrats for Life operatives held an event at Hillary Clinton's Democratic National Convention using my pro-life nonprofit's name, "Whole Life," to advertise a "seamless garment" agenda that equated the pro-life movement with the fight against "climate change." Other examples abound.

How should we react to all this? Some are tempted to write off "Catholic social teaching," to cede it to the statists who use it highly selectively to support a growing secular government that actually targets Catholic institutions for destruction — from the Little Sisters of the Poor to pro-life pregnancy centers, from Catholic adoption agencies to faithful Catholic schools.

But we cannot make that mistake. Catholic social teaching is a rich, intellectually vibrant and philosophically rigorous tradition of reflection on politics, economics, and society that includes the writing of scholars, saints, and popes who were both. It's a treasure chest of insights we draw on as laymen to fulfill our vocation: applying Christian ethics in new and unforeseen contexts, using the principles of Catholic social teaching drawn from the gospel of Jesus Christ as our lighthouse in the storm.

In a year that pitted Donald Trump against Hillary Clinton, we know that the world needs more attention to principles, not less. Our rudderless, secularized society is prone to hysteria, from the worldwide grief over the shooting of a gorilla who menaced a child to the claim that those unsettled by the influx of angry Muslims into the West are suffering from a mental illness called "Islamophobia." Without a solid grounding in a truthful theory of man that defends his dignity and freedom, we have no good answer to the next media-driven moral panic.

Catholic social teaching offers precisely that grounding in clear and luminous principles that can be applied in any situation — from the savannas of the developing world to the teeming cities of Europe, the United States, and Asia. Honed by trial and error over centuries by the finest minds in the world — from Augustine to Dante to Thomas Aquinas and Leo XIII — Catholic social teaching sees man in three dimensions, realistically notes his limits thanks to the Fall, and always keeps in mind that his eternal destination is Heaven. It was Catholic social teaching that rejected social Darwinism and socialism in the nineteenth century — and racism, Communism, and ultranationalism in the twentieth. It was Pope St. John Paul II who diagnosed before anyone else the rising "Culture of Death" that has yielded tens of millions of abortions; hundreds of thousands of tiny, embryonic humans frozen in a technological limbo at fertility labs; the marriage bond attacked by lax divorce laws and new, false forms of marriage; and finally, the rise of "gender ideology" that denies the reality that God made man and woman and saw that it was good (see Gen. 1:31).

No other intellectual tradition has such a sterling record of seeing through the ideologies of elites to the ugly consequences for society's weakest members. Only Catholic social teaching keeps a firm eye on man's dignity, and that keeps Catholics closely attuned to how popular trends and fashionable innovations will impact the least of our brothers. That's why I am proud to say that my life's calling is to spread appreciation for genuine Catholic social teaching, whose core principles I tried to lay out in *The Race to Save Our Century*:

- The dignity of every person as an image of God
- The existence of a transcendent moral order by which we judge each nation's laws
- The need for the state to protect the free institutions of civil society, from the family to the Church, and all the "little platoons" in between
- The need for solidarity, for concern for every person as our moral equal
- The centrality of a free, humane economy that develops human potential and lifts up the poor

It's my prayer that such luminous truths can inform our future.

Fr. James Martin Burned the Bridges to My LGBT Friends

September 2, 2017

This week I had two old friends drop me. One's female, one's male, and each lives with same-sex attraction. I'd never been preachy with them. I'd answered their questions honestly, when they asked me what I believe. And we respected each other.

That's a lot harder now.

Why? Because Fr. James Martin, S.J., adviser to Pope Francis, is claiming that Catholics can and should approve of same-sex relationships. Now neither of these friends wants to speak to me. They think I have the option of accepting their sexual lifestyles, but I'm just willfully refusing out of a mindless nostalgia for old social norms.

Every day has its fashionable heresy. In the 1930s in Europe, that was vain and wrathful nationalism. In the 1960s and '70s, it was envious liberation theology.

In today's Zeitgeist, it's sexual issues that are holding Christians' good names hostage, even their livelihoods. That word *Zeitgeist* in its literal sense means "Spirit of the Age," but perhaps it's more fruitful to call it the Spirit of the World, or the Prince of this World.

He knows what he wants and how he can typically get it. In past ages, he spoke to our vanity, wrath, or envy. But in this lackadaisical age, the Tempter has lowered his sights. He tries to lure us away from the fullness of Christian truth by speaking to baser, more elemental appetites: our lust, but even more, our sloth.

He goads and threatens us to look at our neighbors and shrug. What business is it of ours if people sink into sad and sinful lifestyles? It's not worth getting called names like "bigot" and "hater" to warn perfect strangers against that. (So long as they don't frighten the horses, you know.)

We have plenty of pastors eager to christen such lukewarm indifference as "pastoral" charity, "dialogue," or "welcoming." In reality, it's spiritual laziness.

Each of us shares a little differently in the brokenness of Creation, the bitter harvest of Adam's sin, whose side effects Jesus didn't come to wipe out all at once but to suffer along with us and sanctify. The greatest temptation for Christians has always been to pretend otherwise — to imagine that Jesus' mission was to eliminate all pain and sacrifice. That urge goes all the way back to Peter, who tried to stop Our Lord from completing His mission on the Cross.

Remember what Jesus said to him? "Get behind me, Satan!" (Matt. 16:23). It's an ancient error to mistake the grove at Gethsemane for a brand-new Garden of Eden; to try to replace the Cross with some rainbow-colored maypole.

I know these truths all too well because I long wallowed in our postmodern sexual brokenness. Still today I am tempted by sloth to shrug at sin, to keep shallow friendships in place, and to win the bored applause of the public. But with God's grace, I fight against it. It was only that grace that pulled me out of the ditch in the first place.

So let me tell my story.

I was an atheist until I was in my late twenties. I felt nagging doubts about this arid, airtight worldview. But I strategically delayed giving them any further thought until . . . my testosterone levels began to decrease a little. Finally, I couldn't fend off any longer my conviction that God existed, and His name is Jesus.

But I kept my new faith secret for more than a year. Why? Because I was still sleeping around. I didn't believe I could stop it. The women were all "consenting adults," so I couldn't bring myself to see the harm in it. I prayed for help but felt like it never came.

Of course I was fooling myself, first of all about the harm I actually caused. There were broken hearts, STDs, and at least one abortion. Men who choose to live promiscuously don't know how many of their "partners" choose to have an abortion — perhaps without even telling them. Some won't find out until the Day of Judgment.

I say all of this to make it clear I am no church lady. I've struggled and still struggle with sinful inclinations and wrong habits. But thanks to clear and persuasive spiritual formation and God's patient grace, I came to understand that chastity is real — that it's a central Christian virtue. I've fought to practice it within my marriage and model its importance for my children.

So I understand what it means to be tempted and fail in matters of sexuality. That's why I've never been "hawkish" on homosexual issues. I've followed the Church in her teachings, but I've left it to others to preach that part of the Gospel.

Until now.

Fr. James Martin is one of the most media-savvy priests in America. He pals around with Martin Scorsese and appears on network TV. And now he's using that fame and influence for evil. As Joseph Sciambra wrote in *The Stream*, Fr. Martin is building bridges to the LGBTQ community with thin, rotten pieces of wood; with half-truths and lies.

This prophet of apostasy endorses the shrug of indifference that most straight Christians have toward the struggles of their brethren with same-sex attraction. He's saying that faithful Christians like Sciambra are wasting their time. There's no need to struggle. Just "go with the flow."

Contrast that with Cardinal Robert Sarah, or the pastors who drafted and signed the Nashville Statement. I thank God for them. They know how challenging Christ's teaching on sexual morality is, especially in our culture today. When your inclinations and the media and the law sing in harmony, there is just one discordant note: the gospel. It's unchanging, unchanged, a stark tone that calls us back from our selfish passions.

I love my friends who have same-sex attraction, as I love other sinners and love myself. We're sinners all. And I hope beyond hope that all my friends and I can live lives of chastity, peace, and joy. I know how challenging that is. It is for me. And because I'm a modern Christian, I suffer from the sin of presumption. I feel that God loves us all and forgives us all and we will all be redeemed regardless of how we live. That is how I feel.

But I also think. And my thoughts cause me to doubt. I worry about my friends' relationship with God and their eternal destiny. I worry even more about the despair and loneliness that I see in the "gay community."

Fr. Martin is lying to my friends. He is lying to your friends. He is lying to young Catholics with same-sex temptations who long to live chaste and holy lives. When a pastor with such credentials and such a platform joins the world and its Prince's chorus, countless young people will inevitably take this as an endorsement of their temptations.

Fr. Martin is piling up millstones and chaining them around his neck.

The Christchurch Terrorist's Attack on Western Civilization

March 17, 2019

Last week's slaughter of innocents at a mosque in Christchurch, New Zealand, was so devastating and so hateful . . . it reminded me of my visits to the Middle East and Africa and of the unspeakable crimes ISIS committed against Muslim, Yazidi, and Christians in Iraq and Syria.

During one trip to Iraqi Kurdistan, I joined a former Iraqi official. He oversaw military technologies under Saddam Hussein. He's a Muslim: Sunni on one side of his family and Shia on the other. He grew up in Kurdistan. He jokes that he's a "Sushi" Muslim. A dignified and magnanimous man, he has friends of all religions and ethnicities.

While we were driving toward Mosul, we passed by village after village that had been leveled by ISIS and U.S. bombs. We stopped at one decimated Yazidi town that was only beginning to recover in the wake of ISIS occupation. There, we met a man who introduced us to his young daughter. She had just been recovered from captivity, the Yazidi father told us.

"Allahu Akbar," my friend softly exclaimed, out of force of habit. The girl recoiled, and her father asked him not to say those words in her presence.

Realizing that the girl's abusers had made the phrase hateful to her, my friend excused himself and walked just out of sight. Following behind, I found him fallen to his knees, weeping.

"Jason, you have no idea how painful it is that my prayer would frighten a little girl!" he said.

By the grace of God, he was right. I had no idea.

And by the grace of God, the monster who attacked the mosque in Christchurch did not try to use our Christian faith to justify his crimes. But he did try to use something else dear to us. And he threatens to make it hateful in the ears of victims: our Anglo-American political tradition.

It's only by twisting Western political philosophy that anyone can make it illiberal or hateful. It's the system of ideas that gave us the Magna Carta, the United States Constitution, and, later, the abolition of slavery in both Britain and the United States.

This same tradition of thought gave us the UN Charter of Human Rights and the assertions of human dignity against the illiberal and exclusionary hate of the Nazi regime at Nuremberg.

All of these documents stem from the same liberating and humane political philosophy that has always stood against any faction that threatened to pit man against man.

And in that political philosophy, we also hear echoes of the blessings of true and tolerant religion. As Thomas Jefferson famously put it, "all men are created equal," and "they are endowed by their Creator with certain unalienable Rights."

The so-called manifesto of the Christchurch terrorist is riddled with self-aggrandizing claims about defending the "West" and "our culture" against "invaders." He even claimed to take "revenge" for historical attacks on the "European people."

But for all his claims of defending the West, he is the true invader.

His ideas, as much as his actions, are illiberal and run directly counter to the benevolent type of "liberalism" that makes the West worth fighting for.

The illiberalism of the Christchurch terrorist is precisely what must be fought in any defense of the liberal West. It's no better than the supremacist and hateful pseudo-religion of the ISIS terrorists who sought to tear apart the people of Iraq and Syria.

But illiberalism threatens to overtake and rule both sides of the political spectrum in the West, dividing us along lines of class and color, seeking always to destroy the human dignity of the "other."

Some time after my trip to Iraqi Kurdistan, my friend visited America to attend a mutual friend's funeral. At first, he was nervous, especially when passing through security. How would Americans treat him? Would he be met with suspicion? Scorn?

But after a brief stay, he told me how much he felt at home in America. He knew he would never become an American citizen. But he told me "after just a few weeks here, I know what it is to be an American. And now, I will be an American in my heart everywhere I go."

In less than a month, he had discovered what is precious in our Western way of life. He had discovered the Anglo-American political tradition. That golden thread that links us to our liberty-loving forefathers.

For the sake of all, we must cherish it.

Close the Real Concentration Camps . . . the Ones in China

July 13, 2019

You probably haven't heard about the concentration camps in China. Mainstream media have instead bombarded you with misleading images of temporary immigrant holding facilities in America.

Leftist politicians have been crying out on social media and posting photos of themselves weeping by chain-link fences in Texas or Arizona. They have been calling on people to abolish ICE and to #CloseTheCamps. We can agree that extending help to the vulnerable is never wrong. But we can and must argue sanely on how best to help migrants at the border — and ask whether a long, unsecured border is really safe for America to have. Safe for Americans, or safe for migrants.

Calling on the United States to "close the camps"? That's a cheap, hyperbolic propaganda campaign. It conflates short-term processing facilities meant to handle a sudden migrant influx with some of the worst hells on earth in history. There is literally no comparison.

Pretending that the United States is running "concentration camps" is crassly insulting — not just to our intelligence but to our consciences. It mocks the survivors who lived through the terror of Nazi concentration camps. And it cheapens the suffering of those in China's real concentration camps today. As you read these words, some three million Uyghurs and other Turkic peoples sit behind barbed wire, under guard. It's the largest mass incarceration of any group since the Holocaust.

Likely you haven't heard about this massive crime. The MSM isn't keen to tick off the totalitarian government of China. That might cost them millions in future revenue.

Instead of risking their ties with China, MSM outlets focus on what powerful Democrat politicians feed them. You've likely heard of Rep. Alexandria Ocasio-Cortez's tweet claiming that American holding centers are concentration camps.

Her buddy Rep. Ilhan Omar agreed with her. Omar wrote: "These are camps and people are being concentrated."

MoveOn.org organized "Close the Camps" rallies across America at the local offices of Congress members. *The Progressive*, a Leftist publication, wrote the following on July 9, 2019:

> We are calling on all people of conscience to shut down the concentration camps on the US-Mexico border through any nonviolent means necessary.... Doctors say children are being detained in "torture facilities."

Torture facilities? Those of us who know actual history remember what that means. Jewish children really were detained in torture facilities — then used in medical experiments by the infamous Nazi Dr. Josef Mengele. Men like Mengele amputated limbs. They injected children with typhoid. They performed fatal blood transfusions and committed countless other horrors. In today's America? Some migrant children wait with their families in crowded holding centers, which sometimes run out of toothbrushes.

The Progressive doubled down on its moral squalor. It wrote:

> Unless people step up to stop them, concentration camps always get worse. Today it's refugees; tomorrow it could be Muslims, journalists, political opponents, and anyone who doesn't think or look quite right.

Shameless. Absolutely shameless. Muslim Uyghur families are, in fact, being sentenced to life in concentration camps for not "looking right." Their children are being kidnapped and shoved into child prisons. There the Party indoctrinates them into good little Communists. Their parents never see them again. Is anything remotely comparable happening in America?

The politicians manufacturing outrage don't even believe their own agitprop. If they did, they'd believe the United States an evil country — one that hates migrants enough to "torture" their children. If that were true, then Reps. Ocasio-Cortez and Omar should be screaming at migrants not to come near our borders. Can you imagine Jews flooding into Germany during Hitler's regime?

But these politicians are not warning migrants to stay away from our "concentration camps." Instead, they call for more mass migration, even open borders. In other words, if the United States really had "concentration camps," the Left would be the faction helping to fill them with innocent victims.

So much cynicism. So little concern for actual victims. Philosopher René Girard warned the world against Victimism. He chose that word for people who feign concern for the vulnerable as a means to grab political power.

We know that such politicians don't really care. If they did, they would be organizing rallies for millions of Uyghurs and other Turkic peoples in real concentration camps. But nary a word. Instead, the Left and the media sit silent while many Americans remain uninformed. And China's camps fill up with victims.

The mostly Muslim Uyghurs are a persecuted population of Turkic people. The Chinese Communist government labels them as the enemy of the people and the state. Uyghurs are the indigenous, Indo-European, and Turkic people of the former East Turkistan Republic. China invaded and occupied their country in December 1949. They renamed it Xinjiang, which means "New Territory" in Chinese.

Eurasian in appearance, the Uyghurs identify as culturally, linguistically, and ethnically Central Asian (Turkic), rather than Chinese. Originally, the Uyghurs were the dominant ethnic group in the area. Then the Chinese government started flooding the region with Han Chinese migrants. Why? To ethnically and culturally dispossess the Uyghurs.

We don't even know how many Uyghurs China holds in concentration camps. Somewhere between one million and three million. All this since just 2017. Uyghur adults in concentration camps face:

- Communist brainwashing
- Public humiliation
- Rape
- Forced abortions
- Starvation
- Routine execution

That, American friends, is what happens in actual concentration camps. In case anybody cares.

Uyghurs face savage religious persecution. Uyghur children disappear into boarding schools that are referred to as "kindergartens." Leaked videos show highly guarded, brightly colored, dystopian reeducation centers. The children there learn to hate their parents' religion and race. They sing of their love for the atheist Communist government imprisoning their families.

Uyghurs who live outside the concentration camps aren't free. They live in a constant state of censorship and religious oppression. Even though there are mosques in East Turkistan, they are empty. Nobody dares to make himself a target. It is merely to keep up appearances that China doesn't bulldoze them. Uyghurs are prohibited from reading the Quran or speaking or singing in their native tongue. They are forbidden to fast through Ramadan.

Swarms of police guard every city street. Tens of thousands of cameras equipped with facial recognition and other intelligence technology watch most locations. Surveillance apps on smartphones are spying too. Anybody can prove an informant.

China makes arrests at night, swiftly and quietly, to preserve the appearance of a peaceful society during the day. Groups are rounded up and escorted to "reeducation" camps for contrived offenses or no offenses at all. Things such as "looking" Uyghur. Or having a beard. Or publicly praying.

Traveling to countries like Turkey or Afghanistan can land somebody in one of the many concentration camps networked throughout East Turkistan. The Chinese government calls them vocational training centers. China doesn't even bother to hold show trials before locking people away.

Arrests only increased in the last few years. The pretext? China's fight against "violent radical Islamism." That's a lie. Instead, follow the money.

China's government is fixated on a massive infrastructure-building program that stretches from East Asia to Europe. It is called the Belt and Road Initiative (BRI). The BRI is a massive project that will link Beijing with about seventy countries and make trading more efficient and profitable — and it runs straight through the Uyghur homeland.

The BRI would create highways, railways, and pipelines — and make border crossings smoother. The goal, of course: to expand China's influence and economy globally. Many neighboring countries stand to benefit. Is that why even Muslim countries mostly stay silent?

Uyghurs have been resisting Chinese nationalism for generations. China cannot afford any uprisings for independence like that of East Turkistan's neighbors in Kazakhstan. So China wants to eradicate the national identity of the Uyghurs and the other Turkic peoples of East Turkistan. That will keep the BRI safe, and the profits rolling in, to fund China's massive military expansion. Aiming to compete with the United States, China is arming faster than Hitler did in the 1930s.

We live in an era of information wealth. Satellite pictures have captured images of the concentration camps/prisons and "kindergartens." We cannot say we did not know about these camps (as many Germans claimed). There is no excuse. The world is turning a blind eye to this modern Holocaust. Even Muslim countries such as Pakistan and Turkey, who boast about their role in the protection of Muslims, are doing nothing.

Our own media distracts us with "fake news" like American "torture facilities." If the world can turn a blind eye to the suffering of millions, nobody is safe. It sets a terrifying precedent. You might be next. We challenge those politicians who cry about American "concentration camps" to put their money where their mouth is and stand with us. Back the Uyghur Human Rights Policy Act, now before Congress.

Let's #CloseTheCamps, all right. The real ones. In China.

We Must Stand at the Foot of the Cross and Preach Freedom to Slaves

January 20, 2021

Two events, seemingly far apart, converged for me and marked both high points and low points for my life. First, the efforts of the Democrats and the Never Trump Republicans to make the January 6 march on Washington sound like the Fascist March on Rome. The mainstream media is trying to tie the conservative groups that rallied to protest election fraud to the small number of rowdies who barged into the Capitol.

Elites wish to use a tiny percentage of troublemakers to tar a peaceful demonstration and then to exploit the violence by roping in every effective conservative group in the country, and Clarence Thomas's wife, as "seditious" potential terrorists. But the evidence wasn't there. Because it isn't true.

Second, on January 19, Secretary of State Mike Pompeo took a long, long overdue step. He certified officially on behalf of the U.S. government that China is engaging in a genocide. The evidence is there. Because it's true.

China has long occupied the nation of East Turkistan, and in recent years, it has ratcheted up its vicious persecution of Uyghur Muslims. We've long known that China puts Uyghurs in concentration camps — and that it forces Uyghur women to have abortions.

More recently we learned that China steals and sells Uyghurs' kidneys and lungs on the world black market, and that Uyghurs toil as slaves for suppliers of Nike, Apple, and dozens of other rich corporations. Now in a piece of bitter historical irony, we learn that Uyghur slaves are ... picking cotton. No joke. The Chinese Communist Party really is that shameless.

What brings these two incidents together for me? That's easy. When I spoke to a crowd of Trump supporters in D.C. on January 5, my subject was the Uyghurs. I was calling on the U.S. government to take the step that Mike Pompeo just did.

America needs to be on record as a nation in denouncing this historic crime against human dignity and religious freedom. I'm proud that now we are, and I am grateful to the Trump administration for putting us on the right side of a question that will be posed on the Day of Judgment: "When I was in a prison camp, did you speak for me?"

In many, many other ways, the Trump administration has stood with the vulnerable and the abandoned:

- Preborn children worldwide
- Victims of human smuggling through our broken southern border
- The Little Sisters of the poor refusing to hand out abortion pills as the price of tending the dying
- Christians in the Middle East trying to recover from past administrations' imperial follies
- Blue-collar workers seeking a decent wage
- Black and Hispanic Americans seeking real, responsive representation in government
- Soldiers who hope to come home from endless, directionless wars and occupations that previous administrations sent them to suffer through

The list is quite a bit longer. But I think I can prove my point more easily by pointing in the other direction. All the most powerful, privileged, and smug organizations on earth ranged against Trump and his voters:

- Deep State prosecutors willing to illegally wiretap and frame innocent citizens because of their politics
- Trillion-dollar companies that profit from slave labor in China
- Global Big Tech monopolies that demand special legal carve-outs and censor-free speech
- The abortion industry, which profits from trading in death and despair
- Privileged radical dilettantes who play at revolution from behind the ornate gates of their lavish, exclusive neighborhoods, and titter as our cities burn

In other words, The Hive. The inbred Woke elites who do very well, thanks very much, from crony capitalism, selling to spoiled Ivy League students Che Guevara shirts made of cotton picked by slaves of Communist China (to choose just one image that might help put things in focus).

I feel privileged that I was able to speak about vulnerable people hunted by the government for their religion — the Uyghurs — to an audience of "Deplorables" in America. At least the elites deplore them and wish to silence, cow, and disenfranchise half the country. If it comes down to a choice between the oppressor and the oppressed, I pray I will always know the right side to choose — and stand with them, to take the heat from the media, the politicized prosecutors, and the vicious pressure groups that label pro-life groups as "hate groups."

You and I might have to suffer far worse before this is done. We must stand together, with the imprisoned Uyghur and the pregnant teen, with the exploited immigrant and the jobless worker, the weary soldier and the persecuted nun. My organization, the Vulnerable People Project, was founded for this very purpose. My book *The Race to Save Our Century* predicted a crackdown was coming. It laid out a program for resistance and renewal. We must form a Coalition of the Forgotten and not be shamed or silenced until the world learns to remember.

Could Our Prayers Save This Century from Genocide and War?

March 17, 2021

Ahead of Pope Francis's visit to Iraq, the Western media's fanfare over the "historic" event may have struck some as premature.

In a previous column, I offered a perspective that would have otherwise been left unsaid: skepticism. The papal journey came late, and only after years of strife in Iraq and silence from the Vatican. What if the pope failed to substantially address Iraq's troubles, and the West's part in bringing them about?

In fact, I called on Pope Francis to apologize to the people of Iraq. First, on behalf of the Western nations who plundered and abandoned them in turn. Then for the Western Christians — starting with their pontiff — who failed to intervene.

But then something important happened. Something that, in a way, proved me wrong and also made Pope Francis's journey truly live up to its "historic" billing.

On day one of the papal visit, the pontiff stated: "I come as a penitent, asking forgiveness from Heaven and our brothers for so much destruction and cruelty."

Imagine! Pope Francis, the most prominent leader of Christians in the Western world, drew the attention of one billion people from the outside world and shined a light on the people of Iraq. It was as if Pope Francis had sensed the worries of the region and generously moved to share them. And the positive effects are already showing themselves.

My Iraqi friends tell me of a great feeling of renewed hope. They hope even for the beginnings of a long-overdue solidarity. Will the people of the Western world who followed the pope's visits to scenes of genocide at last start to care?

The pope's penitence — and his recommitment to those living under threat of violence in the Middle East — was unspeakably important. In fact, it was urgent. And such acts of solidarity will remain urgent for the foreseeable future. Why? Because no matter how soon they come, they're late.

Pope Francis's words to the Iraqi people were inspiring. But they also should remind us of just how great the stakes are. Francis was elected in 2013, just as John

Zmirak and I were finishing work on our book *The Race to Save Our Century.* The book argued that the twenty-first century was on course to be even bloodier than the twentieth — and hence the bloodiest in human history. This would happen unless the world changed course and adopted an unrelenting respect for the incomparable dignity of every human person, as the image of God.

We wrote that, just as the genocides and democides of the twentieth century began with strife among ancient peoples with differing faiths, so would ours. That very year, we saw the rise of ISIS and the beginning of a campaign of genocide against Kurds, Yazidis, Iraqi Christians, and other minorities.

And now, running parallel to these atrocities, we see the rise of China. As if to claim the mantle of the Nazis and the Soviets, the Chinese Communist Party (CCP) has already begun its own twenty-first-century genocide.

Under the rule of the CCP, the Uyghur Muslim people of East Turkistan are rounded up, robbed of their faith traditions and their families' integrity, and kept in concentration camps by the millions.

We now have confirmation that Uyghur prisoners are systematically raped and subjected to forced abortions. They're even cut open alive for organ harvesting — their body parts sold for the financial benefit of the CCP.

The world needs what John Paul II called a "Great Campaign" of solidarity with the vulnerable. We must shine a light on all who would violate the dignity and worth of any human person — from the Yazidi child in the Levant to the Uyghur woman in the Chinese concentration camp.

"How we have prayed, in these years, for peace in #Iraq!" Pope Francis tweeted at the beginning of his visit. "God always listens. It is up to us to walk His paths."

That's right. Pray, of course. But also walk. Use the graces you receive in prayer. And there are many opportunities on the horizon for us to walk on behalf of the vulnerable. But it will require us to break free of the shallow conventions of political speech that tend to reign as the dark clouds of genocide gather.

The monopoly mainstream media has referred to the persecution of the Uyghurs as a "complication" for U.S.-China trade negotiations. No, it's far more than that. We must frame it as an opportunity for America to help free the Uyghurs.

With the China Olympics approaching, we will have a similar opportunity: to bring the whole world's attention to the cruelties that the CCP will sweep under the rug.

And in our own private lives, we can do another meaningful thing almost every day. We can refuse to rely on consumer products made by slave workers in China. These products currently dominate many corners of the American market, including religious articles.

Speak up for peace publicly, even if it puts you at odds with your neighbors. Tell people about the plights of the vulnerable. Let's become the first generation of people in modern history to fully halt a genocide in real time — before it's accomplished. Let's turn the phrase "never again" from a wistful hope to a rock-solid promise. Maybe add to it: "Not on our watch."

The McCarrick Scandal Has Only Just Begun

August 4, 2021

In May, the Chinese Communist Party (CCP) arrested a Vatican-appointed Catholic bishop, Joseph Zhang Weizhu, along with seven priests and a number of seminarians in the Diocese of Xinxiang.

It was disturbing news, but not surprising. The genocidal CCP, which currently holds millions of Uyghurs in camps and ferociously oppresses devout Christians, Buddhists, and Muslims alike, has always been an enemy to the Church. And since the Vatican struck a deal with the Communist regime in 2018 — ostensibly to appease it for the sake of the Church in China — such attacks have only increased.

More alarming, in a way, was the fact that most Catholics in America never heard about the May arrests at all. Why not? Because the Western Church refused to mention it. I heard about it through my channels in the world of human rights advocacy. I did not hear any prominent members of the Church hierarchy speak a word of it.

Fast-forward to just last week, when we got one of those pieces of news that stirs the whole Catholic Church. Several Catholic friends texted me all at once. "Finally!" "Did you hear?" "Great news, Jason!"

Ex-Cardinal Theodore McCarrick had been charged with the sexual assault of a sixteen-year-old in the 1970s. It's heartbreaking what McCarrick did to the boy, now a man bravely standing up for himself and others like him.

Three long years after what Catholics call "The Summer of Shame," when allegations against McCarrick first emerged, I'm not surprised that many are now feeling a sense of relief.

Justice, you might think, is finally being served. Perhaps the formal charge against McCarrick even represents a glimmer of hope that the Church can now begin to regain her former glory in the eyes of the public. "Let's get McCarrick's day in court over with," we might even be tempted to say, "so we can return to normal."

But it's that temptation that compelled me to write this piece. Because it's a temptation that we have to resist. In fact, as much as we might long for an end to the whole ugly saga of "Uncle Ted" McCarrick, it's actually important for us to hope and pray and advocate for the scandal to continue.

Let me explain.

McCarrick wasn't just any cleric. He was Pope Francis's American kingmaker, able to handpick trusted friends for positions of influence in the hierarchy of the Church. More to the point: He also played a role in brokering the now-infamous — but little-understood — Vatican-China deal in 2018.

As the Catholic News Agency reported that year:

> Over 20 years, Archbishop McCarrick traveled to China on at least eight occasions, sometimes staying in a state-controlled Beijing seminary, often serving as an unofficial bridge between the Vatican and Chinese government-appointed bishops until 2016.
>
> Prior to allegations of sexual abuse and harassment becoming public this summer, the former cardinal had been an outspoken proponent of a deal between Chinese President Xi Jinping and the Church under Pope Francis, according to Chinese reports.
>
> "I see a lot of things happening that would really open many doors because President Xi and his government are concerned about things that Pope Francis is concerned about," McCarrick told *The Global Times*, in an exclusive interview in Feb. 2016.
>
> The interview quoted McCarrick as saying that the similarities between Pope Francis and Xi Jinping could be "a special gift for the world."

Which brings us back to the mass arrests in May. As I mentioned, we've seen a sharp rise in such incidents since the Vatican sealed its mysterious deal with China. So you would think that Catholic leaders living in America would speak out more adamantly than anyone.

But instead, our most influential clerics haven't said a word about it.

In June, I attended the International Religious Freedom Summit in Washington, D.C. Cardinal Timothy Dolan of New York was one of the speakers. In front of the Chinese Christian refugees and Uyghur escapees from CCP concentration camps who came to testify, Dolan made no mention of any of China's crimes against religious freedom.

Why the silence? We don't know for certain. But perhaps we know who does: McCarrick. Are you starting to see what I mean when I say we must work to ensure that the McCarrick scandal "continues"? In a way, McCarrick's sex scandal, horrific in itself, might prove providential — if we have the will to take it by the horns. After all, as an architect of the Vatican-China deal, McCarrick is not only responsible for the horrific rapes he himself allegedly committed. Nor should he merely be tried for covering up clerical sex crimes in the United States. Think bigger. The McCarrick scandal is an international scandal, involving a secret deal between the Vatican and America's foremost adversary, China, that has encountered practically no public criticism of its abuses by American clergy.

Remember: McCarrick is a master cover-up artist. After decades of serial sexual abuse, he had dozens, perhaps hundreds, of fellow clerics keeping mum for him. Why? And how might such a man go about paving the way for a secret Vatican-China deal over the course of twenty years?

Even after the McCarrick sex scandal initially broke, the best that many of McCarrick's longtime confidants and collaborators in the Catholic hierarchy could muster were a few mutterings about being shocked, while their eyes darted around the floor in front of them during TV interviews that looked more like damage control than any kind of reckoning with the scale of McCarrick and his network's crimes.

We must ensure we get more out of the McCarrick scandal this time around.

Because what many thought of as a story about a dirty old man and his victims could turn out to be a far more substantial story of ecclesial betrayal and interntational intrigue.

Catholics, Our Moment Is Now

June 26, 2020

In 2013, *The New York Times* published a bleak essay titled "The End of a Catholic Moment," mourning the loss of the prestige and influence Catholics had had in America only a few years earlier.

In 2005, Republicans built their party platform on Catholic social teachings, Democrats anxiously sought the approval of Catholic "values voters," and the mainstream media broadcast Pope St. John Paul II's splendid funeral with such reverence that it "almost felt like an infomercial for the Catholic faith."

That "Catholic moment" was over. But another soon came with the election of Pope Francis. Almost immediately, journalists and public figures the world over celebrated a sort of springtime for the Catholic Faith and the dawn of a new golden age.

Just two years later, Pope Francis made history by performing the first-ever canonization of a Catholic saint on U.S. soil: that of St. Junipero Serra. Republican Speaker of the House John Boehner wept on live television during the pope's address to Congress. Democratic leaders Joe Biden and Nancy Pelosi joined the pontiff in reverencing a statue of the new saint.

As you've already learned from the events of the past week, that "Catholic moment" was just as fleeting as the last. But in fact, I would argue that neither was a true Catholic moment at all.

As Catholics, we need to come to understand, and to accept with gratitude, with wonder and awe, and with firm conviction, that the true Catholic moment is never when the world welcomes our Faith with cries of "Hosanna."

No, the Catholic moment is when the Faith is nailed to the Cross.

In this Catholic moment — and this truly is the Catholic moment! — we need to have faith in Our Lord's heroic mission, which was ultimately accomplished almost completely alone, amid darkness and earthquakes, on Good Friday.

Through the dedication of a few faithful Catholics, He offers to accomplish great things in this world. And if we have the courage to rise to the occasion, He may even help us to preserve this nation for our children.

In the lead-up to the Battle of Lepanto in 1571, Islamic forces bent on world domination had killed countless European Christians. Thousands of others had been led away to serve as sex slaves. Muslim forces had demolished and burned churches and committed unspeakable acts of humiliation and torture as a warning against any who would resist.

Just a few decades after the Reformation, Christian Europe was divided and in disarray. It seemed unlikely to the enemy that a united force would ever come against them. Dismayed Catholics and Protestants alike were weak at the knees, unwilling to do anything to draw the Muslim's attention to their own countries and towns.

But by the grace of God, a few Catholic men had the wisdom to recognize the situation for what it was. This is what the Catholic moment looks like.

These men refused to stand by as their churches were desecrated and their families enslaved. Under the leadership of the young Don Juan of Austria, outnumbered by at least one hundred ships, they defended Europe against the violent piracy of her would-be slave masters.

After the fact, the whole Christian world celebrated. The Battle of Lepanto had changed the course of history. As Catholic scholar Michael Novak once wrote: "The air of Europe that October tasted of liberties preserved."

Today, we see our families and friends in the grip of confusion. We see our Catholic neighbors suffering despair. Some scenes from late nights in American cities are even starting to look like early tremors of violence that began in Mosul just a few short years ago.

But each of us needs to see our Catholic moment as clearly as Don Juan of Austria and his men saw theirs.

Symbols and monuments like the statue of St. Junipero Serra are reminders of the same transcendent moral order our forebears in the Battle of Lepanto defended — the moral order that kept our "liberties preserved."

And when Black Lives Matter leaders like Shaun King threaten to tear down statues and stained-glass windows of Jesus Himself, we know it's time for Catholics to be vigilant.

We must defend our monuments because we know that assaults on these pillars of the transcendent moral order always lead to assaults on the human persons whose dignity they represent — the dignity of creatures made in the image of God.

When I saw the statue of Junipero Serra fall, I thought of my trips to Iraq.

I have stood in the rubble of churches that were still smouldering after ISIS set them on fire.

I've walked through village after village where every Christian symbol was destroyed. It was a matter of course that, in these places, it wasn't just the symbols that were destroyed but thousands of our neighbors as well.

We cannot let that happen here.

Why I Gave Afghans Coal for Christmas

December 29, 2021

Like most Americans, I watched with shock and horror at the Biden regime's reckless and criminally negligent withdrawal from Afghanistan. It sentenced the Afghan people to a horrible fate at the hands of the Taliban and their terrorist allies. Biden's decisions also seriously hurt the United States' reputation in the world with friend and foe alike.

Before the feckless withdrawal, it had been years since an American died in action in Afghanistan. The United States had ceased combat operations there in 2014 and was able to maintain leverage over a strategically crucial country while keeping a minimal troop presence. Our Afghan contingent was far smaller than those we keep in South Korea, Germany, Japan, or even Djibouti.

But Joe Biden, with his vast and murky ties to Chinese intel that our FBI won't investigate, threw America's leverage away in a matter of weeks. As I wrote previously, among a litany of other outrages, Biden handed tens of billions of dollars in U.S. military equipment to a terrorist regime closely allied to Red China.

On a moral level, Biden did something far worse. He abandoned thousands of American citizens, Afghan allies of America, and Afghan Christians to a regime based on rape, torture, and terror. As a U.S. infantry veteran, this struck me with special horror. I know what happened to South Vietnamese who aided our old war effort, and I couldn't believe that we were subjecting thousands more of our allies to such a fate.

Through my Vulnerable People Project, I've been trying to help these people get out of Afghanistan to neighboring countries and safety. My special focus has been Christians, since the gospel went viral among the peoples of Afghanistan during the two decades of religious freedom we helped to guarantee there. Now all those people have targets on their backs.

The Biden State Department hasn't just refused to help. It actively frustrated our efforts and those of other private agents, such as Glenn Beck's organization. You'd almost think that Biden was trying to win the goodwill of the Taliban by offering up as scapegoats the people we should be protecting.

While I am still involved in complex efforts to help Christians and other vulnerable Afghans escape, my organization is trying something simpler now. We want to help these targeted Afghans survive through the winter. To do that, they need something simple. They need coal. You and I might think of that as an old-fashioned fossil fuel, or something that Santa leaves in stockings for bad kids. But it's something quite different in the icy mountains of Afghanistan. It's the difference between life and death.

Aiding me in this effort is an extraordinary man named Prince Wafa. No, he's not Afghan royalty. He's an American citizen and former translator for the U.S. military. He escaped Afghanistan just a few weeks ago. But he's looking back at all those left behind and trying to save them too. Wafa told reporters:

> This situation is urgent. Parents are selling their children for food and are desperate for basic survival needs. I understand because I was trapped in Afghanistan. During my crisis, a friend of mine in the United States saw Jason Jones appear on a news segment on *EWTN News Nightly*. Jason's organization was our last hope.
>
> VPP and my local congressman, Rep. Darrell Issa, were there for me when my wife and I were vulnerable. Now that I'm free, it's imperative that we save others. So I have to pay it forward. The power of one news story helped me get the right connections, cell phones, and money so that my life and my family's life would be saved. I want to do the same by driving awareness to this urgent need for resources.

With Wafa's help, the Vulnerable People Project was able to get coal, food, firewood, and other urgent winter essentials to some 1,600 Afghan Christians and other vulnerable minorities. Our work isn't finished by a long shot, however. It's a long winter over there, and the country is still run by terrorists.

It's my prayer that American citizens realize the deep responsibilities that come with vast national power. President Trump understood that, which is why he did not enact a sudden, reckless pullout from Afghanistan. Joe Biden — or the secret committee that actually governs in his name — severely damaged American interests and soiled our national honor with the cut-and-run abandonment of that country. It's just one of dozens of un-American policies and decisions that have lashed America since a controversial and still contested election.

One way we can push back against what team Biden is doing to our country and our world is to mitigate the damage. The Vulnerable People Project is my way of doing that. Afghan Christians shouldn't have to die for the sake of Joe Biden's presidential participation trophy.

The Christian Canary Dying in the Coal Mine That Is India

March 18, 2024

The Indian church has two open secrets. Most Westerners, already discombobulated by the enigma of India, are puzzled even further when they learn the content of these secrets.

Secret no. 1: The Indian church is a first-century apostolic church, independent of Rome. It was planted by St. Thomas the Apostle, who landed on the Malabar coast in AD 52, where he founded seven churches and baptized six of the highest-caste Hindu priestly families.

Even the Roman pontiffs had no idea of the antiquity and apostolicity of the Indian church. When Patriarch John visited Pope Callixtus II in 1122 and said he was from Hulna, St. Thomas's burial site in India, the pontiff could not believe that there was a church in India.

Secret no. 2: A significant portion of Northeast India is predominantly Christian. The mostly mountainous region of eight states and more than two hundred tribes experienced an unprecedented explosion of Christianity in the early part of the twentieth century.

Missiologists and anthropologists agree that the gospel has been the "single most important catalyst" revolutionizing the Northeast tribals in every area, from literacy to the emancipation of women.

Most remarkably, even though it was Western missionaries who brought Christianity to the tribes, the churches of Northeast India are fiercely independent and proudly indigenous, blending their own treasured heritage with the import of Western music and culture.

Throw a stone in Nagaland, Mizoram, or Meghalaya, and it will hit a quartet of Christians singing hymns in four-part harmony. On Easter Sunday, choirs all over Northeast India, robed in colorful tribal costumes, burst into joyous strains of Handel's "Hallelujah" chorus.

Oddly, while Northeast India's vibrant Christianity has remained a mystery even to most Indian Christians, it has been a bitter pill for India's Hindu ethno-nationalists to swallow. This cluster of Christianity has presented an almost unassailable bulwark to their totalitarian goal of a pan-Hindu India.

The idea of an exclusive Hindu nation comes largely from Vinayak Damodar Savarkar's 1923 book *Hindutva: Who Is a Hindu?* — a work that has been seminal in spawning violence and militant Hindu hatred against Christians and other religious minorities in India.

Savarkar's invented metanarrative of Hindutva ("Hinduness") consists of nation (*rashtra*), race (*jati*), and civilization (*sanskriti*). At the core of Savarkar's paradigm is the idea of India as *pitrubhoomi* — literally Fatherland — interpreted by Savarkar as "holy land."

Historian Tanika Sarkar, in an essay in *Public Hinduisms* (2012), explains how the ideology of Hindutva conjoins "nation with faith, and, in the same move, makes the land of India the property, in a literal sense, of Hindus alone."

Since Christians, Jews, Parsees, and Muslims do not fulfill the criterion of India as their "holy land," they cannot be regarded as Indians, notwithstanding the antiquity of their religious presence in the land.

The tribal Christians of Northeast India, however, fail the test of "Indianness" on all four counts! On land, the very inclusion of tribal territory into India after independence from British colonial rule has been fiercely contested.

On ethnicity, the "hill people" of the Northeast are racially different from most Indians, enjoying closer ethnic ties to the peoples of China, Nepal, Bhutan, and Sikkim than to the "plains people" of the Indian subcontinent.

As for Savarkar's criterion of a Hindu *sanskriti*, nothing could be more remote from the proudly indigenous tribes than identifying with Hindu "civilization" or "culture." This is a marked difference from other Indian Christians, particularly Catholics, who have happily enculturated within a Hindu culture — some to the extent of a troubling syncretism.

The flames of these four religio-cultural-racial-territorial factors are stoked by a political element: the pan-Indian, Hindu-political Bharatiya Janata Party (BJP) and its Hindu activist grassroot confederates like the paramilitary Rashtriya Swayamsevak Sangh (RSS). These exclusivist groups are treated like outsiders in the tribal Christian belt of Northeast India.

Not surprisingly, Hindu extremists emboldened by India's Hindu, ethnonationalist prime minister, Narendra Modi, are mounting an ethnic and religious cleansing of tribal Christians in Northeast India — a mass extermination that has been in the planning for decades.

The epicenter of the carnage is Manipur. Christians here aren't the majority, as in the neighboring states of Nagaland, Mizoram, and Meghalaya; nevertheless, they constitute 41.29 percent of the state's 3.2 million people and make the Kuki-Zo tribes a soft target for Hindutva.

It was American Baptist missionary William Pettigrew who brought the gospel to the Kuki and Naga tribes in 1894. Pettigrew's evangelizing efforts provoked hostility among the Hindus, and the state banned missionary work among the Meitei community.

Since May 2023, Hindutva forces have destroyed or burned hundreds of churches, killed more than two hundred tribals, displaced more than seventy thousand, and systematically targeted Christian schools and seminaries. These are official figures — Manipur church leaders say the reality is far worse.

Hindu mobs gang-raped and paraded naked several Christian women. A dossier contains records of twenty-two female victims of rape, torture, assault, arson, and murder.

The Kerala Catholic Bishops' Social Harmony and Vigilance Commission, which carried out an inquiry into the Manipur riots, confirmed that the sectarian violence had been "well-orchestrated" and "targeted the Kuki tribe," 90 percent of whom are Christians.

"Shockingly, today, there is barely a Church that is still standing in the Imphal valley, except a few of those where the non-Zomi-Kuki tribals go for worship. Definitely, this is the first [time] in Indian history that this many places of worship have been vandalized, burnt or demolished," Samast Christi Samaj said in a press release.

"In terms of cruelty, not even infants, children, elderly and infirm have been spared. Cases of rape, mob-lynching, burn[ing] to death, caging in gunny bags, gagging and beating to death are reported to be tactics employed," the statement added.

This week, Manipuri martial arts champion Chungreng Koren pleaded with Modi to visit the state. "Violence is happening in Manipur. It has been almost a year.

People are dying and many people are in relief camps. Modi ji, please visit Manipur once and restore peace in the state," Koren begged.

Not once has the Hindu extremist prime minister, who was hugged by Pope Francis when he visited the Vatican in November 2021, visited the strife-torn region.

Worse, the top leadership of the Catholic Church in India has bought into the Hindu fiction and is playing Neville Chamberlain by attributing the Hindu-led persecution of Christians to ethnic rivalries.

"This is a tribal conflict," Cardinal Oswald Gracias, archbishop of Bombay, asserted in a video statement released by the Archdiocese of Bombay in August 2023. "It is given a religious twist, but it is not a religious conflict between two religions. It is between two tribes."

Just as the Islamic genocide of Nigerian Christians is portrayed by the Nigerian government and the mainstream media as a "herders-farmers clash," the well-oiled Hindu propaganda machine is pushing the false narrative of an ethnic conflict, in which the Christian hill tribes are the perpetrators and the largely Hindu aggressor Meitei community is the victim.

More Hindu disinformation justifies the pogroms against Christian tribals, claiming that the violence is the result of illegal influx from an open border with Myanmar, poppy cultivation by the hill tribes, forced conversions, anti-Hindu attacks, and Kuki militants sparking violence.

The mainstream media is also resorting to moral equivalence by claiming that both groups have been equally affected and that the Kuki-Zo are illegal immigrants to Manipur and not indigenous tribals after all.

The disinformation campaigns, designed to bamboozle the Western press and international human rights organizations, even claim that the Meitei is a tribe and hence deserve the same rights given to the indigenous tribes — which includes the exclusive right to buy and sell land in the hill districts.

A big chunk of Manipur occupied by the tribals has vast reserves of oil and natural gas, which Meitei-dominated governments, in league with oil companies, have sought to encroach on. The Christian tribals will "not allow governments to give contracts to companies to extract oil," a minister from the Manipur Legislative Assembly testified.

Manipur is the Christian canary in the Indian coal mine. If the forces of Hindutva succeed in eliminating the Kuki-Zo Christians, they will continue their Nazi-like expansion and proceed to purge the followers of Jesus in other states of Northeast India.

The world needs to halt this saffron juggernaut. Indian Catholic bishops must stop feeding the BJP crocodile. Pope Francis, who has been as silent as an urn full of ashes, must speak. Protestant leaders need to pressure Western leaders to shame Modi into decency.

The second-century theologian Tertullian famously said that "the blood of martyrs is the seed of the Church." The good news is that the Hindu-led persecution of Christians in India is only furthering what is arguably the most incredible rise in conversions from Hinduism to Christianity in the two-thousand-year history of the Indian church. And that is no secret.

Hypocrisy Is the Road to Holiness for Most of Us

September 30, 2024

Again I looked and saw all the oppression that was taking place under the sun: I saw the tears of the oppressed — and they have no comforter; power was on the side of their oppressors — and they have no comforter.

— Ecclesiastes 4:1

A French wit once remarked: "Hypocrisy is the tribute that vice pays to virtue." That quip expresses a profoundly Christian insight. Every last one of us is a sinner, and the greatest saints saw that most clearly. Look at St. Paul, who called himself "the foremost of sinners" (1 Tim. 1:15).

That wasn't posturing or false humility but the fruit of a conscience made more sensitive by God's grace, a conscience that looked back and inward at the real flaws it saw. That's why Mother Teresa confessed her sins each and every week ("Because I need to," she said). But Joe Biden and Nancy Pelosi breeze through life without a twinge of guilt. It must feel nice …

Apart from becoming absolutely perfect, there's only one way on this earth to avoid some taint of hypocrisy, and it's the path that modern people seem to prefer: Abandon all standards so you cannot possibly fall short of them. Lower the bar so far that it's impossible not to clear it.

Replace the standard of "What is right?" with "What seems to work at the moment," and WHAM: You're immune to the charge of hypocrisy. Instead, you've made yourself a conscienceless sociopath. That seems like a poor trade to make, but it's the one modern political thinkers accepted in the wake of Machiavelli, whose impatience with empty talk of "virtue" led him to embrace cynicism instead.

The political system that people made out of Machiavelli's embittered stance got the fancy name "Realpolitik," but all it amounts to really is "whatever you can get away with." That's hardly a philosophy worthy of the name.

Most of us don't go full Machiavelli, but instead we pick and choose. We maintain high ethical standards and strive to practice empathy for some people and groups, but not for others. We decide which sets of people deserve to be treated according to Christian ethics ... and which ones simply don't. They don't get to fly up in the first-class, Golden Rule section. We shove them back into Realpolitik coach, where we grant them the same treatment any pagan would. We rightly speak up for victims of abuse when they happen to fall inside our "circle of concern." But when we see innocents who belong to other groups suffer, we shrug and quote Frank Sinatra:

> That's life (that's life)
> That's what all the people say
> You're riding high in April, shot down in May.

Just a few exquisite examples of the double standards we practice:

- The Democratic party is quick to demonize blue-collar Americans who complain about the mass influx of unskilled immigrants it permitted when the Biden administration opened our borders. Where are the pro-immigrant activists when it turns out that some 320,000 immigrant children have gone missing and are likely being exploited?
- Neoconservatives of the Dick Cheney and David French stripe (who now back Kamala Harris) claim to be concerned about the lives and freedom of people in Ukraine. So why are they opposed to any ceasefire deal that might stop the slaughter, which has already claimed a million casualties in a war that never should have happened — except that Western policymakers torpedoed a compromise peace deal?
- Conservative Catholics praise the anti-globalist, pro-natalist policies of Hungary and Russia. And rightly so. But they fall suddenly silent when you point out that both countries are blocking Christian Armenia from getting the weapons it needs to stop a vicious jihad waged by Azerbaijan against Christian civilians.
- Christian Zionists rightly condemn the vicious attacks on civilians committed by Hamas. But when you point to the mass destruction of Christian churches and communities in Gaza by poorly trained IDF soldiers, they shrug: "collateral damage."

- The United Arab Emirates pours money into groups protesting the conditions of Palestinians in Israel's occupied territories. But it's also pouring weapons in a vicious civil war in Sudan, helping Arabized jihadis victimize black Christians and Muslims who soon will face a full-on famine.
- Turkey speaks up at the slightest hint of Islamophobia in Europe but keeps mum about the ongoing genocide waged by its ally China against the Turkic-speaking Uyghurs, who languish in concentration camps.
- Iran, which claims to be the global champion of Muslims, viciously mistreats Hazara refugees from Afghanistan, making it illegal even to sell them bread when they're starving.

As head of the Vulnerable People Project, it's my job to practice empathy toward anyone who needs it — even if he's not part of one of my favorite religious or ethnic groups. I've written here about how my work on behalf of Afghans abandoned by Biden's surrender and civilians starving in Gaza forced me to confront my own prejudices about people from that part of the world.

I'm not going to tell you that you should actively prefer people radically different from you, that you ought to care about foreign Muslims more than American Christians. Or that you should dump your own kids in pagan, dangerous public schools out of a sense of "solidarity" or something like it — as *Christianity Today* now teaches.

That's the woke gospel of Victimism, which seeks to virtue-signal like the worst Pharisees whom Jesus scorned. Instead, I want to urge everyone to be a slightly better class of hypocrite. Don't embrace grim Realpolitik for one group, and the Golden Rule for another. Even if you do, quite naturally, care more for suffering people who share your faith or citizenship, don't stop at that. Challenge yourself to remember the common humanity we share with every soul God has created. Don't callously embrace policies for alien strangers that would appall you if you had to endure them. In other words, "Do unto others as you would have them do unto you."

The eventual deathbed convert Oscar Wilde had a famously complex relationship with the moral law. But in one of his plays, he included a line that I think could inspire us here: "We are all in the gutter, but some of us are looking at the stars."

I'll repurpose that line this way: We are all hypocrites, but some of us are looking at the Cross.

Chapter 5

BEAUTY

Andrew Breitbart: A White Plume over the Battle

March 10, 2012

When I first met Andrew Breitbart just a few years ago, it was in passing. We walked through the hallway of some swanky hotel where a small group of conservatives gathered. Everyone else was in his best suit for the occasion, except for me — I hate wearing ties, and never do, but this time I felt embarrassed and underdressed.

Then Andrew breezed in, wearing cut-off blue jeans, flip-flops, and a white button-down, and immediately I felt better. (I figured out later that he had a natural talent for letting awkward people know that they were welcome.) A friend introduced us, and before long, a group of learned, accomplished leaders in political and even spiritual causes had flocked around Andrew and hung on his every word. This wasn't because he was famous (some of them were, too). It was because of who Andrew was, what he cared about, and the passion for human dignity that pervaded the work he did.

Andrew, at various times, worked at different points along the political spectrum — not because he lacked core principles or bent with the wind as an opportunist. No, as I came to know him, I realized that Andrew's life, public and private, was knit tightly together with an integrity that astounded me, and it won him lifelong loyalty even from people whose ideas he no longer shared.

What made Andrew run? Andrew loved people, and so he loved justice, and so he hated bullies. That simple statement sums him up.

What got Andrew involved in media politics was watching the Clarence Thomas hearings — which he saw clearly as an unjust, cowardly ambush of an independent black American. And the spectacle made him sick. Andrew couldn't live with himself if he let a bully go unchallenged. If he saw someone using money, power, or information to hurt an innocent person — be it a conservative jurist or a closeted gay actor being blackmailed — Andrew would show up in the victim's kitchen, reassuring him and showing him how to defend himself.

Andrew was everything modern liberals aspire to be (and some really are): passionate, funny, tolerant, brave, and a doer of justice. That was clear to all who knew him, and that is why top-notch journalists, famous pastors, senators, and billionaires alike wanted to talk to Andrew, why even people who differed with him starkly knew he deserved their trust.

I'll embarrass myself a little now and say that meeting Andrew for the first time was like running into Bob Marley or Bruce Lee — the kind of moment you don't forget. When I got back to Los Angeles that day, I was running from room to room telling my staff that they had to meet Breitbart, though I couldn't exactly say why. I'd invited him to our office in Glendale for lunch, sure that he'd be too busy ever to take me up on it.

Then one day Andrew just stopped by and said, "Can I take you and your posse to lunch?" I don't remember a thing that we talked about that day, but I remember the look on everybody's faces. I have the mental picture burned in my brain: They all just beamed with joy. It's not because they were starstruck (we work in the movie business).

There was just "something about Andrew." He loved people and loved life, and you couldn't help loving both things just a little bit more in his presence. That is what I will miss, really miss, about Andrew.

I am part of a large, charmed circle of people who knew Andrew and loved him. Fatally busy as he always was, he always carved out time for his friends and his family. I remember he seemed to take on a special, distinctive tone of voice with each of his closest friends. When he mentioned his lovely wife, Susie, I knew all I needed to know about their marriage from the tender way he said her name. His longtime business partner, Larry, was also his closest friend. A wise mentor of mine once warned me: "Never do business with a man who doesn't have old friends." Andrew had many, across every professional and ideological line.

Last year, Andrew and I were invited to serve as extras in the movie adaptation of Ayn Rand's atheist opus, *Atlas Shrugged*. I used to be an objectivist myself and had dreamed since I was a teenager of appearing in such a film. So we spent the day surrounded by actors incarnating James and Dagny Taggart, Hank Rearden, and the rest. Andrew and I spoke not of the movie but of its theme: the dignity and worth of every individual man and woman. That was a point that Ayn Rand insisted on.

But where did that dignity come from? How do we know we are more than brainy apes? At this point, Andrew and I began to talk not of John Galt but of God.

A couple of months ago, Andrew called me and asked if I wanted to hang out, work from his home, and grab some lunch. When I got to his house, he was in the middle of a battle on Twitter with some nitwit. I went to the back lanai and set up shop. When Andrew came outside, he didn't want to talk about our work but about the land. He pointed toward the military cemetery behind his house. "My realtor said that the graveyard lowers my property value. He's dead wrong. It's what gives this house its value. The men who are buried there are the reason we have our freedoms. Right now, you and I are in the company of heroes."

And right now, Andrew is.

If Life Is Sacred, Then Labor Is Dignified

September 6, 2015

As we take a day of genuine leisure from our labors in the form of family time, reading, self-improvement, or tending to our hobbies, it's worth reflecting on what work really means.

First of all, work can be joyful, just like working out at a gym or playing a rigorous sport. These three activities are connected because they affirm the goodness of our existence in human bodies, as amalgams of flesh and spirit. As John Zmirak wrote last week at *The Stream*, one of the darkest and deadliest temptations to which human beings are subject is to see our bodies as worthless or even wicked, and our willful intellects as the only important thing about us. To the Gnostic, the body that you were born with is not a precious gift from the Creator, but a creaky and fragile Rube Goldberg that constrains your boundless spirit. It is of no significance, really, compared with your "freedom of choice." Hence the political label "pro-choice" as an alternative to "pro-life" — because for some people, sheer arbitrary choice is more important. They don't want to live without it, and they're willing to kill to keep it.

To them, human beings who don't yet have, or who seem to have lost, the power of choice aren't even people, really. They're "products of conception" or medical "vegetables," whose bodies we may treat as we choose to. That Gnostic path, which seems at first like the high road, leads only to boundless pride and fathomless cruelty. If you would be "as god," you will surely end up just like the fallen angels — and among them.

Work is also intrinsically dignified. It marks us off as persons who take seriously our responsibilities to ourselves, our families, and the broader human community — who pull our own weight; who, as long as we are capable, care for ourselves and contribute to the well-being of others. Some people mistake the meaning of man's Fall as suggesting that work was imposed on us as a curse. Far from it. We had already been hard at work when the Serpent came on the scene. We were tending the Garden of Eden and playing peaceful steward to happy Creation. When he goaded us to grasp the power of God to "know" both good and evil, that piece of human hubris made it bitter to us. Suddenly work could be painful, dreary, repetitive, and taxing to the spirit.

But God thought work important enough that He pressed it upon us as a necessity: "In the sweat of your face you shall eat bread till you return to the ground, for out of it you were taken" (Gen. 3:19). That wasn't really a punishment so much as an instance of tough love: Only through work could we begin to discipline our wild, rebellious spirits. It would be through our work that we could show our love and dedication and begin to prepare ourselves to accept divine redemption when it was offered. So the worker pope, St. John Paul II, wrote in his first encyclical, *Laborem Exercens.*

Because we are fallen, we try to squirm away from God, even from His blessings. The dark side of politics down through the ages could be summed up, briefly, as one group of people trying to force all the others to do their work for them, so they can live in idleness. The aristocrats of Egypt, the warrior caste of Babylon, the "free" slave owners of Greece, the senators of Rome with their armies of conquered captives and a lazy mob in the capital, hungry for bread and circuses. All of them saw "work" as a hot potato that they would toss to somebody else, and each of them had a story about how "real" human life did not entail breaking your back to make things or honestly trade them. That was for the lesser beings, whom even Aristotle rationalized were "natural slaves." True liberty, for the master class, consisted in accepting the fruits of others' labors and dilettantishly playing with ideas and objects of art.

The coming of Christ turned all of this on its head. Or rather, we might say, man had been standing on his head through all his history, and Christ planted us back on our feet. The Second Person of the Trinity was the hard-working son and apprentice of an independent businessman — a contractor, a carpenter, whose skill and sweat with a lathe was what brought customers calling, not his royal blood. Jesus preached to sweaty workers and stinky fishermen, and Christ's most potent apostle was a tentmaker named Saul.

When the Church's high moral code attracted aristocratic followers, who had looked in vain among pagans for traces of old Republican Roman virtue, there was indeed a danger that they would corrupt the Christian creed with their inherited veneration of slothful delectation. And indeed, uncritical embrace of Aristotle would lead many Christians astray on this point.

But much more potent than old Greek books was the example of the monks. It was St. Benedict who demanded of his followers that they work long, difficult days; he even taught them to think of their daily work as a form of prayer. So it was his monks, and those inspired by him, who painstakingly recopied every ancient book we still have; who cleared the forests and drained the swamps and built beautiful, durable abbeys.

We today need to remember more than ever the inner dignity of work. Not just brain work but arm work and back-breaking work of the kind that mows our lawns, digs out our sewers, puts out our fires, defends our country, and enforces its laws. Increasingly, our dominant chattering classes have taught us to view the latter kinds of work with an aristocratic sneer. They think of the people in our army and police uniforms almost as alien mercenaries or highly intelligent drones. Meanwhile, tens of millions of Americans are locked into cycles of intergenerational dependency on welfare, which deprives them of the character lessons and hard-earned self-respect that honest work brings.

My grandfather served his country as an infantryman in World War II and Korea and then came home from those freezing battlefields to work as a tool and die maker for Ford. My father worked in a factory, volunteered for the U.S. infantry during the Vietnam War, and then returned to work in a lumberyard. He moved on to serve as a shoe salesman at Marshalls, where he worked his way up to the office of corporate vice president. I myself was a high school dropout who joined the U.S. infantry and then emerged to work through college at stores like Home Depot and to wait tables and build movie sets until I got my bachelor's degree and drifted into the white-collar world. And do you know what my biggest worry is? That I cannot quite fill the shoes of my father and my grandfather. Their work shoes. But I will try.

Why I Use a Surfer Symbol to Sum Up Solidarity with the Vulnerable

February 27, 2016

I travel a lot, far more than my wife and kids would like. It's demanding to spend so much time on airplanes, in buses, in rental cars on lonely roads driving hundreds of miles between public speeches or meetings. I would much rather be back home fishing or grilling in sunny Hawaii. I could pitch in more with homeschooling the youngest of my seven children in the values that make life mean something — rather than nothing. That is what kids soak in from the culture if you don't pay close attention.

But it's that very culture I'm fighting, the culture of Nothing. Nothing makes it worthwhile to sacrifice yourself, to make lifetime commitments, to welcome new life or take loving, patient care of the old and dying. Nothing brought you into this world, and Nothingness is waiting for you when you leave it.

Nihilism is a fancy philosophical word for what's really a dank, adolescent surrender, a juvenile, cynical shrug at the complex wonders, the extraordinary mystery, pain, and beauty of human birth, life, love and death. It's a cheap defense mechanism you use when you're scared to get hurt, to lose something that matters — so, to harden yourself, you pretend that nothing does. Pretend that for long enough, and you will mean it.

The culture that rules in movies and books, in schools and too many churches, has soaked in this life-sucking poison, and so I schlep from airport to airport trying to offer the antidote. It's not my own invention. I'm not a philosopher or prophet but an ordinary guy who lost a daughter to the violence of our culture of Nothing — and who decided to do something about it. What I chose to do was to push back against the deaths of the innocent, in the womb or in refugee camps, in the ghetto or on the killing fields of Darfur or ISIS-controlled Iraq. Wherever death comes for the innocent, I want, in some sense, to be there; I want my words and actions to place me in solidarity with the victims. That's what I think it really means to be human.

What's special to me about the place where I live, Hawaii, is that its native culture embodies, more deeply than any I have seen, the importance of solidarity — of opening your heart and even your home to those in need. For centuries, Hawaiians have answered the tragic fact that sometimes families break up, or parents die, or young teenagers get pregnant, through a beautiful institution they call *hānai*. As mainlanders would understand it, it amounts to an adoption, but without any of the legal strings and psychodrama that often encumber it elsewhere.

It's really simple: Hawaiian culture sees people not as liabilities but as assets, so if there's a person who has lost his important attachments and needs to make new ones, a family will offer to *hānai* him, to accept him as one of their own. A baby whose young mom isn't prepared to care for him, an old man without any relatives, a teenager whose dad goes to prison — any one of them might find himself *hānai'd* and suddenly be a part of a whole extended family, with all the privileges and obligations that come with it. In the rest of America, that's what the federal government is for.

This spirit of generous welcome is also expressed by the greeting *aloha*, and it resonates throughout Hawaii — a place where the country's Queen Emma once went door-to-door collecting money to build a hospital for the poor. (The Queen's Medical Center is now one of the leading hospitals in the Pacific.) But the piece of Hawaiian culture that for me sums up its embrace of life against death, of solidarity with the vulnerable, is the *Shaka* sign now favored by surfers around the world.

As I learned when I first moved here as a seventeen-year-old, this sign comes from an act of solidarity with the suffering: A train conductor used to ride each day through the cane fields and wave at the toiling workers — whose dull day was broken only by the back and forth of the train. One day, that conductor was injured in an accident and lost three fingers on his hand. The field hands missed his daily greeting and wondered what had happened to him. When the man came back to work and passed through the fields, the workers cheered. He waved at them again, with his newly maimed hand. The workers waved back, but first made their hands look like his — showing just the thumb and pinkie. And ever since, the *Shaka* has been a sign of solidarity and friendship.

I wish I could have been there to see the look on that train conductor's face. I am sure it's the same look I got from persecuted Dinka in Sudan when I showed up as part of a mission to dig them wells. It's the look that Middle Eastern Christians get when they learn that some Western Christians realize that they exist and are working for their safety. It's the same face of wonderment, of surprise at the basic fact that other human beings care about them, that teenage moms have in crisis pregnancy centers when volunteers sacrifice themselves to welcome both mother and baby. It's the spirit of *hānai*, of *aloha*, and I have to spend a lot of time outside Hawaii helping to share it with the world.

So when I meet with TV stars like Hoda Kotb of the *Today* show, or pro-life politicians like Ted Cruz, or donors, or volunteers, or activists, I always snag a selfie with both of us flashing the *Shaka* symbol. It is my hope that someday the *Shaka* will be the universal gesture of solidarity with the vulnerable, a "peace" symbol that really means something.

A Resurrection Movie: *The Vessel*

March 26, 2016

This weekend, we feast the final victory of life over grim death, and forgiveness over sin. It's a story we tell each spring, fittingly at the time when vegetable life, in the form of tiny green shoots, starts pushing up from the thawing earth. When animals start to court. When the whole teeming sea of God's creatures on this fallen earth pushes back against the death that man's sin earned us. We alone, of all the life on earth, were not created for death.

And in a lovely emblem of that, Jesus Himself could not be contained by the grave but burst forth on His own power and broke the gates that our sins had built outside Heaven. As John Henry Newman once wrote, Christ's life was too strong for death. That's the life He offers us, if we will take it. Do we dare? Or are we too attached to the "way things work," to the grinding, familiar routine of our fallen, self-wasting desires?

That's the question that's asked by one of the most powerful films I've seen in years. It came to my attention because its executive producer, and champion, is the brilliant Terrence Malick, whose recent films (*The Tree of Life, To the Wonder*) have posed sharp questions of faith and meaning — the issues that Hollywood usually prefers to squirm away from. This new film, *The Vessel,* stars Martin Sheen, who divides his career between high-budget commercial movies and small films that resonate with his deep Christian faith.

This is no happy-clappy, "gather your pals from Young Life or Theology on Tap" kind of movie. There's a place for films like that, perhaps during "ordinary time," when we aren't marking solemn, glorious feasts of our common faith. No, *The Vessel* is sober and thought-provoking, lyrical and beautiful. It has the rich palette of colors and artful camera angles of a South American film, but you don't have to squint at subtitles. It was filmed in the old-world parts of Puerto Rico, and all dialogue is in English. The issues it raises are timeless and universal. They have been with us since our first parents found the body of their son Abel, the first human death ever recorded.

I can't imagine how they reacted, but *The Vessel* gives us a hint. It's the story of a coastal town that has known death, and known it abundantly: Ten years ago, a tidal wave struck its school and washed every child in town out to sea. Since then, no couple has dared to conceive a baby, no one gets married, and all the town's women dress exclusively in black. It's not so much a culture of death as one of mourning, where people have lost any sense that life has purpose or meaning and don't know what to make of the God who let all this happen. It's a town frozen in amber, where families bereft of hope seem as if they're waiting around to die.

Then a miracle happens. A small, strange miracle that seems quite unrelated to all the suffocating grief, but a miracle nonetheless. A young man, Leo (Lucas Quintana), is out by the water saying goodbye to his childhood friend, the latest young man who intends to leave the dying town and move to the city. They've been drinking, and a tussle lands them both in the waves. Both men are too drunk to swim, and they drown. But three hours later, as his mother and neighbors grieve him, Leo comes back to life. No one knows why, but the whole town comes to believe that he has been marked by God. He becomes a figure of hope to the town, and the beautiful woman he'd always secretly loved, Soraya (Aris Mejias) wakes up from her own dream of grief over her husband, who was drowned along with the children. She falls in love with Leo, and her new love awakens her back to life. She digs out of her closet all the colored dresses she used to love and starts to wear them — to the horror, at first, of other women in the town.

More signs of life begin to stir. The town's pastor, Fr. Douglas (Martin Sheen), notices that more people are coming to church, hopeful that God has given them a sign He still is interested in the village. Best of all, a young couple comes to Fr. Douglas and announces that they now want to have a child. It seems that from Leo's drunken accident, and its mysterious outcome, the seeds of new life have been planted.

But this is no fairy tale. The dark burden of grief that the town has labored under won't be banished without a struggle — a passion, really, though one that happens after the resurrection in the story. (It's almost the Easter narrative in reverse.) The pastor realizes that the people of the village have made young Leo a kind of idol. They even think that he has the power to raise the dead to life. When that turns out to be false, they think that Leo has betrayed them. They turn on Leo and Soraya, turning them into the scapegoat for all the suffering they have been through. It is up to Fr. Douglas to hold them back and redirect his suffering flock to a fuller, richer faith.

I don't want to give away the film's joyful, uplifting ending, and I haven't done justice to the power with which this story is told. Suffice it to say that the film works through all the steps by which a "scapegoat" (such as Our Lord) is blamed for society's suffering, as the Christian literary critic René Girard explained in a lifetime of world-famous scholarship and writing. As Girard discovered — and the discovery is what made him into a Christian — it is only the unique suffering and redemptive work of Jesus that can put an end to the sterile cycle of blame and recrimination that poisons our fallen world. The film ends with a vision of what reconciliation and forgiveness look like in flesh and blood.

The Steve Bannon I Know

November 17, 2016

You might not be surprised to learn some deep lessons about authentic Catholic social teaching from a conference at the Vatican. Except if that person you were learning them from was then the head of Breitbart.com and is now Donald Trump's chief strategist. That's right, Steve Bannon — who is now the victim of an appalling character smear by Leftists and Never Trump globalists in the GOP — gave one of the most profound and enlightening talks in recent Vatican history, in 2014.

I myself am not surprised. Years before Bannon took over Breitbart.com, I met him at the Ritz Carlton in Hollywood, in the company of a major movie producer. Before he brought me to meet Bannon, my producer friend told me that Bannon had been a banker at Goldman Sachs. So what I expected to meet was a snooty, amateur triathlete with a bland personality and pale, uncalloused hands. Instead, I encountered the big personality and talent that is Steve Bannon.

I was a little intimidated at first; here was someone who was clearly afraid of nothing, equal parts brashness and magnanimity. We started talking business, but it wasn't long before somehow we were discussing the Armenian genocide. At the time, I was working on *The Race to Save Our Century,* and twentieth-century horrors weighed heavily on my mind. But they also weighed on Bannon's. Indeed, almost every time we'd ever get together to nail down some detail of a media project, Steve would end up regaling me on the danger to Christian minorities in the Middle East and Africa, or the horrors of abortion and what we must do to stop it. Not your average Hollywood business lunches.

If you read Bannon's Vatican speech, what you meet is a man almost obsessed by concern for the fragility of freedom and peace in our fallen world. Someone consumed by care for the vulnerable among us and unafraid to confront their powerful oppressors. Steve is tough, like the sheepdogs described in *American Sniper* — tough enough to defend the defenseless. He once joked about learning from Lenin, but Bannon won't break eggs to make human omelets, as Lenin did. No, he will break the omelet makers — the Islamists and globalists who recklessly threaten the innocent.

So if you're committed to genuine Catholic social teaching — to peace, open markets and the sanctity of human life, Steve's your man. I met him through someone we both loved, Andrew Breitbart. Together, two Catholics and a Jew, we would sketch out new ways to promote the prophetic ideals of justice too often forgotten in our post-theist world.

Though Andrew is gone, I am sure he is smiling down at the sight of Bannon in the corridors of power, standing at the right hand of the incoming president — who will no doubt hear from Bannon about the evils of Planned Parenthood, the plight of Yazidis, Christians, and Jews in the Middle East, and the need to smash "crony capitalism," which threatens our nation's growth. I hope that Catholics rally to Bannon now, as he goes through his current crucible. We will find no better friend of all the causes dear to our hearts — and the Heart of Our Lord.

Moana Is a Classic Disney Film, with a Surprising Pro-Life Message

December 22, 2016

If you're seeking a Christmas weekend movie that every member of your family will enjoy, look no further than *Moana*. It's exciting, funny, and moving, with great songs and memorable characters — all the elements you'd expect from Disney films of past decades.

One of its stars, Nicole Scherzinger, brings a special bonus: On top of her fine acting and beautiful singing, Scherzinger is an outspokenly pro-life actor. That's rare enough in Hollywood, but Scherzinger takes real career risks for her convictions: On the eve of *Moana*'s release, she spoke out passionately on the subject of abortion.

She told the *Daily Mail* (UK) that she herself was the product of a crisis pregnancy, conceived when her mom was only eighteen. To women in situations like her mother's, she said: "I just want to . . . encourage everybody to keep your babies." Let us encourage you to go see *Moana*, which deserves to succeed — and drop Disney a line about your support for Nicole Scherzinger, who is doubtless catching heat for her outspoken stand.

The film itself is a beautiful retelling of a classic Polynesian folktale that explores the origin of evil — and traces it, poignantly, to parents' rejecting the life of their child.

In this myth, the world of islands and ocean that Polynesians knew — and explored in heroic journeys across thousands of miles of uncharted seas — was once a tranquil, Edenic place full of harmony and abundance, the gift of a nature goddess called Te Fiti. It was from her heart, a gleaming pounamu stone, that she drew the power to give life and raise new islands in the ocean where people might live.

But a demigod named Maui craved this power, and to gain it, he stole her heart. So far, it sounds a lot like the story of the Serpent tempting Adam and Eve in the Garden. But Maui isn't Satan. He isn't evil and envious, but lonely and insecure — because, we find out in the course of the story, his own human parents rejected him at birth and threw him in the ocean to drown. Saved by the gods ("Though my parents threw me away, the gods thought I was worthy of protection," he says), he spends his life doing good deeds for men — sometimes misguided ones.

It turns out that Maui had planned to share Te Fiti's power with mortal men, to gain the love he desperately craved, which his parents denied him. What happens instead is ugly: Having robbed nature of a gift that is rightly divine, Maui finds that he brought down a wave of destruction, want, and pestilence. Te Fiti no longer gives life, and the islands are dying one by one. So Maui is less like the Serpent in Genesis than like Adam: foolish, rebellious, and finally penitent.

The story begins when the young Moana learns that her beloved island is next. The wave of death that Maui set loose in the world washes up on its shores. The coconut trees start to wither, and the sea is emptied of fish. Moana learns, through a series of entertaining plot twists, that she must sail alone to hunt down Maui and force him to return the godlike gift that man was never meant to have.

While we don't want to shoehorn this traditional Polynesian tale into a modern or Western frame, there is enormous resonance here for us in our times. If we think of the gift God gave us of taking part in the creation of new human beings, we can see how man's attempt to impose his own control over this solemn, sacred process has distorted and poisoned our culture. Birth rates have plummeted all around the world, and philosophers actually question whether it is moral or not to have children. Radical environmentalists look at the precious feet of newborns and think of their "carbon footprints." What they miss, of course, is that the only real reason people care about the environment is to leave a decent world for their offspring. Take that away, and people live only for the moment.

Couples who have missed the chance to have families when they are young turn to artificial techniques like IVF — which leave behind thousands of tiny, frozen babies in labs all around the world, which scientists want to harvest for spare parts and experiments. Add to that the global tragedy of abortion, and you'll see that this Polynesian story isn't exotic or quaint. It is potently relevant to Americans today, and Christians who care about the sanctity of life. See it with your kids, and use the story as a teaching moment to let them know about how too many modern people are grasping at godlike power — at the price of precious innocents whose lives God really has entrusted to our power and our protection.

Mark Moses Was a Mensch

January 1, 2017

Governor of Hawaii David Ige offered public condolences to a bereaved family and ordered that flags be flown at half-mast throughout the state. Former Hawaii State Representative Mark Moses has gone to his eternal reward.

These are the proper rituals to observe at the passing of a U.S. Marine, a tireless public servant, and a great man. But as I attended his funeral and offered my own sympathies to his wife and children, I couldn't shake the feeling that so much more should be done in honor of Mark Moses's legacy.

In my mid-twenties, I was looking for purpose and direction. I'd met a lot of good men in the military, and I looked up to them, but they each had a disorienting mixture of virtues and flaws. I desperately needed a role model, and I found one in Mark Moses.

He was the first complete man I'd come across. He was a man of stark practicality, but he cared deeply for his community. He was a civic-minded public figure yet also a devoted family man. He was the very opposite of an ideologue — you couldn't fit his positions neatly under Progressivism or Conservatism or any other capital-lettered "ism" — but there was nothing ambiguous about his worldview either.

If I had to sum him up in a word, it would be the word that, to this day, makes me think of him whenever I hear it: Mark Moses was a mensch. And it's because he was a mensch that he lived up to his robustly Jewish surname, Moses.

When Mark was considering me for the role of chief of staff, he said to me, "I'm a city planner, and you're a visionary. Your head is in the clouds, and mine is in the streets. We'll make a good team." It was a compliment that would stay with me during my time in his office — partly because it wasn't flattery. For him, hiring a "visionary" to help him serve his district was every bit as practical as hiring a plumber to help fix a leaky faucet.

As a recent political science graduate, I was brimming with ideas — a lot of them good but none of them tethered to the day-to-day realities of tending to the needs of the people in Hawaii House District 42.

Mark would patiently listen to me ramble on about political philosophy or religion. Then he'd laugh a good-natured laugh, brush my ideas aside, and bring the conversation back down to street names, stop-sign locations, Little League baseball fields, and school buildings.

He led by example, and I came to admire his unwavering, nose-to-the-grindstone attention to the simple worries of his community. "Rep., you're a great politician," I remember saying to him. "Why don't you run for mayor — or even governor?" But he already had his work cut out for him in District 42, and he would never think of leaving it behind unfinished.

There was nothing abstract about his work. His mission was as primal and focused as the task of plowing and sowing a field to feed a family. He just wanted to see his community built up for his own family and others just like his. That's why he was so happy to be where he was, in the statehouse. He never looked up from his work, his community, and his family long enough to get aspirations for higher office or for wider recognition or fame.

In fact, rather than trying to outdo his would-be opponents (he was a Republican representative in a sea of Democrats), he worked hard at being respectful, honest, and cooperative with everyone in the community. He would often dispatch me to help out at various Democrats' offices. "Jason, I'd like you to go and lend a hand at another office today. Get to know them, help them put their documents together for committee, and just be useful to them. They have more work to get done today than we do here."

Twenty years ago, I visited Mark Moses's deathbed.

Decades before it finally took him, he was already battling Lupus. When I walked into his hospital room, he asked me directly if I thought he was dying.

"Sir, I should call your family. I think you need to spend this time with them."

After a pause, he chuckled weakly. "I'm not going to die," he said with a wave of his hand. "Now get out those papers. We have a lot of bills to get through." As I worked alongside him that night at Tripler Medical Center, it struck me how appropriate it was that this seemingly invincible man was called "Moses."

Though Mark was a committed Jew, he never fancied himself a "visionary." He didn't see himself the bearer of some enlightened ideology. He was just another tribesman of District 42, with all the same reasons to flee Egypt as any other person — but with an added dose of responsibility to seek the promised land with care and competence.

He was the complete man, and his compass was intact.

There's an old phrase used to describe high-minded men who lack character and work ethic: "The man is too heavenly minded to be any earthly good." Well, maybe what made Mark Moses a mensch was being so earthly minded that Heaven couldn't help but take notice and bless his endeavors.

Make no mistake: Men like Mark Moses are the real visionaries. It's just that their visions aren't in the clouds but imprinted here on earth, in the city streets that occupied Mark's mind for all those years, in places like Kapolei, where I now live. His vision wasn't only hoped for but worked for. And after all the devoted attention he and others like him paid to this community, to building proposals, parks, and schools, a vision has become a reality.

It's no coincidence that Kapolei is now known as Oahu's "Second City." Mark was one of the driving forces behind this town's becoming the fastest-growing urban center in the United States.

I used to chuckle a little at his scrupulous plans, his daily labors, his tireless efforts to gain resources — all for a city that didn't really yet exist. But now my family and I live in a housing development in Kapolei that didn't exist when I first worked with Mark. I drive my kids to karate and ballet classes at businesses that didn't exist, on roads that didn't exist. I do my writing and my research at a library that didn't exist — the second-largest library in Hawaii!

I still can't shake the feeling that so much more should be done to honor my mentor's legacy. We Little Leaguers, library-goers, and homeowners owe a debt to Mark Moses's part in the world we live in, and it's a debt that we can never repay.

But what we can do is keep ourselves grounded and care deeply for our neighbors' well-being, just as he did. Take advantage of the good groundwork that people like Mark Moses lay for us and our families, but do so gratefully and — most importantly — preserve it.

These are the proper rituals to observe at the passing of great men.

Unplanned: The *Uncle Tom's Cabin* of the Pro-Life Movement

February 25, 2019

When Harriet Beecher Stowe wrote the novel *Uncle Tom's Cabin,* could she have guessed its impact? That slavery would die less than fifteen years later?

When I watched a screening of the new film *Unplanned,* due for release March 29, I was filled with hope and conviction. I thought: "This film might turn the tide on abortion."

Unplanned is the true story of Abby Johnson. She was an ambitious Planned Parenthood employee who went on to become a heroic defender of women and preborn children.

The film tells the truth about abortion so movingly that it earned an R rating. So a fifteen-year-old girl can get an abortion without even her parents' knowledge but can't walk in alone to see *Unplanned.*

Unplanned can be the *Uncle Tom's Cabin* of the abortion issue. And today's pro-life movement can be the movement that drives its success.

Historians credit *Uncle Tom's Cabin* with spurring the anti-slavery movement to victory. But that credit extends beyond its author. It also goes to those who published, promoted, and simply bought and read the book.

It's thanks to countless Abolitionist heroes that *Uncle Tom's Cabin* became the bestselling novel of the nineteenth century — and the second-bestselling book of any genre, after the Bible.

Today the pro-life movement is the largest, most diverse social and political movement in history. It's stronger every year. A recent Marist poll reports a stark sea change in recent months:

> Americans are now as likely to identify as pro-life (47 percent) as pro-choice (47 percent). Just last month, a similar survey conducted by The Marist Poll found Americans more likely to identify as pro-choice than as pro-life by 17 percentage points (55 to 38 percent). Democrats moved in their pro-life identity from 20 percent to 34 percent.

Part of this shift in opinion? It's because people are seeing what pro-choice politicians really want: abortion for any reason at all, up to the very moment of birth (and sometimes after), in fifty states of the union. I guess some thanks are due to Virginia Gov. Ralph Northam, for admitting that he backs infanticide.

Our movement steadily gains new members from every background and walk of life. It unites people you would never expect to converge.

But we do converge, on the protection of the most vulnerable member of the human family, the child in the womb.

We are millions strong, and this is our *Uncle Tom's Cabin* moment.

I've always believed in the power of movies. They can change hearts and minds and even shape the laws of a nation. That's why I founded the pro-life/whole-life organization Movie to Movement.

As an executive producer of the film *Bella*, my hope was to inspire women to choose life. After *Bella*'s release, we received more than a thousand messages from mothers who said our movie spoke to them during their pregnancies and moved them to choose life.

Emboldened by the success of *Bella*, I went on to work on the productions of over ten films and the marketing of over fifty, including *Voiceless, Sing a Little Louder*, and *Crescendo*. Over the years, my hopes and ambitions grew.

I began to hope I could be the man who would make the movie that would end abortion.

But when I watched *Unplanned* last week, the thought of another anti-slavery hero humbled me.

God didn't want me to make this movie. He wanted a Planned Parenthood Employee of the Year to make this movie. Just as He wanted John Newton, once the captain of a slave ship, to write the hymn "Amazing Grace."

Although we didn't get to write the song, what a privilege it is that we get to sing along.

The abortion syndicate knows how powerful movies are. That's why virtually no outlets in the MSM even reviewed the last powerful pro-life movie, *Gosnell*. It quickly went to video — and you should make a point of frustrating the censors by watching it. But if you want to really drive them crazy, help make *Unplanned* the hit it richly deserves to be.

How You Can Plant the Seeds of the *Next* Notre Dame Cathedral

April 17, 2019

Few of us were thinking clearly on Monday. Christians and lovers of beauty suffered poleaxed astonishment at the burning of Notre Dame. It's too early to know if it will be rebuilt correctly(that is, exactly as it was before the fire). Or if the multiculturalists dominating France and Europe will pervert the building into some "multi-use, multi-faith" structure that mocks the reason for Notre Dame's founding: to be a witness to the Incarnation of Jesus, through His Mother. It's too soon to know if arson was involved. Paris authorities claimed in less than twenty-four hours to have ruled that out. How convenient, given the political explosiveness of any other conclusion. As FaithWire reported of France:

> In the month of February alone, some 10 incidents of vandalism and desecration of Catholic churches were reported across the European country. According to Anglican Mainstream, on average, two French churches are desecrated every single day.

We don't know if the near destruction of France's most iconic historic building — which survived the Revolution and two world wars — will spark a renewal of patriotism, faith, or love for tradition. We certainly hope for all three. France won't last much longer, politically or demographically, without them.

We face so many known unknowns. But here's one thing we do know. The spirit that built Notre Dame, in an age when Vikings still raided France's borders, and Saracens threatened its coasts, is the spirit of the future — if we are to have one. It's the faith that life has meaning, because Someone meant us to live and died to redeem us. And the hope that plants an olive tree that our sons and grandsons can harvest. And the love that drives us to want and welcome children, whatever the cost, as new souls whom God has seen fit to entrust to our protection.

No great art has ever emerged from genuine despair. There are no cathedrals of cynicism that anyone would visit. The "interesting," minor works that emerge from anguish, dread, and angry rebellion? They rarely age well. Is there anything more dreary to read today than Voltaire's sophomoric *Candide*? Are there any buildings more soul sucking than the brutalist monoliths that fashionable collectivists imposed on us in the '70s? Does anyone go to the concert hall to hear modern composers dismantle the tonal system?

Great works need greatness of soul, or magnanimity. Souls need bodies. That means we must welcome life, with all its messiness and suffering, its confusions and failures. As Huxley foresaw, in a Brave New World where mere pleasure and comfort were the highest goals, there would be no need or hope of art — or love or memory. Just a dull, sub-erotic numbness that we designate as "pleasure," between the test tube and the tomb.

Artists are only human. Sometimes they're prodigious sinners. Often they point to darkness and strife from which we'd rather avert our eyes. But every one of the great makers was united in this: He rejected shallow hedonism as a philosophy of life.

One way we can respond to the very great evil of Notre Dame's near-destruction is to fertilize the soil from which such artworks grow. We must prayerfully, faithfully nurture a genuine Culture of Life. As I wrote the day after the fire:

> Yesterday, I watched in horror as Notre Dame Cathedral in Paris was suddenly engulfed in flames.
>
> This beautiful landmark, which has been standing for half of Christendom, appeared to be lost forever. However, miraculously, it is still standing today.
>
> When my friend, actor Eduardo Verastegui, was on a tour of Notre Dame in 2009, he learned that the Christians who built the cathedral envisioned a work of art that would last until the Lord returns.
>
> As we reflected on the story, we were inspired to create a work of art that would be a landmark sharing the dignity of the child in the womb until our Lord returned. *Crescendo,* the short film we produced, was inspired by Notre Dame.
>
> Like the witness Notre Dame bears to God's longing to repair His relationship with the human family, I believe the Lord is calling each of us to do a beautiful work that will last for generations to come. That vision begins by

> cherishing the weak, protecting the vulnerable, and doing everything we can to preserve life, liberty, and the pursuit of happiness for us and our posterity.

Crescendo did more than inspire people with the tale of a famous crisis pregnancy. It raised more than $6 million for crisis pregnancy centers. Those little, humble facilities are more like Notre Dame in their way than many more lavish buildings. They help women say yes to God, say yes to life, as the Virgin Mary once did, in equally troubling circumstances.

By all means, pray and donate to help rebuild Notre Dame. But your work in defense of life lays the foundations for the Notre Dames of the future, for the symphonies, poems, novels, songs, and paintings that arise only from a culture unafraid of life and steeled for suffering — preferably by faith in a Lord who suffered with us and for us.

One last note of hope we can offer. The spirit that built Notre Dame still burns today. Eduardo Verastegui is one of its torchbearers. As Fox News reports:

> The world's biggest statue of Jesus is coming to one of the most dangerous parts of Mexico.
>
> Eduardo Verastegui, a prominent Mexican Catholic actor and pro-life advocate, plans to build the statue called "Christ of Peace" at a towering 252 feet, nearly twice the size of Rio de Janeiro's Christ the Redeemer, which stands at 125 feet in Brazil. The current record holder is Christ the King statue in Poland, which is 172 feet high.
>
> Promoters say it will show "a message of faith, love, hope, and peace" to Ciudad Victoria, the capital of Tamaulipas, a state that borders Texas along the U.S.-Mexico border. The state has recently been rocked by violent confrontations between security forces and drug dealers, but Verastegui said the purpose of the project is to leave a legacy of peace in the region.

Goodbye to a Good Dad

August 12, 2019

Two weeks ago today, I left home for what I knew was going to be a great adventure: meetings with "the beautiful people" in Napa, filming a TV show in Washington, D.C., and a movie in Rome, and then on to Istanbul.

On the last day at the Napa Institute conference, I got a phone call that the man who raised me and my brothers and sisters, the most gentle man I have ever known, was fighting for his life. By the grace of God, I was able to be with him for the last days of his life. Taking the night shift, I was by his side from 9 p.m. to 5 a.m.

My pop, Al Malekovic, was a loving and simple man. He told me his only fear was never to see his "babies again." When he couldn't drift off to sleep, he would say the names of all his children over and over.

You should know that the man I call Pop is the biological father of only two of my brothers. But he loved all seven of us as his own and signed the birth certificates of five of us. On my last night with the man I call Daddy Al, we prayed the Rosary, talked about why God allows suffering, and when he was sleeping, I would meditate on all of my memories of Al, starting with the earliest I could remember.

He entered my life before I was two. My first memory is Al carrying a huge cardboard box up the stairs. He has a big mustache and on his head a hat that old Slavic men wear.

"Jase! I got us a Zenith color TV! It's made in America." Dinner almost every night was the same thing: hamburgers on Wonder bread with a pickle and hash browns. Al would ask each of the kids, "Do you want one piece of cheese or two on your hash browns?" The question was asked with pride. He was happy we could be so decadent to have two pieces of cheese.

When I was in the fourth grade, he took the family to Red Lobster for the first and last time. The trip to Red Lobster was all the evidence I needed to know we were rich. Only rich people can afford lobster. That and our stay at a Holiday Inn. It had a pool with lights. At night it would glow a bright aqua green. The hotel had an arcade, and on every floor, there was a vending machine.

Al's religion was baseball, and my religion was football and martial arts. Al never missed a game or tournament from Pop Warner on and would watch most of my practices. He would lean up against his rust-orange clunker drinking beer, watching us practice, then drive off without a word before practice ended so I could ride my bike home with my friends.

The other adults in our life may have been thoughtless and destructive. But Al was always working to keep us happy. And although he struggled with alcoholism until his early fifties, he never said a mean word to any of us. He was never harsh or cruel. He was always "present" for us. Every afternoon when he left for work — he was a bartender at the legendary Gino's Steakhouse in Harvey, Illinois — my heart would break.

As his children began to have children, Al would continue to play the role of the quiet caregiver. Practically deaf and blind, he would make the trip to Hawaii every year. He'd spend months helping my wife with the children when I would be on my trips. Al insisted on doing this at his own expense even though he lived off a small retirement from his twenty years of working as a custodian at an elementary school. When Big Al kicked the booze, he'd had to leave his profession as a bartender behind.

Several years ago, I asked my wife for a password to one of her accounts. "It's Malekovic2005," she said. I found this amazing because my passwords have always had Malekovic in them. (Note to self: Change passwords.) Then last year, I asked my son Max for his password, and he told me, "Malekovic."

Al Malekovic was more than a father to those of us who lived under his roof. Countless friends of my siblings and I see Al as a father.

People often ask me, "Where do you think your love and commitment to protecting children come from?" I would always answer, "I don't know. Isn't it natural for men to want to love, nurture, and protect children?" But as I sat next to my dad meditating on our life together, the obvious struck me. "It was Big Al. Big Al taught me how to love."

Social Media Bullying and Porn Made Gen Z into "Snowflakes"

December 21, 2019

The Stream senior editor John Zmirak interviews *The Stream* senior contributor Jason Scott Jones about *No Safe Spaces,* the exciting new documentary.

JOHN ZMIRAK (JZ). I watched *No Safe Spaces,* starring conservative radio host and author Dennis Prager and the world's biggest podcaster, Adam Carolla. It's a wonderfully well-made, gripping exposé. It shows how young people, especially students, increasingly reject our Constitution. You're helping to get the film to college audiences. Can you tell us more about it?

JASON JONES (JJ). A majority of people surveyed under age twenty-six don't approve of the First Amendment itself. They think that speech that they hate amounts to "hate speech." And it shouldn't be legal. Colleges, social media giants, and the Mainstream Media ought to collude in repressing it. The government shouldn't protect it and maybe should even punish it.

That has me worried. The best thing about America, about the whole Anglo political tradition, is freedom — not license. Developing the virtues and living up to the dignity God implanted in every human being whom He made in His image. Protecting yourself and your family from violence. Exercising your basic political rights to speak out. Freely practicing your religion in the public square. Arguing frankly and courageously about ideas. These are the core values our soldiers and sailors, airmen and Marines fought for over centuries. They're the things that people in less happy parts of the world often say they want. Think of the Uyghurs in China, the protestors in Hong Kong, the Kurds, Yazidis, and Christians fighting Islamist gangs in Syria.

These values are the beating heart of freedom. They're what you and I wrote about in *The Race to Save Our Century*. To see young people afraid of such freedoms is heartbreaking to me as an American and as a parent. My sons and daughters will have to live in the society that results.

JZ. A big theme of the film is that education is meant to strengthen young people, to build up their intellectual and emotional immune systems. Can you talk about that?

JJ. In a liberal society, we don't educate people by hammering precepts into their heads until they're zealots. We teach our system's basic principles but expose people to angry, even extreme critiques of it. That way, they learn how to answer such critiques, maybe learn from them, while remaining committed to freedom. Nassim Nicholas Taleb speaks of antifragility as the natural outcome of that.

By the grace of God, people become stronger by repeatedly encountering challenges and questions. So respecting the dignity of the human person also produces a stronger society. I want a society that allows people to reach for God. Freedom makes that possible. Totalitarian, dogmatic, theocratic societies cramp the human person, prevent the person's authentic search for God. A Muslim friend of mine, an Iraqi general, told me what was unique about America to him. He didn't see Muslims anywhere but saw Islam everywhere, because he saw people reaching constantly for God.

Intellectual challenges, clashes of culture, religious questions and answers. These are the things we need to help our young people to welcome, by giving them solid grounding in our own beliefs and culture. By teaching them logic, rhetoric, history, and other crucial disciplines that let them courageously face a world full of differences, deceptions, even threats. Without that grounding, they're clay in the hands of the secular culture. It wants to shape them into fragile, reactive, and finally obedient consumers. Tame voters whom elites can command via memes, group shaming, and propaganda news reports.

As Dennis Prager says, "America is meant to be the ultimate safe space," where each of us can freely speak and learn. That's the natural outcome of our liberal tradition and the antifragility it produces.

JZ. *No Safe Spaces* shows that our society seems to be aimed at doing the opposite of making young people strong.

JJ. Absolutely! From helicopter parenting to suppressing sex and cultural differences in primary school to censoring free speech in college. We're treating kids like fragile "snowflakes" who will melt down at the first hint of heat. Unprepared to face challenges, they freak out and sometimes turn violent when someone as mainstream as Ben Shapiro disagrees with them.

In some areas, we have overprotected this generation and treated them like the "boy in the plastic bubble." But in other, more crucial arenas? We've left Generation Z completely vulnerable, failed to do our one job of guaranteeing for them a decent, safe childhood and adolescence. If Generation Z has a lot of "snowflakes," whose fault is that? It's ours. We've been running the snow-making machine.

JZ. What exactly do you mean?

JJ. We've offered the current cohort of students, Generation Z, a much less safe life than you and I had. Even though we were riding bikes without helmets, sitting in cars without seatbelts, breathing our parents' secondhand smoke, and eating Chef Boyardee. But we were much, much safer in the important ways than the people heading off to college today.

We didn't grow up with smartphones that let bullies photograph every dumb-looking thing we were wearing. Or the stupid looks on our faces when we tripped and fell. Then post it on Instagram to everyone in our school, even our neighborhood. If you threw up after a high school party or got an ugly mullet, there was zero chance of it becoming a meme that thousands of people laughed at. Ugly gossip, degrading nicknames, dirt about our families — none of that went to a worldwide audience via Facebook.

Being a young person nowadays is in some ways like being a celebrity, with paparazzi following you everywhere. Waiting for you to screw up so they can pounce and share it with the world.

Unless you've stuck your head underground for the past five years, you've likely noticed the growing reams of stories detailing the apparent correlation between the Internet, smartphone technology, and a striking rise in mental illness in young people. San Diego State University psychologist Jean Twenge has written about this in detail, noting how youth depression and anxiety and suicide attempts have surged since 2009. This, of course, is when smartphones began to take over the world.

It wasn't till I watched this film for the tenth time and talked to college students about it that I realized the truth. This isn't a generation of snowflakes who want college to be a safe space because they're weak. It's a generation that has never had a safe space in its life.

JZ. What's the other main area where we've left young people cruelly vulnerable?

JJ. Pornography, of course. It's everywhere, pouring through every sixth grader's smartphone, whether we realize it or not. My friend Destiny Herndon-De La Rosa wrote about it recently in *The Dallas Morning News*. Her sixth-grade daughter was traumatized that her boy classmates were watching rape porn and laughing at it — then sending it to her and other girls as a joke. Did you and I have to deal with garbage like that?

The porn that's out there now isn't centerfolds of adult models. No, you'll find instead sadistic videos of trafficked girls. Thousands and thousands of videos, which boys can spend hours clicking from one to another. The websites figure out what pushes their buttons and send them to similar stuff, always a little bit "edgier," more perverted. How is that affecting them?

We're just starting to find out. Pascal-Emmanuel Gobry published a major essay on the crippling effects of regular porn use. Not just the collapse in real-life male sexual performance but even the decline of desire — the virtual disappearance of dating in countries like Japan, for example. He also points to brain research that shows an atrophy in crucial areas of the brain, associated with addiction to online porn. We're not protecting our kids from that.

We let them grow up traumatized by the ugliest, nastiest videos that the Marquis de Sade could have dreamed up, badgered and humiliated by online shaming, gossip, and groupthink. All of this the Left (and many libertarians) pretend is what the First Amendment was meant to protect.

No wonder these kids feel fragile. Big surprise that they want to be protected from something. Sadly, the only thing our culture is willing to "protect" them from is … dissenting ideas, other people's religious beliefs, political arguments — the very things, in other words, that our Constitution was written to protect.

When Gen Z kids bitterly say, "Okay, Boomer" to dismiss the opinion of anyone over the age of twenty-six … this is the source of that bitterness.

So I hope people see this film, to see just how much damage the wrong kind of freedom has inflicted on young people and the extent to which this has driven them to fear and reject true freedom, of the kind our Founders wanted.

Rebuke Injustice with the Force of Law: *Divided Hearts of America*

September 22, 2020

In the desert, the devil tried to tempt Jesus Christ Himself by trotting out Scripture quotes. Even the best maxims, from divinely inspired authors, can be misused and turned to evil. That's what I recall when putative "pro-lifers" choose the eve of a life-changing election to suddenly remind us "Politics is downstream of culture." Sometimes they'll get really philosophical and muse, "Give me the songs of the city, and I care not who writes the laws."

As someone who has spent the past twenty years making, producing, and distributing films that affirm the sanctity of life and defend the vulnerable, I have an answer: "Ya think?"

It took decades of solemn movies decrying racism and thousands of news stories in the national press to shame white Americans about segregation and legal racism. Those culture-moving productions helped prepare the way for the Civil Rights Act of 1964.

But what should a black American have said to someone who told him, in that era, not to support that law — because culture, not law, was crucial to rectifying injustice? What did civil rights leaders think of those who opposed anti-racist laws, insisting instead on only "building anti-racist culture"?

We actually have the answer. Rev. Martin Luther King's "Letter from Birmingham Jail" was aimed at "white moderates" who denied their black fellow citizens the remedy of law. Instead, they should rely on "changing hearts."

As Rev. King wrote, the

> great stumbling block in the stride toward freedom is not the White Citizens Councillor or the Ku Klux Klanner but the white moderate who is more devoted to order than to justice; who prefers a negative peace which is the absence of tension to a positive peace which is the presence of justice; who constantly says, "I agree with you in the goal you seek, but I

> can't agree with your methods of direct action"; who paternalistically feels that he can set the timetable for another man's freedom; who lives by the myth of time; and who constantly advises the Negro to wait until a "more convenient season."

I agree with Rev. King. Today the roadblock holding us back from protecting unborn children is not so much the abortion profiteers, like Kermit Gosnell and Planned Parenthood. It's the tepid, half-convinced pro-lifer who doesn't really believe what his words plainly say.

If you believe that abortion is the killing of innocent children, of course you want the law to ban such a wicked, cruel practice. If you believe it isn't, then why should you even want the culture to discourage it? Why not leave women alone?

Perhaps the cruelest possible stance to take is this halfway position. You claim that abortion is not quite so bad that you want the government to ban it. You want to let almost a million women per year go ahead and do it. But then you want movies, TV, books, and social media to make them feel terrible about having done so.

Pro-choicers have followed this logic to its endpoint. That's why they're goading women to "shout their abortions." If it's such a wholesome, natural practice, why not shout it — the way people shout their everythings these days, from their favorite microbrew to their sex-change operations.

But the natural law written on the human heart says otherwise. And not many women are actually happy or proud of having abortions. Millions have broken hearts. Our job as pro-life advocates isn't to rub salt in their wounds. It's to use the law to stop the abortion industry from carving up more human hearts, as we use the police to stop thieves from holding up banks. The law is a powerful teacher and ought to serve the powerless.

That's the purpose of humane art — to change enough hearts so that we can change the laws and stop the cycle of heartbreak. And that's why I'm proud both to be active in this year's presidential election, and of my latest work with Movie to Movement. At this crucial time for our nation, we have just released a powerful new film.

Divided Hearts of America reminds our nation at this critical time of the importance of America's Declaration principle. Our country's existence wasn't justified on self-interest, raw power, or mindless tribalism. No, the men who risked bankruptcy and hanging to declare its independence explicitly made their case for a whole new country on theological grounds. Man is made to be free, with rights no one may tread on, because he's the image of God.

Abraham Lincoln, who did more than anyone to apply this principle universally to all Americans, said sagely that the Constitution was a sturdy, well-crafted frame. But the artwork it protected was the Declaration of Independence.

The central truth of America, which drove its Founders, abolitionists, suffragettes, civil rights activists, and pro-lifers, is simple, profound, and timeless. Man is the child of God and, as such, shares in His inviolable dignity. Each innocent human life is the Ark of the Covenant: Touch it and die.

Will We Kneel to the New God, Equality? Or Will We Rebel, like Harrison Bergeron?

November 5, 2020

As you read this, President Trump's lawyers are fighting the Democrats' voter-fraud coup d'etat. We're not experts in election law, so we can't tell you whether their fight will prevail or if the Democrats will finally reap the reward for four long years of unpatriotic "Resistance." Will the coalition of Deep State spies, media monopolies, urban vote fraudsters, and arrogant elites cancel yet another election? We don't know. We recommend prayer and fasting for the sake of our troubled country.

But what if it works? What if the fix is in? How should we deal with that very real possibility? How can we stand it? Should we just write off politics altogether, withdraw from the world as best we can?

To answer that real temptation, we suggest the great short story "Harrison Bergeron," by Kurt Vonnegut. The premise of that story is simple, laid out in its first few lines:

> The year was 2081, and everybody was finally equal. They weren't only equal before God and the law. They were equal every which way. Nobody was smarter than anybody else. Nobody was better looking than anybody else. Nobody was stronger or quicker than anybody else. All this equality was due to the 211th, 212th, and 213th Amendments to the Constitution, and to the unceasing vigilance of agents of the United States Handicapper General.
>
> Anyone whose intelligence was much above normal had a little mental handicap radio in his ear. He was required by law to wear it at all times. It was tuned to a government transmitter. Every twenty seconds or so, the transmitter would send out some sharp noise to keep people . . . from taking unfair advantage of their brains.

The hero of the story, a fourteen-year-old boy named Harrison, gets himself in trouble with the law. He rebels against this nightmarish future America. He flouts its totalitarian efforts at imposed equality. He rejects a world where good-looking people must wear hideous masks, and athletic people wear crippling weights. Harrison thumbs his nose at the "handicappers" who drag everyone down to the lowest common denominator.

It's obvious why this story is applicable today. The Democrat candidate for vice president, Kamala Harris, makes that obvious in a video she released. In it, she insists that the government's job is to impose equality of results, not opportunity. She calls this enforced sameness "equity."

Now blatant voter fraud and media blackouts may impose such a regime in America, via a presidential candidate directly indebted and subject to blackmail by our enemy, Communist China.

Will we rebel like Harrison? If so, we must count the cost. In the story, Harrison mounts a personal revolt in the most public, symbolic fashion. He interrupts a televised ballet performance, where the lovely, graceful dancers clunk around in ugly masks and crippling weights. Harrison announces that he rejects the regime of egalitarian tyranny. He strips off his humiliating costume and grabs one beautiful ballerina. He tears off her mask and handicap weights. Then together, they perform just one exquisite, perfect dance routine — to show the world what excellence really looks like.

Before Harrison's revolt can awaken a spark in any other unquiet spirits, the Handicapper General herself storms into the studio and onto the stage. She shoots Harrison dead and his dance partner too. And the world goes back to normal.

That's how ideology works. When exceptional men and women stand against it, it summons all its power and tries to destroy them. That's what the Left did to Donald Trump and those who support him, from Gen. Mike Flynn to Nicholas Sandmann, from Kyle Rittenhouse to Carter Page. It's what Twitter did to *The New York Post* for reporting on Hunter Biden. Look for a Biden administration to break Tony Bobulinski for exposing the Biden ties to China. And if you cross the Deep State, the Bidens, or their enablers, will try to break you too.

Are you ready to pay the price, to carry the cross? Or will you take the safe, peaceful path and hide? There's a lot of great stuff on Netflix. Uber Eats will still bring you nachos. You can't speak your mind or live out your faith in the new America, but you're perfectly free to climb into a bottle. Vent your frustrations on video games, once they confiscate your guns. Wave farewell to your kids as they drift away from you, to the new church of Woke social justice with forty-seven genders. Just wear the nice mask that hides your face and repeat the happy slogans that mask your thoughts.

"The King Is Dead, Long Live the Queen!" Dave Chappelle Challenges the Puppet Masters of the LGBT Movement

October 26, 2021

The role of the jester is to challenge the king and to speak uncomfortable truths to him that no one else dares to say.

But to do that, you first have to know who the king is. And when I watched Dave Chappelle's 2019 special "Sticks & Stones," I thought he'd done something absolutely brilliant: He'd become the first comedian to recognize that there was a new king.

See, at the time, most comedians pointed all their jabs at the long-dead kings of the past. The white racialists, like Planned Parenthood founder Margaret Sanger, who dominated the American and European intelligentsia in the early twentieth century. The cynics who promoted a shallow veneer of "patriarchy" and "patriotism" in postwar America and used the very real threat of Communism as a foil for empowering thoughtless corporatists and power-hungry politicians, while suppressing artists and innovators.

That's why so much of today's standup aims at the easy targets: the white Southern conservative, the Trump supporter, or the devoutly Christian middle-American. Because those modern tropes — while their real-world embodiments are, in fact, relatively powerless today — serve as vague personifications of the archetypal power broker of the past.

Dave Chappelle is more than a comedian. He's also a teacher.

Instead, Chappelle called out the current king: leaders of causes like the LGBT movement. He had the insight of a true jester and recognized the "alphabet people" for what they really were: not marginalized upstarts just vying for the right to live out their eccentricities but calculating executives and political moguls trying to use a sympathetic cause to further empower an already-powerful elite.

"The king is dead, long live the king!" That's what I told my friends after watching the 2019 special. I thought I was being pretty clever.

But then came this year's special, "The Closer," which made me realize that Chappelle's insight and instinct as a jester go even deeper than I thought.

Chappelle brought up DaBaby early in his set. The rapper got into hot water shortly before Chappelle was slated to record the special. Specifically, DaBaby was being "canceled" for committing an unthinkable crime: He made "homophobic" remarks during a recent show tour.

Chappelle used DaBaby's plight to hammer home just how unmistakably the LGBT movement rules over America today. You see, DaBaby once "killed a n***a" at a Walmart, Chappelle said, and "nothing bad happened to his career. Do you see where I'm going with this? In our country, you can shoot and kill a n***a, but you better not hurt a gay person's feelings."

And here's where Chappelle pulled the mask off the king. "Is it possible for a gay person to be racist?" he asked. And then the feint: "Of course it is. Look at Mike Pence."

Now, does Chappelle really believe former vice president Mike Pence is gay? No, it's a joke. But like every other syllable in Chappelle's masterful set, the joke was meticulously planned — and it served a purpose.

I mentioned how too many comedians today use easy targets as the butt of their jokes. Chappelle knows that, so he served up a joke to fit the mold. But who was his real target? It's as if he set up the easy, conventional target of a white-haired, Midwestern conservative, and — in the split second before the joke landed — slipped in the true king: the LGBT mogul.

The puppet masters of the LGBT movement have gone hard after Chappelle, accusing him of hating and fomenting violence against "transpersons." That's an unmistakable lie. In his set, Chappelle went out of his way to differentiate between the LGBT political machine and transgender individuals like his dear friend the late comedian Daphne Dorman.

In fact, he defended Dorman against the thoughtless cruelty of the LGBT movement — which tormented Dorman to the point of suicide for not fully conforming to the movement's ever-changing marching orders.

But while it is a lie, the movement's campaign to punish Chappelle does prove the truth of his assertion; that they are, in fact, the king. And that true bravery isn't to be found among those who hide behind the king's skirts but among those who confront him and stand in solidarity with those of whom he says: "Off with their heads!"

Days after Netflix released "The Closer," a group of pro-trans activists held a walkout protest against Chappelle. They demanded that Netflix remove the special. More broadly, they made clear that dissenting voices like Chappelle's should have no place at all in American public life.

A single counterprotester joined the crowd holding a sign that read simply: "We like Dave. Jokes are funny." The activists assaulted the man, tore his sign off the stick he'd attached it to, and then shouted, "He's got a weapon!" pointing to the stick.

Shouting those words and pointing toward someone in a crowd with a police presence is, in my view, exactly what it looks like. If they wanted him dead, they wouldn't have done anything differently.

Moments later, they also shoved up against the counterprotester. In a particularly striking visual from someone's camera phone, you can see a small woman with a crew cut cornering the guy — a stocky young man who stood well over six feet — while several of her friends hem him in with shouts and noisemakers.

This is not the behavior of an endangered minority pushing fearfully back against some powerful representative of "systemic" white power. These protesters — all of them white, from what I could see — are the systemic power.

They're aristocrats — courtiers to the king. You can see it in their cocksure actions, which you can tell they feel confident will bring no negative consequences back on themselves.

(Can you imagine if the roles were reversed? No one, however "transphobic," would forcibly tear an LGBT sign from a protester, then shove and scream at him or her. The consequences would be ruinous for the aggressor, and we all know it.)

And it wasn't just this one protest. All the centers of cultural and political power have spoken in unison in response to Chappelle's special: "Off with his head." And again, it obviously isn't individual, vulnerable transpeople who have the power to marshal the global media against black artists. No, it's just the king and his henchmen.

And as I've watched the reactions to Chappelle, I've been struck by one central fact. The worst of the attacks come from . . . whites.

One white man identifying as a woman published a column saying he's taking away Chappelle's "black card." Another — the white producer of the Netflix film *Dear White People* — called Chappelle "dangerous." GLAAD — a massive political firm headed by a white Episcopalian from Staten Island — accused Chappelle of "inciting hate and violence," literally a potential criminal charge.

The trans movement, you see, is really a white movement. And its henchmen, as Chappelle put it, "are minorities until they need to be white again." And: "I have never had a problem with transgender people. If you listen to what I'm saying clearly, my problem has always been with white people."

Dave Chappelle is more than a comedian. He's also a teacher. I truly learned something from Dave Chappelle's "The Closer."

In 2019, I thought Chappelle was the first comedian to challenge the new king. Now I realize that Chappelle is the first comedian to recognize that there is no new king at all. That the king of today is the same white, Western, male king of the past — only now he's wearing a dress.

That's a lesson that I hope the whole world learns. In fact, far from being "canceled" along with DaBaby, I think Chappelle's special should be memorized by eighth graders all over America, and immigrants should learn key passages along with the Pledge of Allegiance in order to become citizens.

"The king is dead, long live the queen!"

Powerful New Documentary *Alive* Depicts Young People Turning from Atheism and Nazism to Christ

April 20, 2022

Fifteen years ago, in my work in the film industry, I had the privilege of working alongside Lucia Gonzalez. Lucia was a young aspiring filmmaker from Spain. She was interning with Metanoia Films, having worked on *Bella*, and was now working with me on *The Stoning of Soraya M*. My heart leapt when my Hollywood publicist friend Alexis Walkenstein sent me a screener link from a new film being distributed by Lucia Gonzalez-Barandiaran and her company Bosco Films.

I've spent many years making and promoting films for the Christian and family market. I've seen a lot of good intentions and pure motives lead people nowhere, thanks to a failure of craftsmanship. I've also seen wonderful films disappear down the well thanks to botched, misguided marketing. At the same time, I've seen mainstream films with toxic messages produced with consummate skill, promoted by clever marketers who knew how to make them into "phenomena." Our culture gets changed by movies like that, and not for the better.

That's why it's such a pleasure for me to come across a film like *Alive*.

It wasn't expensive to make. There are no special effects or exotic and gorgeous locales. Most of it consists of people talking about their lives. While the film is beautifully shot with exquisite music, what elevates it above the ordinary is simple. It's the presence of God.

The film recounts the lives of three young Spaniards and one middle-aged couple. Each emerged from the slick, secular liberal culture of post-Franco Spain — where faith in God is denigrated and dismissed, treated as a relic of an old fascist regime or, at best, a pastime for old folks. Each of these people's stories shows how God's grace gently but relentlessly pressed against his defenses — seeking a crack of humility where He could overwhelm and reclaim the person.

The film was produced by the vigorous Catholic youth movement Hakuna, which operates worldwide. The movement and the movie are centered on the power of

Christ operating via the Eucharist, the sacrament He instituted with His apostles at the Last Supper. For too many Catholics, this vital sign of God's love has become a hollow symbol or a mechanistic accompaniment to ritual observance.

In *Alive*, we see something different. Each of the people who recounts his conversion story here explains how the Eucharist served as the focal point for something quite new in his life: a personal encounter with Jesus, an ongoing dialogue with Him about who He is, what He wants from us, and what He offers in return.

We meet a young medical student who thought that Christianity was something to console sickly old grandmas with little left to look forward to. When he reluctantly accompanied a friend to a "Holy Hour," he met the God he'd long forgotten. Soon he was sneaking off to services, ashamed to tell his secular parents. But his love for God only deepened, transforming this former Nietzsche fan into a humble, joy-filled Christian. God's slow, inexorable work eventually moved him to "come out" to his parents and friends and admit his faith in Jesus. He's now studying for the priesthood.

A college student lost her beloved boyfriend in an auto accident. She was still grieving when an acquaintance reached out to her in friendship. At first, she was resentful. Upon some self-reflection, she realized that she was envious. She knew that there was some special peace and joy in this person's life, which she'd never known. Eventually, she welcomed this new friend and began joining her for Holy Hours spent cultivating a sense of God's personal presence. Over time, this contemplative prayer transformed her life, allowing her to experience the very same sense of meaning and love.

A middle-aged couple who were go-through-the-motions Christians encountered a crisis: at age forty-eight, the wife discovered she was pregnant, and the pregnancy was in trouble. Together, the couple endured a gauntlet of medical professionals warning them that she would give birth to a "monster" and pressuring her to abort. But the two attended a religious retreat together and started seeking out Jesus in the Eucharist. His presence helped them fend off the terror that gaslighting doctors instilled and trust in God's plan for their lives and their tiny child. (We see her, healthy and happy, sitting between her parents during the interview.)

Perhaps most powerful is the story of an alienated teenager, who became addicted to alcohol and intoxicating ideology. Living in a Spain where the liberal establishment detests the nation's heritage and seeks to replace its population with refugees, he reacted by grabbing on to an ugly alternative: the neo-Nazi movement.

It channeled his adolescent anger toward convenient targets and gave him a sense of purpose as part of a "revolutionary" movement. We see him and his friends gathered reverently around a portrait of Adolf Hitler.

God's grace worked through a priest who'd known the young man as a boy. He invited this fervent racist and atheist to join a mission to Calcutta. And for some mysterious reason, the young man agreed. He witnessed nuns from Europe pouring out their lives in service of dark-skinned foreigners — and saw that they were happy. They were experiencing a joy that had eluded him all his life. He wanted to know the source, so he started observing them closely. Eventually he realized that they weren't deluded humanitarians but souls in love with Jesus. And he fell in love as well. Soon he abandoned racist ideology and spent his days tending the wounds of Indian beggars.

This gentle, meditative film filled me with hope. It showed me chapels and churches full of fervent, happy young people on fire with love for Christ. Every Catholic should see it, and so should non-Catholics curious about the Church's sacramental practices and the role they play in cultivating a personal friendship with Christ.

Cabrini Reminds Us That God Isn't Done with America

March 6, 2024

I know too many fellow believers and patriots who have swallowed what some call the "black pill"; that is, they've let frustration, fear, and indignation consume them to the point that, to protect themselves from further disappointment, they now embrace despair. They dwell on each piece of genuine negative news, and each rumor or ominous warning, with almost a perverse glee. Like Job's "friends" in the Bible, they advise us to "curse God and die."

As someone who has for decades worked in the front lines of the pro-life movement and opposed our country's useless wars inside elite GOP circles, nobody could accuse me of being some Pollyanna optimist or of refusing to face the darkness and ugliness that confront us every day. But in the midst of depressing headlines and high-profile betrayals, I hold on to hope. And more frequently than you might think, I'm consoled by genuine evidence that the tide has turned in our favor — that God has not washed His hands of us and that we might turn out like penitent Nineveh, not Sodom.

Sometimes those nuggets of hope come in the unlikeliest shapes. One of them is the career of my friend, the filmmaker Alejandro Monteverde, whose latest work, *Cabrini,* is the gorgeous story of a saint. Powerfully filmed and brilliantly acted, *Cabrini* shows how supernatural faith can overcome the grimmest obstacles our fallen world throws before us.

The young, sickly Frances Xavier Cabrini forms a religious order and crosses an ocean to offer love and care to thousands of new Italian immigrants, in a gilded-age New York City that treats them like disposable, cheap labor at best — and a sinister threat at worst.

That movie opens officially this weekend, though thousands have already screened it. *The Stream*'s John Zmirak reviewed it for *Chronicles* magazine, noting how it highlights the Catholic Church one hundred years ago using her own private funds to heroically minister to legal migrants — rather than profiting massively by trafficking migrants in illegally, on the taxpayers' dime, as our Church sadly does today.

To me, *Cabrini* is the latest development in an astonishing cinematic career. It is the work of a grateful legal immigrant to the United States who loves our country enough to gently but firmly examine even the darkest sides of our history — and affirm that what's noble and good about America can triumph. And will triumph, I think, based on the powerful resonance Monteverde's films have had, one after the other.

The first film was *Bella,* on which I served as executive producer. That film won the Toronto International Film Festival's People's Choice Award. An honest drama, it showed a lonely, broke American woman with a crisis pregnancy finding hope and deciding to choose life. What few people have noticed was what in the film conveyed that hope to her: an experience with a beautiful, loving, and faithful Latino family. In fact, *Bella* was the first American film in history, I think, to make such a family its hero. That film explored one of our country's grimmest realities, our throwaway culture of death, but showed us the way out and through.

Monteverde's second exquisite film was *Little Boy,* set during World War II. That film depicts twin evils that afflicted the United States simultaneously: the hideous reality of Japanese militarism afflicting the peoples of Asia and killing American boys, and the panicked reactions of the U.S. government. That is, the mass internment of thousands of patriotic American citizens and legal residents of Japanese descent, followed by the bombings of Hiroshima and Nagasaki. The film shows how the young son of an American POW suffering at the hands of the Japanese befriends an elderly Japanese-American facing bigotry and possible internment. And yet, for all the evils it confronts, the film is almost a Norman Rockwell painting come to life — a passionate depiction of basic human decency and the basic goodness of America and its system.

Most of you are likely familiar with the next film Monteverde made, which came out just two years ago, after Hollywood sat on it and tried to censor it for nearly a decade. *Sound of Freedom* goes into the very darkest places imaginable, exploring the world of child sex trafficking in our underground economy — a vile abuse now being made vastly worse by America's refusal to secure our southern border. (Indeed, one star of *Sound of Freedom,* Eduardo Verastegui, who also starred in *Bella,* wrote a column for *The Stream* making just that point.) But as always, there is still hope.

Sound of Freedom tells the true story of Americans who risk death at the hands of human traffickers to affirm the truth that "God's children are not for sale."

If immigrants can come to this country and find in it the profound goodness that Alejandro Monteverde has — values that resonate with millions of Americans — then we can't be as far gone as we sometimes fear. In fact, we're on the side of natural law itself, the structure of human nature, and the will of almighty God. That should carry us through the No Man's Land of the next few ugly, partisan months, and whatever crosses we find we might have to carry until they pass.

Steve Bannon Taught Civics in Prison and Now Schools the Reporters

October 30, 2024

What is anarcho-tyranny? Put simply, it means "Anarchy for me, tyranny for thee." It describes a two-tiered justice system that operates to intimidate, punish, and finally suppress political opposition. You could find examples of it all through our fallen history, from the legal codes of ancient Rome that subjected slaves to torture to the Jim Crow laws in postwar America — where black men who looked crookedly at white women could face imprisonment or lynching.

But the most infamous example of anarcho-tyranny as a means of consolidating power can be found in the Weimar Republic. The Nazis employed anarcho-tyranny to extend their control of the German street, such that the conservative government felt there was no choice but to invite Hitler to join them. Nazi thugs would brawl with Catholics, social democrats, Communists, and other enemies — and then, when all got arrested, pro-Nazi judges would set the Nazis free, while imprisoning their victims for the crime of defending themselves.

The Left in today's America is following not the Communist playbook (which often fails) but the Nazi one.

See the George Floyd rioters who walked free while peaceful January 6 protestors still rot in prison, and the settlement our government paid Peter Strzok for subverting it in the lawless false impeachments of Donald Trump. But we don't need to look back years for prime examples. We saw two Trump supporters, Peter Navarro and Steve Bannon, sent to federal prison for defying the illegitimate subpoenas of the lawlessly constituted January 6 committee.

Navarro emerged just in time to give a triumphant address to the Republican National Convention. Steve Bannon was set free yesterday.

At the press conference he held in New York City, Bannon (whom I proudly call a friend) showed us why he's the most important political operative in America — bar none. Looking somehow better after a prison stint than he did before he went in, Bannon faced cameras and a mostly hostile press. And he gave a master class in media, deftly handling loaded, hostile questions from white-knuckled reporters who clearly wished to body-slam him back into a cell. He interrupted their filibustering, trashed their false presuppositions, and kept on his message with a twinkle in his eye.

And that message was important, not just to the Trump campaign but to our country. As an aside, Bannon at one point thanked the prison officials in Danbury, Connecticut, for letting him teach civics to fellow prisoners. And Bannon's whole appearance was, in fact, a civics lesson — one we all sorely need and which sadly went over the heads of the MSM apparatchiks who reluctantly had to report on his release.

Bannon's central message was a crucial one in the civic nationalism that has animated Trump's movement all along. He laid out how our system is rigged to favor callous (and mostly white) elites and penalize the poor. Bannon explained how the open-borders policies of Joe Biden and Kamala Harris were part of a conscious strategy to limit inflation by pushing down the wages "not of financial executives or lawyers, but of the poorest, least skilled Americans." He cited Federal Reserve statements that openly admitted this.

And ordinary Americans in the working and middle classes are catching on, he warned. He spoke of the black and Latino men he met in prison who are serving long sentences for drug possession, who should have been set free thanks to "Donald Trump's prison reform." But the Department of Justice has intentionally defied the law Trump passed and signed (the First Step Act) because actually obeying it would have benefited Trump. Bannon referred to Harris as the "Queen of Mass Incarceration," echoing Tulsi Gabbard's devastating debate takedown that drove Harris out of the Democratic primaries in 2020.

Bannon traced the growing support of black and Latino male voters for Donald Trump to this kind of flippant, dictatorial behavior by the Democrats, and equally to the economic chaos that party has inflicted on our country. Those voters, Bannon said, remembered how blue-collar wages rose faster than white-collar wages, unemployment was minimal, and inflation wasn't an issue — while Trump was in office. Those voters compare how they were doing four years ago with how their lives are going now. That bleak contrast, he said, made Kamala Harris's mindless embrace of "the politics of joy" a bitter joke to millions.

Bannon predicted confidently that America is "going beyond the politics of race, the politics of gender," and entering a new, dramatic era: "the politics of money." In it, alternative media such as his *War Room* podcasts, Elon Musk's new unchained X, *The Stream,* and other uncensored venues will expose how our elites rig the justice system, regulations, immigration policy, and other key aspects of government to benefit themselves — and fleece the man on the street. That's if we can stop Kamala Harris and her plans to pack the Supreme Court while gutting both the First and Second Amendments.

That kind of populist nationalism embraces people of every race, both sexes, all religions, and every lifestyle except one: the cozy existence of powerful parasites, who feel so threatened by Donald Trump that they flooded the Harris campaign with a record $1 billion, and who misuse their power to imprison dissenters like Bannon himself.

Bannon called for Trump supporters to strain every sinew to get out the vote, and called on Trump himself to fully inform voters in real time of the massive efforts by the Left to hijack this election — which he noted now include threats to use Congress to defy the Supreme Court and refuse to certify even an unambiguous Trump victory, on the lame pretext that Trump is an "insurrectionist."

Bannon explained in detail how the chaotic incompetence of the Biden-Harris administration and its naked capture by the powerful leaves the Left with only the darkest options: to demonize half of America for daring to complain and to use their control of election offices and courts to simply steal the election — again. But he also promised that they will fail if we all do our part.

A big part of that is prayer. And tonight, I'll be offering prayers of gratitude that Bannon is now back out here fighting.

Epilogue

The Solidarity Gospel

Christ redeemed us from the curse of the law,
having become a curse for us.

— Galatians 3:13

I recently sent a letter to supporters of my organization, the Vulnerable People Project (VPP), about our plans to take action ahead of a predicted famine that could claim half a million lives in Sudan. "That is so awful that it's hard to believe," a donor wrote back. She continued:

> As a fellow Catholic, I have a tough time reconciling that with the many promises in the Bible that God will meet all of our needs. What do you say to people who ask you to explain why God tells us not to worry [because] He will provide, but then millions of people die of poverty?

It's such an important question and one I hear so often that it deserves a public reply.

It's easy for Catholics to dismiss and ridicule the so-called "prosperity gospel" typically preached in certain Protestant communities. It's especially easy for Catholics who've yet to wrestle with the faith and who remain perhaps more aloof from their neighbors in need than the gospel would really allow.

We at VPP have the sorrowful privilege of being in contact with human suffering every day. Like all of us, I have been wrestling with the problem of suffering since childhood. A child doesn't have the kind of sophistication that helps us grown-ups deny the realities our faith insists on, and I'm blessed with a lucid memory of my first childhood prayer.

I was sitting on the avocado-green (don't judge — it was the 1970s) carpeted floor of my grandmother's little apartment, pitting gray and green plastic army men against each other and eating over-easy eggs and scraps of toast from a sundae bowl. *Sesame Street* was playing on the black-and-white TV.

But when a PBS documentary on heroin addiction came on, I was stunned into rapt attention. My grandmother was sitting at the kitchen table doing crossword puzzles; I was surrounded by Axis and Allied soldiers, and the sun flooded into the room, making it the closest place to Heaven on earth. But there, in that little box, I saw emaciated men and women crawling across the bare floors of burned-out houses in Chicago, feebly handling syringes, lighters, and spoons.

My little heart broke. I was terrified, sorrowful, and overwhelmed with guilt. How could I live this wonderful and pleasant life while others lived in such tragic conditions? "God has only so many good lives to give out and so many bad lives to give out," I thought. Never having been taken to church or taught to pray, I said my first prayer on that apartment floor. "God, give me one of those lives," I said, pointing to the TV, "so no one else has to have it."

That straightforward prayer, innocent and unassuming, acknowledged suffering as a fact rather than treating it as an academic question. So the prevalence of human pain — even frightening agonies and abject abuses — was for me a given. As it is for all of us before we are taught to forget.

It would be decades before I accepted the Catholic Faith. But when I began to explore Christianity as a young atheist, I discovered one Scripture passage that was at once comforting and confusing: "I saw all the oppressions that are practiced under the sun," said King Solomon. "And behold, the tears of the oppressed, and they had no one to comfort them! On the side of their oppressors there was power" (Eccles. 4:1).

It is uncanny that the mighty King Solomon, this central figure in Jewish Scripture, saw power in this fallen world as being on the side of the oppressor. And Solomon's insight lays the groundwork for Jesus better than any joyful trumpet-blare verses that false teachers might twist into a promise that the gospel means an end to our heartaches.

The gospel doesn't promise that Christ will relieve man's suffering on earth. Instead, it promises that the Mystical Body of Christ will do what no earthly power ever would: unite itself with those who suffer.

Only one thing is as clear to me as the suffering of my neighbors: that the body of Christ knelt by the side of a woman caught in the act of adultery; that Our Lord made a point of identifying Himself most intimately with the powerless and then commanded that they be treated as if they were Himself; that the King of Kings has chosen the side of the oppressed.

And His choice colors all of human history. From the first years of the gospel's spread, the Body of Christ stood with the slave, with the abandoned infant, with the widow and the orphan.

Centuries later, the Body of Christ instituted its solidarity with the vulnerable in laws and governments. We see it in the Magna Carta's guarantees against arrests and convictions without trial. In the U.S. Constitution's protections for religious freedom and private property. In the abolition of slavery throughout the Western world.

The Body of Christ could also be found sharing in the pain and affliction of Molokai's nineteenth-century lepers, for whom St. Damien gave his life. And in the last century, among the poorest of the poor in Calcutta, where St. Mother Teresa offered her whole strength for their comfort and consolation — allowing herself to be driven into a deep, long, dark night of the soul in the process.

Today, members of Christ's Mystical Body are the loudest advocates for the child in the womb, for religious minorities oppressed by Islamist factions throughout Africa and the Middle East, and for the millions of Muslim Uyghurs hunted and imprisoned by China's atheist regime.

Two weeks ago, when the lives of three people whom VPP had promised to help were in danger, I spent a whole night on a lawn chair in my backyard, weeping.

Around two in the morning, as Texas-sized drops of rain as warm as the air relentlessly splashed my already-drenched body, it dawned on me that the Yazidi we've rescued from persecution, the Afghan allies we've ushered into safe houses, and my heavily surveilled Chinese dissident friends in the West — they all still suffer.

In my tears, I began writing to many of the people VPP has served: "I understand that your suffering isn't over. I'm sure that on many nights, you can't sleep. I am grateful for your friendship and inspired by your courage. Please know I am here whenever you need me."

My little struggle that night motivated me to stay up until morning sending messages like that.

I'll forever be grateful for the clarity that comes with the work of VPP — my team's effort to be present to the vulnerable. For me, there is no abstractness about the problem of the power of evil over our lives. I have dark nights of the soul. I've been despondent and wrestled with acedia. But by the grace of God, I can feel great sorrow with my faith in God and, God willing, my soul intact.

If Catholics ask themselves the probing question my donor asked, it might reveal that the prosperity gospel isn't just the silly idea of a few easily parodied megachurches. It's a universal temptation that can subtly work its way into any Christian heart.

"God is infinitely good and all his works are good. Yet no one can escape the experience of suffering or the evils in nature which seem to be linked to the limitations proper to creatures," the *Catechism of the Catholic Church* states. It goes on to quote St. Augustine: "I sought whence evil comes and there was no solution." The *Catechism* continues, "His own painful quest would only be resolved by his conversion to the living God. For 'the mystery of lawlessness' is clarified only in the light of the 'mystery of our religion' " (CCC 385). In other words, the Church in her wisdom humbly observes what all of us can see and no one can deny: The world is rife with suffering for which there can be no satisfactory human justification.

We fallen Catholics, on the other hand, tend to lack that wisdom and humility as much as any prosperity-gospel Protestant does. So we tiptoe around the problem of suffering, harboring a secret, nervous hope that we might simply get away with never facing it.

When we take that route, we only add to the problem of suffering the further problem of our own indifference to it (at least until it reaches our own doorsteps). And in so doing, we risk losing the heart of the gospel — and our own souls.

Thank God for answered prayers, especially the rash and naive prayer I made as a preschool-aged little boy.

No, this is not a confession of heroin addiction. Assenting to a belief in God in my late twenties and eventually converting to Catholicism in my early thirties, I was startled by how my greatest prayers had all been answered.

I used to joke with my wife that God let me down by not answering my first and most sincere prayer. It was only after I read the works of the great Catholic philosopher René Girard that I realized He had answered that prayer. In a beautiful and strange way, God answered in a way only our good God could.

Through the work of this apostolate I founded before I was Catholic, God thrust me into the service of the most vulnerable people on earth. And "to stand with the vulnerable," writes Girard, "is to become indistinguishable from those you stand with."

About the Author

Jason Jones is a film producer, author, activist, popular podcast host, and human rights worker. He is president of the Human-Rights Education and Relief Organization (H.E.R.O.), known for its two main programs, the Vulnerable People Project and Movie to Movement. Jones was an executive producer of *Bella,* which won several film industry awards, most notably the People's Choice Award at the 2006 Toronto International Film Festival. He was an associate producer of *The Stoning of Soraya M.,* winner of the NAACP Image Award and the Los Angeles Film Festival. He produced the award-winning pro-life short film *Crescendo* with Eduardo Verastegui and Pattie Mallette (the mother of Justin Bieber). *Crescendo* raised more than $6 million in North America to support pregnancy centers and women's shelters. Jones is the author of *The Great Campaign Against the Great Reset, The Race to Save Our Century,* and *The World Is on Fire.*

CRISIS Publications

Sophia Institute Press awards the privileged title "CRISIS Publications" to a select few of our books that address contemporary issues at the intersection of politics, culture, and the Church with clarity, cogency, and force and that are also destined to become all-time classics.

CRISIS Publications are direct, explaining their principles briefly, simply, and clearly to Catholics in the pews, on whom the future of the Church depends. The time for ambiguity or confusion is long past.

CRISIS Publications are contemporary, born of our own time and circumstances and intended to become significant statements in current debates, statements that serious Catholics cannot ignore, regardless of their prior views.

CRISIS Publications are classical, addressing themes and enunciating principles that are valid for all ages and cultures. Readers will turn to them time and again for guidance in other days and different circumstances.

CRISIS Publications are spirited, entering contemporary debates with gusto to clarify issues and demonstrate how those issues can be resolved in a way that enlivens souls and the Church.

We welcome engagement with our readers on current and future CRISIS Publications. Please pray that this imprint may help to resolve the crises embroiling our Church and society today.

Sophia Institute Press® is a registered trademark of Sophia Institute.
Sophia Institute is a tax-exempt institution as defined by the
Internal Revenue Code, Section 501(c)(3). Tax ID 22-2548708.